THE PRACTICAL WRITER

THE RACTICAL

RITER

Edward P. Bailey

Philip A. Powell

Sixth Edition

Harcourt Brace College Publishers

Fort Worth   Philadelphia   San Diego   New York   Orlando   Austin   San Antonio
Toronto   Montreal   London   Sydney   Tokyo

Vice President, Publisher	Ted Buchholz
Senior Acquisitions Editor	Michael Rosenberg
Editorial Assistant	Tammi Price
Project Editor	Elizabeth C. Alvarez
Production Manager	Jane Tyndall Ponceti
Art Director	Sue Hart
Cover Image	Ann Trusty

ISBN: 0-15-501787-X
Library of Congress Catalog Card Number: 94-77138

Address for Editorial Correspondence: Harcourt Brace College Publishers, 301 Commerce Street, Suite 3700, Fort Worth, TX 76102.

Address for Orders: Harcourt Brace & Company, 6277 Sea Harbor Drive, Orlando, FL 32887-6777. 1-800-782-4479, or 1-800-433-0001 (in Florida).

Printed in the United States of America

5 6 7 8 9 0 1 2 3 4 039 9 8 7 6 5 4 3 2 1

PREFACE

Eighteen years ago, we sat down with pen in hand, yellow legal pad in front of us, and some ideas we were enthusiastic about.

Much has changed since then: Now we sit before computers that have the power entire print shops had two decades ago. The pen and yellow pad are gone. But the enthusiasm remains. And each time we work on a new edition, we are surprised anew at how much we agree with our younger selves, how little fundamentally we wish to change in a book that has been good to both of us.

We still feel that readers appreciate the kind of clear structure that *The Practical Writer* teaches. And we still feel that students appreciate a step-by-step approach to learning that structure and all that goes within it.

So what does *The Practical Writer* do? And what have we changed for this edition?

WHAT DOES *THE PRACTICAL WRITER* DO?

We begin by presenting the fundamentals (organization, support, unity, coherence) one at a time—in a tightly structured one-paragraph essay. The paragraph, we've found, is a unit large enough for students to demonstrate their understanding of the fundamentals and small enough for them to work with toward mastery. At this point, we don't overwhelm them while they're learning the fundamentals by making them struggle to find support; instead, we ask them to write about personal experiences and the people and things they know well. We encourage them to be colorful, interesting, and—above all—specific.

We then move through several longer stages of writing to a 1,000- to 2,000-word research paper. By the time students complete the research block, they can write a serious paper—the kind they will have to write in other college courses and beyond them—with a less mechanical structure than we required earlier. We still offer a model, of course, but it becomes a guide rather than a goal.

The last two topics of our book, punctuation and expression, are not part of the step-by-step approach. Students can study these chapters whenever they're ready for them. They aren't typical handbook material, though, because we've been careful to select only what first-year students need to learn, leaving out the skills they probably know and those they're not yet ready to apply.

Finally, we try to avoid the "scholarly" style of writing and to speak personally to students, as though we're talking to them in class.

WHAT HAVE WE CHANGED FOR THIS EDITION?

As usual, we've worked to keep the fundamentals in place and to update where necessary. Specifically

- *We've brought the research section up to date.* Keeping up with the "computerized library" is nearly a full-time task these days—exciting things keep happening. We can all now simply sit in a small room at a computer terminal and have almost inconceivable access to the world's knowledge.

- *We've rearranged the four chapters in Part Four, "More Patterns of Development."* We've tried to order the chapters the way most teachers might like to use them: starting with comparison and contrast and moving to cause and effect, classification, and then process. We've also completely rewritten the process chapter to make it less restricted to technical writing.

- *We've broadened our brief discussions of "practical writing."* These sections explain how particular chapters are useful beyond first-year English. In the last edition, these sections concentrated on connections between the writing our book teaches and writing in the world of work. Now we show that this book also has direct relevance to other courses students may be taking.

- *We've deemphasized techniques of layout.* In the last edition, we showed that even a five-paragraph essay can benefit from headings and indented lists. We still include that information, but we present it as an alternative rather than as the primary approach. For example, the title of Chapter 10 has changed from "Techniques of Layout" to "Alternative Techniques of Layout." Throughout, you'll continue to see some essays with these techniques and some without. Instructors, in other words, now have more options.

- *We've revised about half the exercises.* We've also added some exercises that ask students to write about what they're learning in other courses.

- *We've added an appendix on commonly confused words.* This appendix covers such problems as *affect/effect* and *imply/infer.*

As a final word, we continue to express appreciation to our students, colleagues, and publisher. We'd also like to express our thanks to our reviewers: Professor Delois Cook, Talladega College, Talladega, AL; Professor Doris Johnson, Jefferson State Community College, Birmingham, AL; Roger Haley, New Mexico State at Alamogordo, Alamogordo, NM; Victoria Bursey, Cuesta College, San Luis Obispo, CA; and Kathleen Tickner, Brevard Community College, Melbourne, FL. Thanks also to our editors, Michael Rosenberg and Tammi Price. Both have been unusually helpful in thinking through the revisions for this edition.

Edward P. Bailey, Marymount University
Philip A. Powell, Burke, Virginia

CONTENTS

HOW THIS BOOK WORKS

The Practical Writer is intended for typical first-year college students, who perhaps lack knowledge but don't lack intelligence. We assume that these students can learn quickly and well from a step-by-step approach to the fundamentals, good examples to follow, and carefully designed exercises.

We begin by presenting the fundamentals (organization, support, unity, coherence)—one at a time—in a tightly structured one-paragraph essay. The paragraph, we've found, is a unit large enough for students to demonstrate their understanding of the fundamentals and small enough for them to work toward mastery. At this point, we don't overwhelm them while they're learning the fundamentals by making them struggle to find support; instead, we ask them to write about personal experiences and the people and things they know well. We encourage them to be colorful, interesting, and—above all—specific.

We then move through several longer stages of writing to a 1,000- to 2,000-word research paper. By the time students complete the research block, they can write a serious paper—the kind they will have to write in other college courses and beyond them—with a less mechanical structure than we required earlier. We still offer a model, of course, but it becomes a guide rather than a goal.

The last two topics of our book, punctuation and expression, are not part of the step-by-step approach. Students can study these chapters whenever they're ready for them. These chapters can be studied any time, whenever your students are ready for them. They are not typical handbook material, though, because we've been careful to select only what first-year students need to learn, leaving out the skills they probably know and those they're not yet ready to apply.

Finally, we try to avoid the "scholarly" style of writing and to speak personally to students, as though we're talking to them in class.

A MODEL FOR WRITING

The One-Paragraph Essay (Stage I)

This part of the book shows you how to write a good one-paragraph essay.

Although you seldom see one-paragraph essays in publications, you'll find them remarkably handy for improving your writing:

- One obvious advantage is that they are short—so you can spend your study time writing a really good one.
- At the same time, they're long enough for you to practice some fundamentals of writing.
- Finally, what you learn about one-paragraph essays transfers nicely to larger themes and even research papers.

In Part One, you'll learn about the simplest one-paragraph essay, which we call Stage I. Later, in Part Two, you'll study the organization for a slightly more sophisticated one-paragraph essay, which we call Stage II.

Part One presents a very tightly structured model for a paragraph. You may wonder if all good writers follow such a structure for persuasive writing. No, of course not. This structure is not *the* good way to write a paragraph, but it is *one* good way. And this way has a very real advantage: it automatically gives your paper organization so that you have one less thing to worry about. You then can concentrate on learning the other fundamentals that experienced writers already know. And by working constantly with this model paragraph, you will learn organization, too—the easy way.

Support for the paragraph's main idea is also easy. Right now, we don't care whether you know how to find facts in the library. We're much more concerned that you can recognize and use good support once you find it. So we make finding it simple. You don't need to go any further than your own mind: you can use either your experiences or your imagination for support. As a result, you can have fun with your one-paragraph essays. They can be intriguing and perhaps humorous.

Writing doesn't have to be dull!

1 Overview of the One-Paragraph Essay (Stage I)

For many years, teachers have given this advice to their students:

- Tell your readers what you're going to tell them.
- Tell it to them.
- Then tell them what you just told them.

Simple, isn't it? Yet, even though the advice is simple, it's also extremely useful. In fact, it serves as the structure—the underlying organization—of much nonfiction writing. After all, most readers appreciate knowing at the beginning what the writing will be about. And they appreciate a reminder at the end giving the writing's overall purpose. That way, all the details in the middle have a context. As a result, readers know where they are in a piece of writing and don't get lost.

You'll find this organization valuable to you as a *writer,* too: it gives you an easy way to get started. You will already have solved the problem of how to organize the overall flow of your writing. You can then move on to the next step in your prewriting process.

This chapter shows you how to apply this simple organization to the one-paragraph essay. Later chapters will show you how to apply it to longer (and even very long) essays, including research papers.

So let's turn now to the basic building block of much good writing: the one-paragraph essay. It has three main parts:

- The first sentence states the idea you want your readers to accept (your main point). We call this a *topic sentence.*
- All middle sentences present specific support for that idea.
- The last sentence rewords the topic sentence—to remind your readers of the point you've just made.

Let's look at these three points another way—as a model.

THE MODEL FOR THE ONE-PARAGRAPH ESSAY (STAGE I)

The model looks like this:

> Topic sentence
>   Specific support
>   Specific support
>   Specific support
> Reworded topic sentence

Now let's look at a "real" paragraph—one that follows the model we've just shown you:

> The Boundary Waters Canoe Area, a wilderness park in northern Minnesota, is a refreshing change from the city. Away from the din of civilization, I have canoed silently across its waters for an entire afternoon and not heard a single noise except for an occasional birdcall and the sound of waves beating against the shore. Also, my partner and I were able to navigate our way through a string of five lakes by following a campfire's scent drifting through the pure air. Most refreshing, the park is so magnificently beautiful that even the voyageurs of old were willing to endure its hardships in order to settle there. The Boundary Waters Canoe Area is thus an ideal place to clear your head of the congestion of urban life.

Look carefully at the first sentence. Do you see that it really does state the main point of the paragraph—the idea that the rest of the paragraph supports?

Now look at the last sentence. Do you see that it is only a rewording of the first sentence? Easy, isn't it?

So the first sentence stated the main point, and the last sentence reworded it. There were three points in the middle—a sentence for each.

Here's an outline of that paragraph:

> Topic sentence   The Boundary Waters Canoe Area is a refreshing change.
>   Specific support   quietness
>   Specific support   purity of the air
>   Specific support   beauty
> Reworded topic sentence   It's an ideal place to clear your head of the congestion of urban life.

The structure of the paragraph is absolutely clear, unmistakable, and obvious. For some writing (fiction, personal essays), an obvious organization isn't necessarily good. But for writing that takes care of the day-to-day business of the world, an obvious organization is usually helpful to readers.

As writers, then, we should take into account what works best for our readers. Getting right to the point with a topic sentence and then providing the support is a very good way to keep our readers on track.

ANOTHER EXAMPLE

Here's another sample one-paragraph essay. It, too, follows the model perfectly:

> Even though I have never really lived there, going to my grandmother's farm always seems like coming home. The feeling begins as soon as I cross the threshold of that quaint little house and tumble into the arms of waiting aunts and cousins. The sense of welcome overwhelms me. Then there are the cozy rooms—the ceilings don't seem higher than six feet—with their crackling fireplaces that make me want to snuggle down into the feather-stuffed chairs. But the memory that always lasts the longest is the smell of Grandma's biscuits and pastries cooking in her coke-fed stove. Yes, only in Grandma's house do I feel the warmth and welcome that always seem like coming home.

Notice that all the middle sentences have to do with the pleasant connotation of "home" in its best sense: feeling welcome, cozy, cared for. Each of those ideas supports the topic sentence.

Again, let's look at an outline of that paragraph:

Topic sentence   Going to my grandmother's farm seems like coming home.
   Specific support   greeting by relatives
   Specific support   coziness of house
   Specific support   smell of home-cooked food
Reworded topic sentence   Visiting Grandma's seems like coming home.

Both sample paragraphs we've shown you have exactly three items of specific support. You may wonder if that's what you should always do. No. Three items seem to work well in both of these paragraphs. But sometimes five or six items are necessary to be persuasive; at other times, one long example will do.

Although the sample paragraphs in the first two or three chapters of this book are good, they are intentionally fairly simple so you can easily see their basic organization. But if you don't fully understand the one-paragraph essay yet, don't worry. The next few chapters explain further.

Also, you can find a checklist for the one-paragraph essay immediately following Chapter 8. You may wish to turn to it now. It gives you a good sense of the material in the first eight chapters.

PRACTICAL WRITING

So far, the one-paragraph essay may seem like only a teaching tool. But as simple as it is, it has significant value in school—and beyond.

Practical Writing in School

In school, you can easily use the pattern of the one-paragraph essay for some of your writing. Simple answers to essay questions on tests can follow this pattern. So can any one-paragraph writing you do in school—whether you're taking a course in English, history, mathematics, physics, computer science, or anything else. Most readers—and we can assure you this includes teachers, too—like to see the main idea up front, and good, detailed support afterward.

For example, in English you might be asked a brief essay question like this: "What is the main feature of e. e. cummings' poetry that appeals to you?" Your answer could be this one-paragraph essay:

> I like the individual freedom that comes through in e. e. cummings' poetry. You can see that freedom right away in the lack of capitalization and normal spacing in his writing. You can also see it in the content: his poems often deal with the carefreeness of spring and the value of the individual. Those are just two of the ways I see the emphasis on freedom I like so much in e. e. cummings' poems.

That could serve as a very brief answer, if that's what your teacher expects on a test. It could be more convincing, of course, as a longer essay with detailed examples for each point.

The next chapter shows you how to use examples. And later in the book, we'll show you how to expand the one-paragraph essay into a full-length essay. You should find that especially useful in your courses beyond this one.

Practical Writing at Work

This structured approach will also be useful after you graduate. Since we wrote the first edition of this book, we've done a great deal of work with business and government writers—lawyers, accountants, auditors, doctors, bankers, military officers, government analysts, computer experts, political scientists, scientific researchers, and others of similar skill. Our main task has been to help these people—usually bright, educated, and successful professionals—express their ideas clearly.

One consistent message we tell them is this: readers in the busy world of work strongly prefer to have the main point up front for almost everything they read. In fact, if they don't find it there—right away—they often skip to the back and start hunting for it.

If you're reading a report from your doctor, don't you want the diagnosis up front instead of three pages later, after all the lab results and all the lists of possible illnesses you might have, but don't?

Suppose you work in an office and have a five-page report to read and comment on for your boss. Where do you, as the reader, want to see the main point? Do you want it at the end? Or at the beginning? Almost all of us prefer the beginning.

Let's look at an example of poor business writing—a memo that delays the main point (a recommendation) until the end. Notice how confused you get trying to struggle with all the details without a main point to guide you.

Memo With the Recommendation Last

Date: July 7
From: Fielding Brown
To: Maribeth Wyvill

The copy machine was broken for three days this month—June 2, 5, and 9. During that time, nobody was able to do any of the photocopying crucial to our work. Also, it had routine maintenance two other days this month—June 15 and 30. Then, too, nobody could use the machine. Finally, Neal and Sharon had a large photocopying project that kept others from using the machine for three other days—June 1, 3, and 4. I recommend, therefore, that we buy a second copy machine because the one we have can't meet our needs.

It's easy to get lost in the facts of that paragraph, isn't it? If you are the boss—the one deciding whether to spend the money—you'd certainly have to read that memo *twice*. The first time you'd be hunting for the recommendation, which doesn't come until the last sentence. The second time, with the recommendation in mind, you'd read to see if the facts served as effective justification.

Writers cannot expect their readers to reread. And few bosses like rereading, either. Wouldn't the memo be better with the recommendation up front, like this?

Memo With the Recommendation First

Date: July 7
From: Fielding Brown
To: Maribeth Wyvill

I recommend we buy a second copy machine because the one we have can't meet our needs. Ours was broken for three days this month—June 2, 5, and 9. During that time, nobody was able to do any of the photocopying crucial to our work. Also, it had routine maintenance two other days this month—June 15 and 30. Then, too, nobody could use the machine. Finally, Neal and Sharon had a large photocopying project that kept others from using the machine for three other days—June 1, 3, and 4. For these reasons, I strongly urge that we buy a second copier.

As you can see, the memo now takes the shape of the model we gave you at the beginning of this chapter.

Practical Writing

Throughout the book, we'll point to the connections between our models and good writing outside your writing course. The connections are strong and important—for your other college courses and for the world of work.

The one-paragraph essay is a valuable little tool. That's why we think of this as a *practical* book—one that can help you many times, in one way or another, throughout your life: thus, *The Practical Writer*.

EXERCISES

A. Outline the following paragraph the same way we outlined the two paragraphs in the chapter:

Three common electric distractions on my desk waste my precious study time at night. The worst distraction is my clock, constantly humming to remind me how little time I actually have. Another interruption is the "high-quality" fluorescent desk lamp that sometimes buzzes, flickers—and then goes out. And, finally, consider that fascinating little invention, the computer, that not only does all kinds of complicated math problems, but also challenges me to games and helps me write letters home. After stopping to worry about the time, fix my lamp, and play with the computer, I am too tired to study, so I just go to bed.

Topic sentence _Three common electric distractions on my desk precious stu waste my_ _time at night_

Specific support _The worst distraction is to remind me how much time I actua my clock, constantly humming_

Specific support _desk lamp that sometimes buzzes, flickers, and then goes o Another interruption is the high-quality flourescent_

Specific support _computer that not only does all And finally, consider that fascinating little invention, th_

Reworded topic sentence _I am too tired to study so I go to bed_

B. Outline this paragraph:

Old, stiff, and weathered, my grandfather's hands show the strenuous way of life he has known as a working man. Many hot summer days tilling the

Topic sentence: There are three things on my desk that waste my study time.
support: Clock
support: desk lamp
support computer

stubborn soil of West Texas have left their lasting mark in the form of a deep and permanent tan. Grandpa's hands are also covered with calluses—begun, perhaps, when he split cordwood for two dollars a day in an effort to pull his family through the Great Depression. Most striking, though, are the carpenter's scars he has collected from the days of building his house, barn, and fence and from the unending repair jobs that still occupy his every day. Although small and battered, Grandpa's hands bring back images of a time when men and women worked from dawn to dusk just to survive, a difficult but respected way of life.

Topic sentence ___My grand fathers ^hands show the strenuous ways of a working man.___

Specific support ___~~tittle~~ tan___

Specific support ___Calluses___

Specific support ___carpenter's scars___

Reworded topic sentence ___My grandpas hands are small and battered.___

C. Outline this paragraph:

The East Wing of the National Art Gallery in Washington, D.C., is a showplace of modern art. Inside, it houses collections of such artists as Picasso and Matisse, well known for their nonrepresentational works. Hanging from the ceiling is a mobile, normally thought of as a dangling toy parents hang above their infant's crib. This one, however, is several stories high and much more impressive to the parents (and children, too). Even the building is in keeping with its contents: it has lots of glass, open spaces, and strange angles and corners. For modern art, this wing of the gallery is an excellent place to visit.

Topic sentence ___The National Art Gallery contains much modern art.___

Specific support ___nonrepresentational works___

Specific support ___hanging mobiles___

Specific support ___building design___

Reworded topic sentence ___It is a great place to visit.___

D. Outline this paragraph you saw earlier in the chapter:

I like the individual freedom that comes through in e. e. cummings' poetry. You can see that freedom right away in the lack of capitalization and normal spacing in his writing. You can also see it in the content: His poems often deal with the carefreeness of spring and the value of the individual. Those are just two of the ways I see the emphasis on freedom I like so much in e. e. cummings' poems.

Topic sentence ___I like e.e. cummings' poetry.___

Specific support ___lack of capitalization___

Specific support ___content___

Reworded topic sentence _Freedom is emphisized in e.e.cummings poetry._

E. Now outline the business memo you saw earlier in the chapter:

  I recommend we buy a second copy machine because the one we have can't meet our needs. Ours was broken for three days this month—June 2, 5, and 9. During that time, nobody was able to do any of the photocopying crucial to our work. Also, it had routine maintenance two other days this month—June 15 and 30. Then, too, nobody could use the machine. Finally, Neal and Sharon had a large photocopying project that kept others from using the machine for three other days—June 1, 3, and 4. For these reasons, I strongly urge that we buy a second copier.

Topic sentence _I recommend we buy a second copy machine._

Specific support _broken 3 days_

Specific support _routine maintenance_

Specific support _two machines neccosary for big projects_

Reworded topic sentence _We must buy a second copier._

2 Support: Examples, Statistics, Statements by Authorities

The first sentence in our model paragraph is the topic sentence, but let's save that for the next chapter. Instead, we'll start with support. Once you understand support—and how specific it must be—you'll understand much more easily how to write a good topic sentence.

This chapter talks about three different kinds of support:

- examples
- statistics
- statements by authorities

EXAMPLES

Professional writers tell us: The secret to good writing—the real secret—is using examples.

Yet many teachers say: One of the biggest problems with undergraduate writing—one that almost all students have—is that they don't use nearly enough examples.

So, here's a chance to solve a problem by learning a secret. Let's begin by talking about two different kinds of examples: *quick* examples and *narrative* examples.

QUICK EXAMPLES

You already know from your everyday experience what a quick example is: a quick example is one instance, one occurrence, of whatever you're talking about.

If you're discussing the meals available at fast-food restaurants, a hamburger is one example—one of several possibilities. You could have named fried chicken, tacos, roast beef sandwiches, or (at the waterfront in San Francisco) even sourdough bread and crabs.

For a quick example to be effective, it must be very specific. If you want to show that Constance Dilettante can't stick with anything, don't say, "She changes her mind a lot." Don't even just say, "She changed her major frequently in college." Be still more specific: "She changed her major from philosophy to computer science to animal husbandry—all in one semester."

Do quick examples really make any difference? We think so. Consider the following:

Sentences *Without* Quick Examples

There were many expensive cars in the school's parking lot during the football game.

You could tell spring was here because of all the flowers in bloom.

Why do lawyers use words that mean one thing to them and something entirely different in ordinary English?

Sentences *With* Quick Examples

There were many expensive cars in the school's parking lot during the football game—*Mercedes convertibles, low-slung Porsches, red Ferraris.*

You could tell spring was here because of all the flowers in bloom: *tulips of all colors, yellow daffodils, and (if you want to call them flowers) even a few early dandelions.*

Why do lawyers use words that mean one thing to them and something entirely different in ordinary English (*words such as party and action and motion*)?

See the difference that quick examples make? They take something rather abstract—cars, flowers, legal terms—and make them much more concrete. It's almost as though the abstract words don't really communicate, don't really find a place to lodge in the brain cells. But the more concrete words—*Mercedes, tulip, party*—do.

Using Quick Examples

When should you use quick examples? How often do you like to see such examples when you read? Pretty often, right? And that's how often you should use them when you write.

Quick examples, of course, don't have to come at the ends of sentences. You could have a paragraph, probably a very short one, that depended entirely on quick examples.

A Paragraph Depending on Quick Examples

Chairs come in many different designs. Easy chairs—designed for people who like to lounge back—usually have lots of padding, perhaps a curved back, and comfortable armrests. Straight chairs usually have minimal padding, a vertical back, and sometimes no armrests. Some contemporary computer chairs, kneelers, have padding for the knees and seat, but no back at all and no armrests. So, depending on their purposes, chairs differ quite a bit.

The topic of that paragraph may not be exciting, but the quick examples—easy chair, straight chair, kneeler—certainly communicate much more than the abstract beginning: "Chairs come in many different designs."

NARRATIVE EXAMPLES

A *quick* example is just one instance, one occurrence. But a *narrative* example is a brief story. A narrative example can really make an impact, so we emphasize it in this book.

Sometimes you want to emphasize an idea to help your readers understand what you mean. So you decide to run a little "motion picture"; that is, you decide to tell a story that will help your readers visualize what you're saying—as though they are watching a short film rather than simply reading words.

For example, if you want to show that shark hunting is dangerous, you could give a quick example by saying, "A friend of mine was once maimed while hunting sharks." Or you could really make your point by telling the story:

With a Narrative Example

I still have nightmares about the time last July when Rocky and I were scuba diving off the coast of Baja California. Rocky spotted a great white shark and tried to shoot it with his spear gun. As he fired, the shark spun suddenly toward him. Before I knew what happened. . . . [Then—poor Rocky—finish the story.]

Can you see that a narrative example really drives the point home?

A narrative example, then, is a specific incident (usually with names, dates, other details). It is not the *kind* of thing that can happen (not "sometimes people get hurt when they try to shoot sharks with spear guns"). It is the story of something that *did* happen (June, Rocky, Baja California, great white shark).

Let's examine another narrative example. You might find a paragraph like this in a magazine like *Time* or *Newsweek:*

Another Narrative Example

Alison Marks, a 23-year-old graduate student in architecture at the University of Colorado, had a blood pressure reading of 180/120 in February. Her doctor prescribed Elavil, which Alison took for three months until she became so busy with exams that she found taking medicine too much trouble. After exams, she still neglected her medicine. As a result, her blood pressure rose so sharply that in September she was rushed to the hospital with a stroke.

Do we care that this patient was an architecture student, or that she was 23, or that she was named Alison Marks? Yes, somehow we do. Alison becomes more real to us, someone we can sympathize with. And, because Alison's case becomes believable and typical, we begin to be convinced that people with high blood pressure should take their medicine. The narrative example has helped convince us.

Now let's apply what we've learned about narrative examples to the one-paragraph essay. Suppose you're sitting in your room trying to write your first college English paper—the one for this course. You remember your professor's words: "I want to see examples—*specific* examples—whatever else you do on this paper." She's told you to write about something that distracts you.

You look aimlessly around the room, your eyes suddenly brighten, and you slap down this sentence:

My roommate distracts me when I try to study.

Now you need some examples. Let's see: she has that tape player going again, she's smacking her gum, and you remember all those dumb questions she asks every few minutes. Here goes:

First Try

Although my roommate is a helpful companion at times, she is a distracting nuisance whenever I try to study. Throughout the evening, her tape player blares in my ears. Even worse, she insists on smacking her gum. She also interrupts me with questions that have nothing to do with homework. At any other time, my roommate is a friend, but while I'm studying, she's my greatest enemy.

"Pretty good," you say. "I think I'll show it to my roommate to see what she—on second thought. . . ."

Now, suppose you're sitting in your room a couple of days later, ego deflated by a bad grade, trying to rewrite that paper. Your examples seemed specific enough to you—record player, gum, questions—but they obviously weren't. You used quick examples when a narrative example might have been more effective.

Instead of presenting a list of things your roommate does to distract you, you could have used a narrative example—a story of something that actually did happen at a particular time and a particular place. In other words, you could have talked about one specific study period. You could have told us not just that her tape player was going, but also what tape she was playing. You could have told us what kind of gum she was chewing. You even could have told us what specific "dumb" questions she asked you. In other words, you could have written this paragraph:

Better Version With a Narrative Example

Although my roommate is a helpful companion at times, she is a distracting nuisance whenever I try to study. Just last Wednesday night, Anna decided to spend the evening playing her "classic" Bob Dylan tapes. While I was trying desperately to integrate a math function, all I could hear was that the answer was somewhere "blowin' in the wind." Even worse, the entire time Dylan was rasping away, Anna accompanied him by smacking and popping her Bazooka bubble gum. I'd finally given up on math and started my struggle with chemistry when she abruptly asked (loudly, of course, so I could hear her over the music), "Do you think any Cokes are left in the Coke machine?" My stomach started rumbling and my throat suddenly felt dry—even drier than the chemistry text I was trying to read. As I dropped the change into the Coke machine, I realized that although Anna is usually a friend, while I'm studying she is my greatest enemy.

Now we can picture you, Anna, and all those distractions. You've told us the *story* (a narrative example) of your evening trying to study, helping us to *see* you and *feel* your frustration. That's communication.

So, remember the secret that all professional writers know: *examples.*

STATISTICS

Examples are an important form of support. They help persuade your readers and make your paper more interesting. Examples alone, though, may not be enough. Sometimes we need something else: *numbers.* Who doesn't love numbers, trust them, believe in them? Give us a statistic we don't suspect is phony, and we are probably convinced immediately. Alison Marks and her trouble with high blood pressure may move us emotionally, but we will more likely be persuaded by a medical report like this:

With Statistics

Recent statistics show convincingly that jogging is saving the lives of many Americans. Of the 12.5 million who jog at least 10 miles a week, 78 percent have a pulse rate and blood pressure reading lower than non-joggers the same age have. Estimates indicate that these joggers can expect to live to an average age of 77—more than three years longer than the average age of their contemporaries. The lesson seems clear, doesn't it?

To be convincing, statistics must be unambiguous. We aren't necessarily alarmed, for example, to hear that 47 of 54 football players were injured in a practice session because we have no way of knowing how serious the injuries were. Perhaps 46 of the players were treated for minor scrapes. We would become alarmed, however, to hear that 47 of 54 football players were hospitalized for at least one night following a practice session. The second statistic defines *injury* more clearly, so it is more convincing than the first.

STATEMENTS BY AUTHORITIES

The last kind of support we'll consider is the statement by an authority, a person who is in a position to know about something. If people we trust tell us something, we just might believe them. But we do so because we trust *them:* their character, their judgment, and their knowledge of the subject.

We would never believe Alison Marks, the architecture student who forgot to take her pills, if she told us that shark hunting is one of the safest sports, but we might listen to her if she told us that patients with high blood pressure should take their medicine. We also might believe the president of the American Medical Association, or a research specialist in high blood pressure, or a cardiologist—people who know what they're talking about.

Who are some people whose unsupported opinions about high blood pressure would not be convincing? We wouldn't trust someone whose character, judgment, or knowledge of the subject is questionable:

- We wouldn't trust the unsupported opinion of the druggist convicted of selling overpriced drugs to people who didn't need them anyway.
- We wouldn't trust the doctor being investigated for gross incompetence by the American Medical Association.
- And we wouldn't trust our roommate, who thinks blood pressure is measured by a thermometer.

The first has doubtful character; the second, doubtful judgment; and the third, doubtful knowledge.

By the way, the use of authority is particularly important when you are presenting statistics. Remember all those impressive figures about people who jog? Guess where the numbers came from. For all you know (and, in fact, for all those statistics are worth), they came from a sixth-grade creative writing class. The point, of course, is that unless the writer tells you the source of the statistics, you don't know whether you should trust them.

Here's a revision of that paragraph showing the use of authorities (in italics), including one citing statistics:

Authority and Statistics

Recent statistics show convincingly that jogging is saving the lives of many Americans. *According to the Congressional Subcommittee on Physical Fitness,* 78 percent of the 12.5 million people who jog at least 10 miles per week have a pulse rate and blood pressure reading lower than non-joggers the same age have. *This committee* estimates that these joggers can expect to live to an average age of 77—more than three years longer than the average age of their contemporaries. *Dr. Hans Corpuscle, chief adviser to the committee,* says that joggers are "the single healthiest group of people in America today." The lesson seems clear, doesn't it?

COMBINED TYPES OF SUPPORT

A paragraph that uses one type of support—such as examples—is often convincing, but many good paragraphs contain several types: a couple of examples and some statistics, or a statement by an authority and an example, and so on.

The following paragraph says that people attend yard sales for entertainment. Can you identify the types of support?

Combined Support

Although you might think that most people attend yard sales for the bargains, the main reason they attend is for the entertainment they find there. For example, consider what happened to my family last summer when we held a yard sale to get rid of some old things before moving to a new place. Many people came, but few bought. Each new carload of people disgorged a new group that would while away an hour or so on a Saturday by caressing the sun-faded curtains, thumbing through ancient *National Geographic* magazines, and carefully considering sweaters eight sizes too small for them or anyone else in their group. Then the group would gather around a folded section of the classified ads and pick the next sale they'd visit. My suspicions about why those people came to our sale were confirmed a few months later by a survey I read in *Psychology Monthly.* The survey showed that seven of ten people who attended yard sales admitted they did so "just for the fun of it." The psychologist who conducted the survey then reached a conclusion I could have told him last summer: "The real bargain that people seek at yard sales, if only subconsciously, is not another frying pan or partially burned plastic spatula, but just a little weekend entertainment."

Notice that the statement by the authority is an effective rewording of the topic sentence, so no separate concluding sentence is necessary for this paragraph.

This paragraph uses all three kinds of support—all invented by the writer. When you are inventing support for exercises, or when you find your support in books or magazines, statistics and statements by authorities are no problem. If, however, you are writing paragraphs based on personal experiences (much like many samples in this section of the book), you will naturally rely heavily on examples. Fortunately, the example is one of the most colorful and convincing kinds of support.

INVENTED SUPPORT

Before you begin the exercises, let's discuss invented support. It greatly simplifies the learning process for you:

- You don't have to struggle to find real support at the same time that you're trying to figure out just what good support is. In fact, you don't have to search any further than your own mind.
- You can be as specific as you like.

But please remember: inventing evidence for a class is just an exercise, a convenience for you and your instructor.

Rules for Inventing Support

Please follow these rules when you invent your support:

- Never write invented support unless your readers know that is what they are reading.
- Never write invented support unless your instructor approves.

If you're careful, you can have fun with your writing. Most of the examples we used in this chapter were invented; you could easily tell that. So try to be imaginative. At the same time, though, be somewhat realistic. Don't, for instance, try to convince us that the Grand Junction School of Cosmetology is noted for its scholarly excellence because it had 13 Rhodes scholars last year. The school may be good, but such an exaggerated figure is bound to raise eyebrows.

PRACTICAL WRITING

Good support has practical value for any kind of writing.

In the last chapter, we showed you a one-paragraph essay on e. e. cummings' poetry. It might have served as a good short answer for a test, but it didn't have enough support to be effective in many other circumstances. So let's add some specific support—quick examples, in this case—to improve it:

I like the individual freedom that comes through in e. e. cummings' poetry. You can see that freedom right away in the lack of both capitalization and normal spacing in his writing. Just look at the way he writes his name—no capital letters! Already he seems like a rebel (as he certainly was). You can also see his emphasis on individual freedom in his content: his poems often deal with the carefreeness of spring and the value of the individual. Consider, for example, the first lines of one of his most famous poems: " 'sweet spring is your/time is my time is our/time for springtime is lovetime/and viva sweet love.' " The value of spring and the individual certainly comes through in those lines, doesn't it? So e. e. cummings' format and content are two ways I see his emphasis on the freedom I like so much.

The examples make a lot of difference in the paragraph's impact, don't they? You can use the same technique—good support—in virtually all of your writing in school, whether you're writing about poetry, computers, or laser optics. All readers need the concreteness that good examples give.

The need for good support also carries over into your writing after you graduate. In fact, a common problem with business writing is that it leaves out the convincing support, relying instead on generalizations.

Suppose you've had some people inspecting your company—the one you're president of. A section of the inspection report provides this generalization with only minimal support:

Poor Support: Only a Generalization

We made many random observations of the workforce. Much of the time, workers were not productive.

"That's interesting," you may say, "but I'm hardly convinced. Where's the proof?" Now let's consider a rewrite, this time adding some statistics:

A Little Better: With Statistics

During June, we made *118 random observations* of the workforce. *At least 78 times,* the workers were not productive.

"Hmmm," you might say. "I wonder what you mean by 'not productive 78 times.' Can you tell me more?"

The inspector can tell more—and should have in the first place. Let's look now at what should have been the first version. This time, it gives not only statistics but some quick examples, too:

Much Better: With Statistics and Quick Examples

During June, we made 118 random observations of the workforce. At least 78 times, the workers were not productive. These are some of our observations:

- After clocking in, about 20 employees routinely left their workshops in company vehicles and went to the cafeteria. Some stayed more than an hour.
- During one five-day period, 9 of 19 employees didn't work a full shift. They arrived as much as 30 minutes late, left as much as 30 minutes early, or both.
- On June 19, about 40 employees returned to the shop area 30 to 60 minutes before the end of the workday.
- On June 20, some employees parked for over 40 minutes behind the library. Others drove company vehicles for long periods without stopping to do any work.

From our inspection, we believe these observations in June are typical of what goes on year round.

The inspectors seem much more convincing now, don't they? So remember: Detailed support is a key to communication at school and on the job.

EXERCISES

A. For each of the topic sentences below, invent (simply make up) a quick example (one sentence), a narrative example (three to five sentences), a statistic (one to two sentences), and a statement by an authority (one to two sentences), as required. Use the sample paragraph on yard sales, which contains invented support, as a model.

1. *Medical technology is a real life saver.*
   Narrative example _Medical technology has taken great leaps over the past century developing medicines such as penecillin and tylynol._

   Statistic _Due to current medical technology the average life is extended by over 15 years._

   Statement by an authority _According to the sergeon general rescent medical technoloy will save 27 lives every ½ hour nationwide._

2. *Home gardening can be rewarding.*
   Statistic _To many home gardening is boring, but it can be very rewarding. For over 80% of home gardeness find in very relaxing._

   Narrative example _Gardening is also a way to relieve stress while doing something that you enjoy._

   Statement by an authority _Many experts agree that gardening can help to reduce blood pressure as well as cholesterol._

3. *Women's [or men's] fashions are changing for the better.*
   Quick example _Chlothes are more comfortable_

than they were in the past.

Quick example Modern materials also provide for longer lasting clothes that dont wear out nearly as quickly.

Statement by an authority Many fashion experts, including Calvin Klein agree that fashion and clothing is headed on the right direction.

B. Follow the same instructions for these topic sentences:

1. *Medical technology is too expensive.*

   Statement by an authority According to govermental medical experts, medical technology for public universities is much too costly.

   Quick example The average medical school can not handle the inflation that is taking place in medical technology.

   Narrative example Most medical schools already account for over 28% of the Minnesota budget, much due to the rise in medical technology.

2. *Home gardening can be dangerous.*

   Narrative example Considering that there are so many unsafe gardening tools, it is very unsafe to garden.

   Statistic Rescent studies have shown that home gardening accidents account for almost 1/4 of all ambulence calls.

   Statement by an authority Experts tell us not to garden at home, but many people still ignore this and garden dangerously.

3. *Women's [or men's] fashions are changing for the worse.*

   Quick example Just look at clothes today, and

compare them to the bell bottoms and dresses of old.

Quick example There is no taste in fashion these days.

Statement by an authority Fashion experts agree that most men would rather be dressed in quality 60's clothing.

C. Invent support for the same topic sentence four different ways:

1. *Today's automobiles are getting safer.*

Statistic There are air bags in almost ~~all~~ 90% of all new cars.

Statistic Anti-lock brakes also provide for safer driving. saving as many as 321 lives a year

Statistic Traction controll helps to reduce accidents in inclimate weather. saving as many as 220 lives in the past 3 years.

2. *Today's automobiles are getting safer.*

Statement by an authority Todays saffey ~~standards~~ experts require air-bags in all new automobiles. for maximum saffey.

Statement by an authority Consumer Reports tells us that anti lock brakes are a must.

3. *Today's automobiles are getting safer.*

Quick example Volvo has just introduced a side air bag for side impact collisroons.

Quick example when deciding which car to ~~buy~~

_____ saftey is a large concern.
_____

Quick example _Many new car buyers look at saftey_
before such things as price, and design.
_____

4. *Today's automobiles are getting safer.*
Narrative example _When driving in snow traction_
controll can mean the difference between
ending up at home safely or in the ditch.
Narrative example _Tougher saftey standars help_
to make newer cars ~~safer~~ safer.
_____

D. Answer these questions about Exercise C:

   1. Which form of support was most effective? Why?
   2. Which form of support was least effective? Why?
   3. What combination of support (statistics, statements by authorities, quick examples, narrative examples) would you recommend for the topic sentence in Exercise C? Why?

E. Look at the paragraph on yard sales at the end of the chapter. Now intentionally destroy the effectiveness of the paragraph: rewrite the good example (the second through the fifth sentences) by making it too general.

F. Now let's reverse Exercise E. Here are some topic sentences followed by examples that are too general. Improve each italicized example by converting the dull generality into a narrative example. You'll need several sentences for each one.

   1. Vacations to other states can be educational. *Last summer, for example, I learned some interesting things.*
   2. Fire can cause tremendous damage. *Once a house burned on my block.*
   3. Books can help young people develop character. *There's one book that really helps a lot.*

G. In Exercises A, B, and C you outlined several paragraphs. Choose the one that interests you the most and use the support you invented to write the paragraph. Appendix A to this book gives you a suggested format. *(over)*

Chris Brewer
English 4th hour
Mr. Hynes
October 20th

Automobile Safety

Todays automobiles are much safer than those of the past. They contain such available options as airbags, anti lock brakes, and traction control. Most new cars are equipped with safety standards to pass the year **2000**. When shopping for a new car most consumers look for **safety**. One magazine, **Consumer Reports**, tells the whole story about automobile safety. Flying is still the safest way to travel, but if you are going to drive todays automobiles are extremely safe.

3 Topic Sentence

Now we move to the first sentence of the one-paragraph essay: the topic sentence.

Think of the topic sentence as the main idea of the paragraph—the point you're making, the generalization that the rest of your paragraph will support.

Writing textbooks try to define the topic sentence with a number of terms: it is the writer's "viewpoint" of the topic, the writer's "judgment" about the topic, the writer's "conviction," the writer's "assertion." Those textbooks are right; the topic sentence is all these things. However, we prefer the term *opinion:* the topic sentence is a precise statement of the opinion you wish to persuade your readers to accept.

Why do we associate a topic sentence with the word *opinion?* An opinion is a judgment that seems true only for the person who believes it. Imagine for a moment that you're telling a friend something you believe—a viewpoint, a judgment, a conviction, an assertion you hold to be true. Your friend replies, "That's just your opinion."

She's not denying that you believe what you say, but she is letting you know that you'll have to persuade her to agree with you. She's placing the burden on you to support your belief so that she can accept the idea as you do.

A similar relationship exists between you (the writer) and your readers. Your topic sentence stands as a statement of your opinion *until* you persuade your audience to accept it fully. Recognizing that the topic sentence is a statement of opinion will help you remember your obligation to support your idea.

Why should the topic sentence be an opinion instead of a fact? If you state your idea and your readers respond with "Oh, yes, that's true" or "That's a fact," what more can you say? Suppose you write this topic sentence:

William Shakespeare wrote *Hamlet.*

In your paragraph, you could discuss Shakespeare or his play, but you wouldn't be trying to convince a reader to accept the topic sentence itself; that Shakespeare wrote

Hamlet is accepted as fact. And statements of fact (or at least what everyone accepts as fact) don't make good topic sentences because they leave the writer nothing important to say. On the other hand, suppose you try this topic sentence:

Francis Bacon wrote *Hamlet.*

Now you've stated an opinion. Unfortunately, hardly anyone believes it. You've crossed into such controversy that you'll really have to work to convince readers to accept your topic-sentence opinion.

Your topic-sentence opinion doesn't need to arouse instant doubt. You don't need to take outrageous stands like these:

Dogs are really man's greatest enemy.

A toupee is better than real hair.

In fact, most good topic sentences generate neither instant acceptance nor instant doubt. Usually, readers have not formed their own judgments, and they're willing to accept yours if you can persuade them. For example, consider this topic sentence:

Today's toupees are so well made that they look like a person's own hair.

The writer is stating what he believes to be fact. Although readers have no reason to doubt him, they are not obliged to believe him either. They probably will agree with what he says once he provides specific support for his opinion. And it *is* his opinion—until he persuades readers to accept it as fully as he does.

When you write a one-paragraph essay, you'll begin with a topic sentence and follow it with specific support (examples, statistics, or authoritative statements). If you structure the topic sentence well and then support it well with specifics, you'll persuade your readers to accept your idea fully. The rest of this chapter shows you how to write a good topic sentence.

A Good Topic Sentence

A good topic sentence has two parts:

- a *limited* subject
- a *precise opinion* about that subject.

LIMITING THE SUBJECT

The first step in writing a good topic sentence is to choose a subject limited enough to support in a single paragraph. If you try to support a large subject in a one-paragraph essay, your argument is not likely to be convincing: your subject will probably demand more support than you can develop in one paragraph. Thus, limiting the subject is the first step toward writing a good topic sentence.

Let's look at a sample. Suppose you begin with a general subject: advertising. Since the topic is obviously too large for a one-paragraph essay, you must limit it. Of the many types of advertisement (television, radio, newspaper, billboard, and the like), you choose one—for instance, magazine advertising.

As you glance at the advertisements in your favorite magazine, three attract your attention. In one advertisement, you see a scantily clad woman holding a tape recorder she wants you to buy. In another, a muscular man is looking manfully at a bottle of cologne. And in a third ad, a couple embrace in delight as they hold cigarettes in their free hands. You see a common element in each sales pitch: the advertisers use sex appeal to make you want the things you see before you. In this way, you limit the subject from *advertising* to *magazine advertising* to *sex appeal in magazine advertising.*

Consider the process you just went through. You might have noticed the lack of color in the tape-recorder advertisement, the large amount of space wasted in the cologne ad, or the small print that obscures the Surgeon General's warning in the cigarette advertisement. Instead, you focused your attention on sex appeal in the ads, thereby limiting the subject.

STATING THE PRECISE OPINION

The second part of the topic sentence tells your opinion about the limited subject. Although limiting the subject is a step toward precision, an opinion about even a limited subject will remain vague unless you tell your readers what your idea is exactly.

The precise-opinion part of the topic sentence is a word or phrase that makes a judgment, such as *dangerous* or *exciting.* But a warning is necessary here, for not all judgment words will express precise opinions. Words like *interesting, nice, good,* or *bad* seem to take a stand but remain vague. What do you really mean when you say something is "interesting"? What have you said about a person you call "nice"? Such vague judgments make imprecise opinions. On the other hand, precise judgments combine with a subject to define an opinion about the subject.

Again, let's apply this theory to our sample case, sex appeal in magazine advertising. So what if advertisers support sales with sex appeal?

You look again at the ads that will support your argument only to find another common element: sex appeal isn't really related to the items for sale. The ads held your attention because sex appeal was connected to nonsexual items. You are irritated because the advertisers are trying to manipulate your senses so that you will buy whatever they advertise. Thus, you are ready to state precisely your opinion about sex appeal in these three advertisements: it is *irrelevant.*

Again, consider the process you used. You had to make a judgment about sex appeal in the advertising; you had to establish your precise opinion about the subject. Because you didn't like the sex appeal in the ads, you might have said that the sex appeal was bad. But what would *bad* mean? Did the sex appeal disgust you? Did it appeal to your prurient interests in a manner not consistent with community standards (whatever that means)? Did the sex appeal in the ads merely irritate you? Just what was *bad* about it?

When, instead, you made the *precise* judgment that sex appeal in some magazine advertisements is irrelevant to the product, you established your exact stand on the subject.

WRITING THE TOPIC SENTENCE

Once you have limited the subject and have decided precisely your opinion about it, you have formed the two basic parts of the topic sentence: a *limited subject* and a *precise opinion* about that subject. You can easily structure a topic sentence by stating the precise opinion in some form after the sentence's subject, as in the following:

For me, dieting is futile.

Dieting, the subject of the sentence, is the limited subject, and *futile,* which follows, is the precise opinion about it.

Now we can write the topic sentence for the paragraph on sex appeal in magazine advertisements.

The sex appeal in many magazine advertisements is irrelevant.

We can see, then, that the basic pattern for the topic sentence is "*limited subject* is *precise opinion.*" Consider these examples:

Arcade video games are challenging.

Restoring old houses is rewarding.

In the first sentence, *arcade video games* is the limited subject and *challenging* is the precise opinion. In the second, you intend to persuade the readers that *restoring old houses* (the limited subject) is *rewarding* (the precise opinion).

REFINING THE TOPIC SENTENCE

Even though this pattern is basic for a topic sentence, you aren't restricted to it. Perhaps the model seems too mechanical. You can easily convert the model to a slightly more sophisticated form. Look at the following topic sentence in the basic pattern:

Overpackaging of supermarket items is seriously wasteful of natural resources.

Here is the same idea in another form:

Overpackaging of supermarket items seriously wastes natural resources.

Notice that the precise opinion *wasteful* (the basic pattern) became the verb *wastes* in the rewritten sentence. Now look at a topic sentence from an earlier chapter:

Even though I have never really lived there, going to my grandmother's farm always seems like coming home.

That sentence almost exactly follows our basic model:

Going to my grandmother's farm is like coming home.

In another topic sentence we may say this:

Hitchhiking is dangerous.

But we may also state the idea more imaginatively:

Hitchhiking has proved to be the last ride for many people.

The important point is that refined topic sentences, such as those above, always can be converted to the basic model: "*limited subject* is *precise opinion.*" When you write a topic-sentence form beyond the model, take a moment to make sure that you still can convert it to the two basic parts.

Whatever the pattern of the topic sentences, the result is the same. When you have limited your subject and precisely defined your opinion about it, you have formed the necessary parts of the topic sentence. You have created an assertion that will guide both you and your readers through the supporting material of the paragraph.

PRACTICAL WRITING

As we discussed in Chapter 1, topic sentences are useful beyond this course. Did the topic sentence about e. e. cummings follow the basic model?

I like the individual freedom that comes through in e. e. cummings' poetry.

No—but we can convert it to the basic model:

The poetry of e. e. cummings is about individual freedom.

So, starting with a good topic sentence can be useful in a college paper about literature. In fact, a good topic sentence is a great start for just about any paper you write on any subject. Think of another college subject, and you'll quickly see that there's usually a need to clearly express your idea—your opinion—about something in that subject. For example:

- *History.* What were the main causes of the Civil War?
- *Astronomy.* What is the probable composition of the Great Red Spot on Jupiter?
- *Chemistry.* What is the most efficient way to identify an unknown substance?
- *Computer science.* What is the best way to network computers over a wide area?

A topic sentence gives focus to your paper, for your reader and for you. Understanding the value of topic sentences should be of immense value to you as a communicator.

EXERCISES

A. Place a check mark by the sentences that would not make good topic sentences because they don't state opinions or because the opinions aren't precise.

   ✓ 1. Spiders have eight legs.

      2. Spiders are beneficial to the environment.

   ✓ 3. Outdoor carpeting is great.

      4. Outdoor carpeting has significant drawbacks.

   ✓ 5. According to the National Weather Service, eight inches of snow fell overnight.

      6. The snowfall turned the city's streets into a nightmare for commuters.

      7. Mirrors tell the truth.

   ✓ 8. Mirrors are nice.

   ✓ 9. Door-to-door salesmen didn't come here at all last month.

      10. Mule deer must be hardy to survive Colorado winters.

B. For these topic sentences, underline the subject once and the opinion twice. Also, circle any subjects that aren't limited enough and any opinions that aren't precise enough.

1. The closet is full.
2. The closet has an unusual design.
3. Chocolate is good.
4. Fatty foods can cause health problems.
5. Many airports have high-tech features.
6. Today's golfers are extraordinary athletes.
7. Summer vacations are wonderful.
8. Insecticides can be harmful to human beings.

9. Firefighters' tactics are based on scientific research.
10. Soccer is great.

C. Limit the general subjects below and then state a precise opinion about each limited subject.

Example:

General subject traveling

Hitchhiking	is/are	a danger to us
(limited subject)		(precise opinion)

1. **General subject** diseases

diabetes	is/are	troublesome
(limited subject)		(precise opinion)

2. **General subject** motor vehicles

motercycles	is/are	exciting
(limited subject)		(precise opinion)

3. **General subject** insects

misquitos	is/are	a bother
(limited subject)		(precise opinion)

4. **General subject** weapons

guns	is/are	necessary
(limited subject)		(precise opinion)

5. **General subject** clothing

hats	is/are	interesting
(limited subject)		(precise opinion)

6. **General subject** food

pasta	is/are	lovely
(limited subject)		(precise opinion)

Breakfast

Breakfast is usually my poorest meal of the day. In the morning I am usually not hungry so I skip breakfast. Breakfast cereal is too expensive. I am short of time in the morning so I do not eat breakfast. Hot cereal is high in salt. Breakfast is my poorest meal of the day because it is a small meal. Therefore, breakfast is my poorest meal of the day.

4 Unity

You know that a topic sentence presents a precise opinion about a limited subject. Now we can go to the next step in good writing: unity.

Think about the word *unity* for a moment. It means *oneness,* doesn't it? So for a paragraph to have unity, it must have *oneness.* More specifically, each idea in the paragraph should clearly support the "one main point," the topic sentence. Normally there shouldn't be any ideas that are irrelevant, that don't support the point of the paragraph.

If, for example, you're writing about the dullest class you ever took, you would destroy the unity by talking about the fascinating lectures and exciting field trips. Or if you want to show that your mynah bird is an ideal pet, the friendliness of the boa constrictor is off the subject and, therefore, irrelevant. In other words, everything you say in a paragraph must support your paragraph.

Can you find the two places in this next paragraph where the writer loses her sense of unity?

Poor Unity

My most frustrating job was cooking for the dorm cafeteria during my freshman year. No matter how hard I tried, I never could cook what the menu said because the food company always delivered the wrong food or brought it late. I also was frustrated because I had trouble estimating how much food to cook. Many times we ran short of hamburgers or had to throw away pounds and pounds of french fries. Sometimes we ate the extra french fries, though, and we'd sit around, joking and having a good time. The worst thing, however, was the condition of my clothes after the meal was over. Even if I hadn't spilled anything (and I usually had spilled spaghetti or something worse), my clothes smelled awful. I'd want to go home to change before going anyplace else. Some of the other students who didn't work in the cafeteria also spilled food and had to change, too. No wonder, then, I thought cooking for the dorm cafeteria was frustrating.

Did you find the two sentences that violate the unity of the paragraph? The first is about eating french fries and having a good time; the second is about other students spilling food on themselves and having to change clothes. Neither of those sentences has anything to do with the main topic of the paragraph: working in the cafeteria is *a frustrating job for you.* Here's a diagram showing what we mean:

Topic Sentence
My job as cook was frustrating.

Support
Wrong food was delivered.

Support
I had trouble estimating amounts.

Support
Had fun eating extra food.

Support
My clothes were messy.

Support
Other students changed clothes, too.

Conclusion
Therefore, my job as cook was frustrating.

Now let's fix the unity of that paragraph:

Good Unity

My most frustrating job was cooking for the dorm cafeteria during my freshman year. No matter how hard I tried, I never could cook what the menu said because the food company always delivered the wrong food or brought it late. I also was frustrated because I had trouble estimating how much food to cook—many times we ran short of hamburgers or had to throw away pounds and pounds of french fries. The worst thing, however, was the condition of my clothes after the meal was over. Even if I hadn't spilled anything (and I usually had spilled spaghetti or something worse), my clothes smelled awful. I'd want to go home to change before going anyplace else. No wonder, then, I thought cooking for the dorm cafeteria was frustrating.

Note the difference: the writer sticks to the subject. All the examples help show that being a cook for the dorm cafeteria was frustrating. A diagram of this paragraph looks unified, showing that all the blocks fit:

> **Topic Sentence**
> My job as cook was frustrating.
>
> **Support**
> Wrong food was delivered.
>
> **Support**
> I had trouble estimating amounts.
>
> **Support**
> My clothes were messy.
>
> **Conclusion**
> Therefore, my job as cook was frustrating.

As you can see, the idea of unity is really simple: stick to the point. Don't be led astray by a word or idea in one of your sentences the way the writer was in the first paragraph. Make sure everything in your paragraph belongs there. That way, your reader won't be distracted—or worse, confused.

EXERCISES

A. Read these paragraphs and underline the precise opinion in the topic sentence. Then identify those sentences that don't help support the precise opinion.

(1) Preparing a house for sale is exhausting work. (2) First, you have to repaint everything—inside and out. (3) Then you have to clean the carpets and floors. (4) Sometimes you find neat things in the house you haven't seen for years! (5) And, last, you have to get the yard completely in shape. (6) So getting a house ready for sale really is tiring.

The irrelevant sentence is ___(4)_____.

(1) Albert Bierstadt was a pioneer as a landscape painter. (2) He desired to paint unusual places so much that he left his home in Europe—in the middle of the 19th century—and moved to the United States. (3) He painted mainly traditional landscapes before he left Europe. (4) He was also a pioneer in that he traveled to the far west of the United States to do his most famous paintings: large pictures of Yosemite. (5) So Albert Bierstadt's drive to paint the unusual made him a pioneer.

The irrelevant sentence is ___(3)_____.

(1) Walt Disney was a <u>creative</u> genius. (2) He created the first animated film with talking characters, the first color animated film, and the first full-length animated film. (3) Surprisingly, he wasn't much of a cartoonist himself. (4) Disney also created the idea of theme parks—including Disneyland and Disney World. (5) He earned a lot of money from his ideas. (6) He really was a very creative person.

The irrelevant sentences are _____(3)_____ and _____(5)_____.

B. In the following examples, provide unified support for the topic sentence. If you need to, invent specific details for your support.

1.

> Topic Sentence
> Maps use colors well.
>   Support for dimensions
>   Support representations
>   Support scales.
> Reworded Topic Sentence
> Therefore, maps use colors well.

2.

> Topic Sentence
> Classrooms need comfortable furniture.
>   Support Children need to rest.
>   Support People need to be comfortable.
>   Support I like to be comfi.
> Reworded Topic Sentence
> Therefore, classrooms need comfortable furniture.

3.

> Topic Sentence
> Breakfast is usually my poorest meal.
>   Support I have no time.
>   Support It is a small meal.
>   Support I am not hungry.
> Reworded Topic Sentence
> Therefore, breakfast is usually my poorest meal.

C. Write a paragraph on one of the topic sentences in Exercise B; use your invented support. Add two irrelevant sentences to destroy the paragraph's unity and underline them.

(Page 33)
(back)

5 Coherence

A one-paragraph essay needs more than unity. It also must have coherence.

The best way to define *coherence* is to look at its opposite: *incoherence*. If a woman runs into a room screaming "Fire! Dog! House!" we call her incoherent. Does she mean that a dog is on fire in the house? Or that the house is on fire with the dog inside? Or that a doghouse is on fire? We don't know. Although the woman apparently has some very important ideas she wishes desperately to communicate, she has left out the essential links of thought. Coherence requires including those links.

This chapter discusses three important ways to achieve coherence in the one-paragraph essay:

- explanation of the support
- reminders of the opinion in the topic sentence
- transitions

These important techniques will help your readers move smoothly from idea to idea within your paragraph. Then, when your doghouse catches on fire, you'll know exactly how to call for help.

EXPLANATION OF THE SUPPORT

Don't assume that your readers are specially gifted people able to read minds. You must not only present support to readers but also explain how it is related to the topic sentence. In other words, you must link your support—clearly and unambiguously—to the topic sentence. The author of the following paragraph does not try to explain his support at all, apparently hoping that his readers are clairvoyant:

First Try

In the early morning, I am easily annoyed by my roommate. I have to shut the ice-covered windows. A white tornado of dandruff swirls around the room. A mass of smoke from cigarettes hovers near the door. No wonder I find my roommate annoying.

No wonder, indeed! The paragraph is incoherent because the author has failed to explain how his support relates to the topic sentence. Does he mean that his roommate is annoying because he does not close the window in the morning? Or is he annoying because he opens the window every night, even in winter, thus causing the writer to be cold in the morning? And who has dandruff, and who smokes? Is it the roommate, or is it the author, who is upset because the roommate does not understand? Readers could conclude that the author is doing the best he can to get rid of the dandruff and that he is smoking heavily only because he is trying to distract himself after waking up every morning in a cold room.

By being incomplete, by not explaining the support fully, the paragraph demands too much of readers. Let's guess what the writer really meant and then revise the paragraph to add coherence.

Second Try

In the early morning, I am easily annoyed by my roommate. I have to shut the ice-covered windows *that John, my roommate, insists on opening every night, even during the winter.* A white tornado swirling around the room *shows me that his dandruff problem is still in full force.* A mass of smoke *from John's pack-a-day habit* hovers near the door. No wonder I find my roommate annoying.

We have now explained that John, the roommate, is guilty of the indiscretions. The coherence is improved greatly, but the paragraph still needs work.

REMINDERS OF THE OPINION IN THE TOPIC SENTENCE

In the preceding section, we learned not to assume that readers can read minds. In this section, however, we will make an assumption about readers: Readers, like all of us, prefer being mentally lazy. They don't like remembering too much at once. While they are reading the support, they like occasional reminders of the opinion in the topic sentence so that they will remember why they are reading that support.

We can remind them of the opinion in the topic sentence with either of two techniques at the beginning of each item of support:

- We can repeat the exact words of the opinion.
- We can use other words that suggest the opinion.

In the sample paragraph about the roommate, we can use the word *annoy* in presenting each example, or we can use words such as *disgusted* or *choking on stale smoke,* which *suggest* annoyance. Notice the reminders in the revised paragraph:

Third Try

In the early morning, I am easily annoyed by my roommate. I *am annoyed* each time I have to shut the ice-covered windows that John, my roommate, insists on opening every night, even during the winter. A *disgusting* white tornado swirling around the room shows me that his dandruff problem is still in full force. A *choking mass of stale smoke* from John's pack-a-day habit hovers near the door. No wonder I find my roommate annoying.

By reminding the readers that each example presents something annoying, the paragraph becomes more coherent.

TRANSITIONS

Each example in the sample paragraph now has a clear explanation of the support and a reminder of the opinion in the topic sentence, but the paragraph is still rough. It moves like a train with square wheels, clunking along abruptly from idea to idea. To help the paragraph move more smoothly, we must add transitions.

Transitions are like road signs that tell readers where they are going. If you live in Louisville and wish to drive north to Indianapolis, you don't want to stop to ask people to find out you are on the right road. You would rather have road signs. Similarly, readers don't want to run into an example that slows them because they don't understand how it relates to the previous example or, worse yet, how it relates to the topic sentence.

In a paragraph, the road sign could be *however* to tell readers that the next idea is going to contrast with the one just presented; or it could be *also* to tell readers that another idea like the preceding one is about to be presented; or it could be *therefore* to tell readers to prepare for a conclusion.

These and other transitions will keep your Indianapolis-bound driver from losing valuable time because he has to stop, or, if he takes a chance and presses on, from arriving nowhere, which is where he may end his trip in a paragraph without transitions.

Common Transitions

To add an idea: *also, and, another, equally important, finally, furthermore, in addition, last, likewise, moreover, most important, next, second, third*

To give an example: *as a case in point, consider. . . , for example, for instance, as an illustration*

To make a contrast: *and yet, but, however, instead, nevertheless, nonetheless, on the contrary, on the other hand, still*

To begin a conclusion: *as a result, clearly, hence, in conclusion, no wonder, obviously, then, therefore, thus*

A paragraph must have transitions, but where should you place them?

CRITICAL LOCATIONS FOR TRANSITIONS

Topic sentence

Transition ———————————————▶

Specific support

Transition ———————————————▶

Specific support

Transition ———————————————▶

Specific support

Transition ———————————————▶

Reworded topic sentence

Sometimes you will find that no transition is necessary between the topic sentence and the first item of specific support because the second sentence of the paragraph is so obviously an example that a transitional expression seems too mechanical. For instance, you might be able to leave out the first transition in this final revision of the sample paragraph about the roommate. The remaining transitions, however, are all desirable.

Final Version

In the early morning, I am easily annoyed by my roommate. *For example,* I am annoyed each time I have to shut the ice-covered windows that John, my roommate, insists on opening every night, even during the winter. I am *also* disgusted by a white tornado swirling around the room, which shows me that his dandruff problem is still in full force. *Most bothersome, though,* is the choking mass of stale smoke from John's pack-a-day habit that hovers near the door. *No wonder* I find my roommate annoying.

Our sample paragraph is finally coherent. We have:

- explained the support
- reminded the reader frequently of the opinion in the topic sentence
- added transitions at the critical locations

You're so familiar with the above paragraph by now, and it's so simple, you may believe the transitions aren't really necessary. Perhaps you're right. But what if you read a paragraph that begins like this?

Poor Coherence

If you've ever bought a pomegranate, you probably know that it's one of the most difficult foods to eat. The juice is delicious and a beautiful ruby color. It drips everywhere, staining whatever it hits. The bitter, inedible pulp seems impossible to avoid. . . .

By now, you're probably lost. If the writer has trouble eating a pomegranate, then why start by telling us how delicious and beautiful it is? The writer knows why, but readers don't because there aren't any transitions. Let's put them in:

Revised for Effective Coherence

> If you've ever bought a pomegranate, you probably know that it's one of the most difficult foods to eat. *Although* the juice is delicious and a beautiful ruby color, it *unfortunately* drips everywhere, staining whatever it hits. *Also frustrating,* the bitter, inedible pulp seems impossible to avoid. . . .

The transitions (and the reminder *frustrating*) make the paragraph easy to understand the first time through.

Good writing shouldn't be an IQ test or a guessing game for readers, so let them know what you're thinking as your ideas shift directions. For now, use the three techniques demonstrated in this chapter, even if they seem mechanical. As you gain experience as a writer, you will learn more subtle ways to link your ideas to each other and to the topic sentence. Your immediate goal now, though, is to communicate coherently with your readers.

Three Techniques for Coherence

- explanation of the support
- reminder of the opinion in the topic sentence
- transitions

EXERCISES

A. Outline this paragraph and indicate the transitions by filling in the blanks below. Merely summarize the topic sentence, the support, and the reworded topic sentence rather than writing them in full.

> A significant change I have noticed in myself since entering college is a fear of mathematics. The mere sight of a 350-page math text, for instance, causes a cold shiver to run the length of my spine. As I cautiously open the front cover of the text, a myriad of complex formulas springs at me, quickly eliminating any trace of confidence I may have had. My dread of math is also strengthened each time I enter the small, dismal classroom. I can find no consolation in watching my classmates cringe behind open briefcases as they prepare to do battle with a common enemy capable of engulfing us all in a blanket of confusion. Finally, my greatest fears are realized as my instructor self-consciously adjusts his glasses and admits that he majored in English and never truly mastered, or even understood, calculus. Then I suddenly realize that the Cartesian plane has snared me in its nightmarish world for another semester.

Topic sentence _____

Transition _____

Specific support_____

Transition _____

Specific support_____

Transition _____

Specific support_____

Transition _____

Reworded topic sentence _____

The opinion the above paragraph demonstrates is *fear.* Circle all *reminders* of that opinion in the paragraph; that is, circle all words that either repeat the word or suggest the meaning of *fear.*

B. Outline this paragraph and show the transitions by filling in the blanks. Again, simply summarize the topic sentence, the support, and the reworded topic sentence rather than writing them in full.

     Since becoming a college student, I have learned many ways to study faster than I did in high school. As an example, I discovered that spending three-fourths of my study time sprawled across a desk in deep slumber has helped me find a sudden aptitude for instantly memorizing five chapters of chemistry the period before a test. Another way I have developed my study skills is reading magazines at the bookstore on free afternoons. When my classmates (and occasionally the professors) ask me to justify this practice, I calmly tell them that the rate at which I study is sure to increase if I study only in the evenings. But by far my most useful device for sharpening my study habits is my custom of writing my girlfriend during finals. What else could teach me to study an entire semester's material in only an hour and a half? So, since becoming a college student, I have developed many ways to study far faster than I ever had before.

Topic sentence _____

Transition _____

Specific support_____

Transition _____

Specific support_____

Transition _____

Specific support_____

Transition _____

Reworded topic sentence _____

The opinion in the above paragraph is *study faster.* Circle all reminder words that either repeat the phrase or suggest the meaning of *study faster.*

C. Using another paragraph in this book assigned by your instructor, underline all the transitions and circle all the reminders.

D. Rewrite this paragraph, adding transitions and reminders of the opinion in the topic sentence. You also may need to add some support to explain fully the relationship of the support to the topic sentence.

> The city of Stockholm is among the loveliest in the world. Slum districts, prevalent in almost all large cities, are nearly nonexistent in Stockholm, having been replaced by government housing. The citizens are careful to dispose of their litter properly and to pick up litter other people may have dropped. Stockholm has a unique layout: it is built on twenty-three islands. Water winds throughout the city. The beauty of Stockholm makes it one of the most alluring cities in the world.

E. Follow the same instructions as for Exercise D:

> Overnight camping can be disenchanting if you are a novice. Whether you hike in (carrying pounds and pounds of food and equipment on your back) or whether you drive (with all the monotony car trips are infamous for), you will probably be tired once you are ready to set up your camp. When you settle back to admire the stars at the end of the day, you will probably be besieged by bugs—mosquitoes and sand flies seem to prefer making their homes in scenic places. When you go to bed, you may find that your sleeping bag, especially if you have a cheap one, is quite uncomfortable. Camping for newcomers can be quite different from a purely romantic adventure.

F. Write a paragraph that convinces readers that *something* (not some*one*) has a particular characteristic. On the final copy, underline all the transitions and circle all the reminders. Make sure you have met the other requirement for coherence by explaining your support fully. (The paragraph in Chapter 1 on the Boundary Waters Canoe Area could have been a response to this exercise.)

G. Write a paragraph that convinces readers of one significant way in which a friend of yours has changed. Use examples from your experience with that person as support. On the final copy, underline all the transitions and circle all the reminders. Make sure you have met the other requirement for coherence by explaining your support fully.

H. Write a paragraph that convinces readers of one important characteristic you like your friends to have. Use examples from your experience as support. On your final copy, underline all the transitions and circle all the reminders. Make sure you have met the other requirement for coherence by explaining your support fully.

I. Think about the other courses you're taking now. Write a paragraph that describes one intriguing idea from one of those courses. On your final copy, underline all the transitions and circle all the reminders. Make sure you have met the other requirement for coherence by explaining your support fully.

J. If you've held a job, try this exercise: Describe one important characteristic that workers need at the place you work (or worked)—patience? stubbornness? endurance? intelligence? something else? On your final copy, underline all the transitions and circle all the reminders. Make sure you have met the other requirement for coherence by explaining your support fully.

6 Tips on the Writing Process

So far, we've concentrated on what the final *product* of your writing should look like—a paragraph with a topic sentence, good support, unity, and coherence.

This chapter will give you a few tips on the *process* for getting there. To do that, we'll answer two questions:

- What is the writing process?
- What is the role of computers in that process?

THE WRITING PROCESS

The traditional way to think about the writing process is to divide it into three parts: *prewriting, writing,* and *rewriting.* Most teachers today think the process is more complicated than that, and we certainly agree with them. Nevertheless, these three parts give us a convenient way to talk about the process in general.

PREWRITING

Prewriting is the process of gathering your thoughts and preparing to write. You choose your topic, refine it, and consider ways of supporting it. You don't have to think your way through the entire paper. In fact, most writers have trouble envisioning the completed paper—even only a one-paragraph essay—before the pencil hits the page. That's why writers do a little writing as part of the prewriting process.

Try some of these strategies to help with your prewriting:

- If you have no idea of a topic, and your instructor hasn't given you one, browse through some popular magazines. Just let your mind wander. You may write about something that isn't even in the magazines, but your browsing will have triggered ideas for you. Even better, browse through an encyclopedia.

- If you still don't have a good topic, talk to your friends. Tell them about your paper and start a general discussion. You might be surprised by how a random conversation can get your mind going in the right direction.
- Once you have a general topic, try refining it into a good topic sentence (remember: a limited subject and a precise opinion). We suggest you actually write it down and then play around with it until it's just right.

Now you need the support. One technique for getting good support—especially if the topic is about your personal experiences or uses invented material—is to brainstorm on paper. That is, spend a few minutes jotting down whatever comes to mind. Don't be judgmental at this point ("That doesn't make sense at all!"). Just let your thoughts flow. When you're through, look at what you have written. Often you'll find something useful.

Another way to get good support is to try a little free writing. That is, just start writing. Don't stop to think and don't stop writing. Make yourself write for perhaps five minutes, saying whatever comes to mind. If you are like us, a lot of absolute nonsense will appear on your page. But buried in that nonsense may well be a few nuggets that will become the actual support in your paper.

These techniques are all standard fare in the writing game—well known and often used. They take a little time, but only a little. And that small investment gets your brain in gear, ready to write.

WRITING

So, you have come up with your ideas. Now is the time to get them on paper. If you already have some on paper from free writing or brainstorming, it's time to bring law and order to the page.

Here are some strategies for the writing stage:

- Make an outline. You don't need a formal one for your one-paragraph essay, but you should have at least an informal one jotted down.
- Next, remind yourself of the rules for the one-paragraph essay so you'll meet the requirements of your assignment.
- Then . . . just start writing. Don't worry about errors and spelling—you can take care of them later. Just try to get the whole thing on paper, warts and all. Your goal here is to achieve a good flow of ideas. Try to write fairly quickly.
- Stop if your ideas aren't working at all, as any further writing will just waste your time. Instead, try some of the techniques of prewriting again. (Or take a break. Not too long, though!)

When you have a complete draft, breathe a sigh of relief. You have more work to do, but the hard part is finished.

REWRITING

In the writing stage, you put a premium on speed—getting everything down on paper. In the rewriting stage, the premium is on care. Few people slap down an "A" paper in one burst of creative effort. Most need to add some polish.

Here are some suggestions:

- First, check for the larger matters: Does your writing make sense? Does it follow the requirements for the one-paragraph essay? Is it unified? Coherent? Interesting?

- Then check for the smaller matters: Have you spelled the words correctly? Is your punctuation correct? Do your word choices seem good? These matters are small, but they can get big fast.

- Read your paper aloud. Don't read silently. Actually say the words. It's amazing how awkward phrases, missing ideas, and poor sentence structure stand out when you actually hear the words. We read this entire book out loud several times when we prepared the first edition. And we're glad we did!

- Finally, set your writing aside. Do something else. Then come back to it. Your mind will be cleared of all the ideas you had when writing, and now you can see your writing through the eyes of someone else—or at least have a more objective view of what you wrote. Then, add the final polish that turns the funny-looking rock into a real gem.

We began by saying the writing process is more complicated than simply prewriting, writing, and rewriting. That's true. The process often loops back and forth. For example, while you're in the writing stage, you might get stuck. That's a good time to head back for a few minutes in the prewriting stage.

Or you might do part of your paper and then set it aside. Before going on with more writing, you might begin (as we often do) by doing a little rewriting. That helps you ease into the actual writing by refamiliarizing yourself with what you've done.

THE ROLE OF COMPUTERS

By all means—if at all possible—use a computer! If you already use one, you know what we mean. And if you don't use one, you can't really guess how beneficial it can be. You would do well to actually try one—you'll see the benefit immediately.

The computer (and we include memory typewriters that act like computers) is effective at all stages of the writing process:

- *Prewriting.* Remember the writing we suggested you do as part of this process—free writing and brainstorming? It's all so easy with a computer. With paper and pencil (or an old typewriter), you soon end up with a page that's more like hieroglyphics than English—and just as hard to decipher. And the physical fatigue—"writer's cramp"—can make you unconsciously decide to take a break and do something less productive but more relaxing.

- *Writing.* The computer shines here. With an old-style typewriter, you have to worry about the ends of lines and making mistakes. With a computer, you don't need to care about those things, so you can concentrate fully on the task at hand: getting good ideas on paper. As a result, you usually get words on paper much faster.

- *Rewriting.* The computer is, of course, famous for what it can do at this stage. Making changes is no longer something to dread, as it used to be in the days of ordinary typewriters. You can make changes with ease. And spelling checkers can help even good spellers who make typos while speeding through the writing stage of the process. Grammar checkers, which are especially useful in the business world, are becoming more useful for college writing.

Try an Experiment

As an experiment, try writing one of your papers using a computer. We ask our students to try at least one paper during the semester using a computer in our computer lab. At the end of the course, we then ask what happened. Almost without exception, students report that learning to write on a computer was one of the most important steps they've taken as a writer.

EXERCISE

Write your next paper using a computer. Use it for all stages of the writing process: prewriting, writing, and rewriting.

The One-Paragraph Essay (Stage II)

In this section you'll learn a slightly more sophisticated way to organize a one-paragraph essay. You'll see later in the book that this new type of paragraph is actually a stepping-stone to larger themes and research papers. Once you learn how to write a Stage II paragraph, the full-length essay will be simple for you to learn.

Overview of the One-Paragraph Essay (Stage II)

So how are Stage I and Stage II paragraphs different from each other? While a Stage I paragraph has only one opinion, the Stage II paragraph has more than one:

- the opinion in the topic sentence (which is the main opinion)
- and the opinions in the subtopic sentences (these opinions help support the main opinion in the topic sentence)

Subtopic sentences are generalizations *within* the paragraph—and they help support the overall generalization: the topic sentence.

Let's look at an example. Here's a Stage II paragraph (we've italicized the subtopic sentences):

A Stage II Paragraph

Old-style computer manuals can be really frustrating to use. *For one thing, the indexes are usually frustrating because they are hard to decipher.* I remember when I was trying to find out how to print my paper: I tried to find the word *print* in the index. Believe it or not, the word wasn't even there. I finally asked the person next to me, who said the term for printing in that manual isn't *print,* instead, it's *concatenate.* No wonder I had trouble! *Aside from the indexes, the general quality of writing in the manuals themselves is frustrating.* The manual for my old spreadsheet program doesn't have any diagrams at all, asking me to visualize what a spreadsheet looks like. And my old word processing manual assumes I know as much as the software developers do. As you can tell, I think older computer manuals were user-unfriendly.

See how the subtopic sentences support the topic sentence? Now let's look at an outline of that paragraph:

Topic sentence Older computer manuals are frustrating.
    Subtopic sentence Indexes are hard to use.
        Specific support One index didn't use the word *print.*
    Subtopic sentence General quality of writing is poor.
        Specific support Spreadsheet program has no diagrams.
        Specific support Word processing program assumes too much.
Reworded topic sentence Older computer manuals needed work.

Notice that each subtopic sentence has the kind of specific support we discussed in Chapter 2. We use examples here (a narrative example for the first subtopic sentence and two quick examples for the second one). But statistics and statements by authorities would do as well.

Notice also that if you remove the subtopic sentences above, you would have a Stage I paragraph. Sometimes the relationship between Stage I and Stage II paragraphs is not so simple. You could add subtopic sentences to the Boundary Waters Canoe Area paragraph in Chapter 1, but you would end up with a worse paragraph because the support is so meager—the paragraph would have more topic and subtopic sentences than support sentences.

Also, some Stage I paragraphs cannot become Stage II paragraphs because they were never divided into subtopic ideas. The sample paragraphs about fearing mathematics and learning to study faster in the exercises for Chapter 5, for example, do not have subtopic ideas, so you could not easily convert them into Stage II paragraphs.

Let's look now at a general model of the Stage II paragraph:

MODEL OF THE STAGE II PARAGRAPH

Topic sentence
    Subtopic sentence
        Specific support
        Specific support
    Subtopic sentence
        Specific support
        Specific support
Reworded topic sentence

This outline is not rigid, of course. Your Stage II paragraph may have several subtopic sentences, and each subtopic sentence may have several items of support, depending on the subject and your approach to it. Consider this Stage II paragraph, for example:

Another Stage II Paragraph

Although apparently just an assortment of oddities from the National Museum of American History, a special exhibit called "The Nation's Attic" struck me as a tribute to American ingenuity. *One part of the exhibit demonstrated the ingenious ways Americans have found to shape everyday items.* For instance, a large collection of sewing accessories—hundreds of thimbles, needle cases, sewing cases, and pincushions—showed how simple things could be made more useful, more beautiful, or more entertaining. *More imaginative, though, were the things made apparently just because Americans wanted to accept the challenge of making them.* There was an intricate model of the U.S. Capitol constructed entirely of glass rods. Someone else had engraved the Lord's Prayer on a single grain of rice. And a group of chemical engineers even had managed to do the proverbial "undoable": they actually had created a silk purse from a sow's ear—just to prove it could be done. *The most interesting part of the exhibit to me, however, was some of the bizarre but ingenious failures among the models submitted for approval to the U.S. Patent Office.* I haven't been able to forget an early attempt at creating an electric razor. The inventor had mounted some razor blades on a rotating wheel so it looked something like the paddle wheel of a riverboat, and this wheel was attached to a small handheld electric motor. There were no guards to control the depth at which the blades cut, so anyone foolish enough to use the razor no doubt would have lost much more than a few whiskers from his face. Still, although I would never have sampled this inventor's work, I had to respect his resourcefulness. This invention, like the other unusual items in "The Nation's Attic," showed the mark of American ingenuity.

Here is an outline of the paragraph:

Topic sentence   "The Nation's Attic" was a tribute to American ingenuity.
Subtopic sentence   Some everyday items were ingenious.

> Specific support   Sewing items.
> Subtopic sentence   Some items made just for the challenge were imaginative.
> Specific support   Capitol from glass rods.
> Specific support   Lord's Prayer on grain of rice.
> Specific support   Silk purse from sow's ear.
> Subtopic sentence   Some bizarre failures were ingenious.
> Specific support   Attempt to create electric razor.
> Reworded topic sentence   The unusual items showed American ingenuity.

You might notice that the last sentence of the sample paragraph ties together the last item of support with all those that preceded it. This is not a necessary attribute of a reworded topic sentence, but it works nicely here.

Notice also that even though a paragraph follows a model, as does the paragraph above, it can still be good writing.

EXERCISES

A. Outline this paragraph:

To play water polo well, you have to learn to cheat. The only way you can keep the ball is by making a few slightly illegal moves. Pushing off your opponent's stomach can give you the elbowroom necessary to make a good pass or score a goal. Likewise, kneeing your attacker in the ribs can keep him from stealing the ball while you are setting up a play. When the opposing team does get possession, the unapproved solution for retrieving the ball is again through cheating. Pulling back on your adversary's leg is an effective means of slowing him down to give you a fairer chance at guarding him. But the most effective method of getting the ball is simply to pull his suit down, which immediately stops all his competitive activity. Fortunately, water polo is played in the water, since it hides the cheating all players must do in order to be successful.

Topic sentence _____

   Subtopic sentence_____

      Specific support _____

      Specific support _____

   Subtopic sentence_____

      Specific support _____

      Specific support _____

Reworded topic sentence _____

B. Outline this paragraph:

　　Giving a good speech takes a lot of work. For instance, it takes hard work just to prepare the content—to write it. Last year I had to give a speech to our entire graduating class in high school. I wanted to impress my friends and their families, of course, but the words I wrote always sounded phony—too "elevated" in tone. I wrote and wrote and rewrote until I finally decided not to be impressive but just to say the good things I felt about the school. I had spent more than hours; I had spent days getting the words right. Once I had the words, the hard part really started: practicing my delivery. I gave my speech to my empty room. I gave my speech to my mirror. I gave my speech to my twin sister. I even gave my speech to my parents! So don't let anybody tell you that giving a speech is easy.

Topic sentence _____

　Subtopic sentence_____

　　Specific support _____

　Subtopic sentence_____

　　Specific support _____

　　Specific support _____

　　Specific support _____

　　Specific support _____

Reworded topic sentence _____

C. Outline this paragraph you saw earlier in Chapter 2:

　　I like the individual freedom that comes through in e. e. cummings' poetry. You can see that freedom right away in the lack of both capitalization and normal spacing in his writing. Just look at the way he writes his name—no capital letters! Already he seems like a rebel (as he certainly was). You can also see his emphasis on individual freedom in his content: his poems often deal with the carefreeness of spring and the value of the individual. Consider, for example, the first lines of one of his most famous poems: " 'sweet spring is your/time is my time is our/time for springtime is lovetime/and viva sweet love.' " The value of spring and the individual certainly comes through in those lines, doesn't it? So e. e. cummings' format and content are two ways I see his emphasis on freedom I like so much.

Topic sentence _____

　Subtopic sentence_____

　　Specific support _____

　Subtopic sentence_____

　　Specific support _____

Reworded topic sentence _____

8 Support: Subtopic Sentences

Subtopic sentences are like topic sentences:

- Both state opinions that need support.
- And both have two parts: the subject (which must be limited) and the opinion (which must be precise).

Topic Sentences and Subtopic Sentences

A *topic* sentence is the main idea of your paragraph. A *subtopic* sentence is the main idea of one part of your paragraph. Theoretically, if you can persuade your readers to accept each subtopic sentence, then they should accept your topic sentence as well.

The precise opinion in each subtopic sentence is usually identical to the precise opinion in the topic sentence. For example, we showed you a sample Stage II paragraph in the last chapter. These were the two subtopic sentences; notice that the opinions in them are identical:

For one thing, the indexes are usually *frustrating* because they are hard to decipher.

Aside from the indexes, the general quality of the writing is *frustrating* in the manuals themselves.

The rest of this chapter shows you three different kinds of subtopic sentences: subtopic sentences that answer the questions "Why?" "How?" or "When?" There are other kinds of subtopic sentences than these, of course, but these three ways can get you started quickly.

SUBTOPIC SENTENCE: "WHY?"

One of the easiest ways to find a subtopic sentence is to state the topic sentence and then ask, "Why?"

Suppose this is your topic sentence: "Vegetable gardens take a lot of planning." If you ask yourself, "Why do vegetable gardens take a lot of planning?" you might come up with these two subtopic sentences:

Vegetable gardens take a lot of planning because the soil needs to be prepared.

Vegetable gardens take a lot of planning because the vegetables need to be planted at specific times.

Here is a possible outline, including the specific support you might want to use:

Topic sentence   Vegetable gardens take a lot of planning.
    Subtopic sentence   They take planning because the soil needs to be prepared.
        Specific support   Soil should be tilled in the fall, after the last harvest.
        Specific support   Soil should be tested in the spring, especially for acidity and nitrogen.
    Subtopic sentence   They need to be planted at specific times.
        Specific support   Last year, I planted the lettuce too late, so that by the time it should have been ready for harvest, it had died from the heat.
Reworded topic sentence   Therefore, you should plan your garden in advance.

In this outline, the subtopic sentences give some reasons why the topic sentence is true; the specific support then gives the concrete support for the subtopic sentences.

By the way, subtopic sentences that answer the question "Why?" always can be joined to the topic sentence with the word *because:*

Vegetable gardens take a lot of planning *because* the soil needs to be prepared.

Vegetable gardens take a lot of planning *because* the vegetables need to be planted at specific times.

You don't have to use the word *because* to join the "Why?" subtopic sentence to the topic sentence, but you can. Whenever you write "Why?" subtopic sentences, you might want to test them by joining them to the topic sentence with the word *because.*

Notice that you can support your subtopic sentences with the same kind of specific support you learned in Chapter 2: examples (quick or narrative), statistics, and statements by authorities.

SUBTOPIC SENTENCE: "HOW?"

Another common type of subtopic sentence answers the question "How?" Notice that the italicized subtopic sentences answer the question "How does rush hour traffic bring out the worst in drivers?":

> Heavy rush hour traffic brings out the worst in many drivers. *Traffic conditions make some drivers overly nervous.* Uncle Billy, usually a calm and careful driver, becomes so flustered in rush hour traffic that he can't carry on a conversation and forgets to check the rearview mirror when he changes lanes. A 1987 study of traffic flow in the Los Angeles area showed that the average waiting time at freeway entrance ramps increased to 1.5 minutes during rush hour because of the number of drivers who were afraid to merge into the heavy stream of cars. *Also, heavy rush hour traffic reinforces the aggressiveness of some drivers.* Often drivers follow too closely during rush hour because they're afraid other drivers might slip in ahead of them. Drivers continue into intersections on yellow lights even though they will get caught there and block cross traffic. A psychologist who has studied driver reactions concluded that "stress conditions of rush hour traffic cause physical and emotional reactions like those of a soldier in combat." Rush hour traffic conditions show many drivers at their worst.

Do you see that these subtopic sentences answer the question "How?" and not the question "Why?" "Why?" subtopic sentences probably would state something about the cause-effect relationship between rush hour traffic and the way drivers present themselves in it; "How?" subtopic sentences, on the other hand, show the results of the traffic on driver behavior.

We need to add a word of caution here. Sometimes subtopic sentences clearly answer "Why?" and sometimes they clearly answer "How?" At other times the questions appear to overlap. In other words, sometimes we can't be sure which of these two questions the subtopic sentences answer. Don't worry. The fine distinctions you would have to make are more fitting for a class in philosophy or semantics than for one in composition. Treat these questions for what they are—a quick and effective way to find subtopic sentences.

SUBTOPIC SENTENCE: "WHEN?"

Another type of subtopic sentence answers the question "When?" For example, to show that your roommate is constantly sleepy, you could ask yourself "When?" The resulting paragraph could be this one (we've italicized the subtopic sentences):

My roommate is constantly sleepy. *He is sleepy in the morning when he gets up.* He fumbles with the alarm clock. He once put his trousers on backward. *He is sleepy when he is in class.* He once fell asleep in Math III and crunched his jaw on the desk. He does not even remember the subject of the lecture he attended yesterday morning in biology. *He is sleepy in the evening.* His typical study position is a comatose sprawl with his head on his desk. He is always in bed by 8:30 P.M. My roommate is sleepy all the time.

Each of the italicized sentences answers the question, "*When* is my roommate sleepy?"

PARALLEL SUBTOPIC SENTENCES

In the examples in this chapter, all the subtopic sentences within a one-paragraph essay answer the same question: "Why?" "How?" or "When?" Your Stage II paragraphs should do the same.

In other words, if you are supporting the idea "Hitchhiking is dangerous" in a Stage II paragraph, don't answer the question "Why?" for one subtopic sentence ("Hitchhiking is dangerous because too many drivers are deranged") and the question "When?" for another subtopic sentence ("Hitchhiking is dangerous at night, when the streets are poorly lighted"). These ideas may both work to support your topic sentence, but they don't work well together. They are not parallel and seem like a mixture of apples and oranges when you are selling only apples.

Once you have outlined your Stage II paragraph, be sure your subtopic sentences answer the same question: "Why?" "How?" or "When?"

EXERCISES

A. For each of these topic sentences, invent subtopic sentences and specific support. Be sure all your subtopic sentences answer the same question: "Why?" "How?" or "When?"

1. *Medical technology is a real life-saver.*
    Subtopic sentence (Why? or How? or When?)

    _____

    _____

    Specific support (quick example)

    _____

    _____

    Subtopic sentence (Why? or How? or When?)

    _____

    _____

Specific support (statistics)

_____

_____

Specific support (statement by authority)

_____

_____

2. *Home gardening can be rewarding.*
    Subtopic sentence (Why? or How? or When?)

    _____

    _____

    Specific support (narrative example)

    _____

    _____

    Subtopic sentence (Why? or How? or When?)

    _____

    _____

    Specific support (statistics)

    _____

    _____

    Specific support (statement by authority)

    _____

    _____

3. *Women's [or men's] fashions are changing for the better.*
    Subtopic sentence (Why? or How? or When?)

    _____

    _____

    Specific support (statistics)

    _____

    _____

    Specific support (statistics)

    _____

Subtopic sentence (Why? or How? or When?)

Specific support (quick example)

Specific support (quick example)

B. If your instructor asks you to, outline the opposite of all the above topic sentences:

1. Medical technology is too expensive.
2. Home gardening can be dangerous.
3. Women's [or men's] fashions are changing for the worse.

Use whichever type of subtopic sentence ("Why?" "How?" or "When?") and whichever type of specific support (examples, statistics, statements by authorities) you wish.

C. In Exercises A and B you outlined several Stage II paragraphs. Choose the one that interests you the most and use the support you invented to write the paragraph.

D. Write a Stage II paragraph convincing us that someone you know has a positive (pleasant, good) or a negative (unpleasant, bad) characteristic. Since you will be writing about someone you know, don't use invented support for this exercise.

E. Write a Stage II paragraph explaining how something you have observed impressed you. The sample paragraph in Chapter 7 about "The Nation's Attic" could have been a response to this exercise. Since you will be writing about something you've observed, don't use invented support for this exercise.

F. Write a Stage II paragraph about one of these topics. Use invented support if you like.

early explorers	the marathon
space travel	soccer
a newspaper reporter	a hospital emergency
exotic birds	cooking away from home

G. Write a Stage II paragraph about one of these topics. Don't use invented support.

a historical event	a recent political event
a book or poem you like	a recent sports event
a place you know well	your pet
technology you like	technology you don't like

H. Think about the other courses you're taking. Choose a focused topic from one of those courses and write a Stage II paragraph based on it. For example, in history, you could give two reasons the Battle of Gettysburg was a disaster for the South. Or in physics, you could tell about two times scientists applied one of Newton's laws for practical benefits. Or in computer science, you could briefly explain two ways modern programming techniques help programmers.

I. If you have held a job, try this exercise. Write a Stage II paragraph characterizing your first day there. Were you nervous? Confident? Frustrated? Confused? Impressed? Something else?

CHECKLIST FOR THE ONE-PARAGRAPH ESSAY

Topic Sentence

_____ Does your paragraph begin with a topic sentence?
_____ Does your topic sentence have a limited subject?
_____ Does your topic sentence have a precise opinion?

Support

_____ Does your support begin with the second sentence of the paragraph?
_____ Is your support detailed enough?
_____ Do all your items of support clearly belong with the topic sentence (unity)?
_____ Do you explain your support fully so the relation to the topic is clear (coherence)?
_____ Does each item of support include a reminder of the opinion in the topic sentence (coherence)?
_____ Do you have transitions at the critical locations (coherence)?

Conclusion

_____ Does the last sentence of the paragraph reword the topic sentence?

Other

_____ Is your paragraph convincing?
_____ Is your paragraph interesting?
_____ Have you checked the spelling of the words you're unsure of?
_____ Is your paper neatly done so it's easy to read?

THREE

The Five-Paragraph Essay

A five-paragraph essay is a handy device for learning to write longer papers. The first and last paragraphs are the introduction and conclusion, two new types of paragraphs most longer papers need. The three central paragraphs provide enough material to justify a full-length introduction and conclusion but still keep the paper short enough to be manageable—for both you and your instructor.

You will also begin writing about more serious topics. So far, you've depended on your own experiences for much of your support; you'll still present your experiences here, but you'll supplement them with occasional support from books and magazines. Of course, we don't expect you to learn the fundamentals of the multiparagraph essay and the fundamentals of documentation at the same time, so we present in this section a simplified system of documentation you can use until you study the research paper in Part Five.

CHAPTER

9 Overview of the Five-Paragraph Essay

Are your paragraphs turning into monsters? Are they getting longer and longer, seeming more like small themes instead of one-paragraph essays? If so, you're ready to take the next step: learning to write the five-paragraph essay.

Actually, the five-paragraph essay is a lot like a Stage II paragraph. This diagram shows you how they resemble each other:

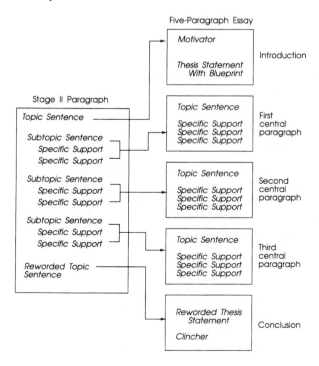

PARTS OF A FIVE-PARAGRAPH ESSAY

A five-paragraph essay has these parts:

- an introduction (one paragraph)
- central paragraphs (three paragraphs)
- a conclusion (one paragraph)

Let's look at each of these briefly. (We'll discuss them in greater detail in the next few chapters.)

INTRODUCTION

An introduction is, of course, the first paragraph of the essay. In a way, the topic sentence of your one-paragraph essay served as an introduction, but now that you're about to write longer papers, you'll want something more substantial at the beginning.

Introductions have three parts: a *motivator,* a *thesis statement,* and a *blueprint.*

Motivator

A motivator is the beginning of the introductory paragraph. Its purpose is simply to get the reader interested in reading more—in other words, in *motivating* the reader.

Thesis Statement

A topic sentence carries the main idea of a one-paragraph essay, right? In the same way, a thesis statement carries the main idea of the five-paragraph essay.

Blueprint

A blueprint is simply a short list of the main points you're about to present in the essay. Since a five-paragraph essay has three central paragraphs, your blueprint will have three points, one for the topic of each central paragraph.

CENTRAL PARAGRAPHS

There are three central paragraphs in a five-paragraph essay, and each central paragraph supports the essay's main point (or thesis statement).

A central paragraph is like a one-paragraph essay, with a topic sentence at the beginning and specific support following. Normally, though, central paragraphs don't have reworded topic sentences.

CONCLUSION

Remember the reworded topic sentence at the end of a one-paragraph essay? That sentence gave your one-paragraph essay a sense of finality. The conclusion—the last paragraph of a five-paragraph essay—also gives a sense of finality. A conclusion has two parts: a *reworded thesis statement* and a *clincher.*

Reworded Thesis Statement

A reworded thesis statement simply does what it says: rewords the thesis statement. It's intended to be a reminder to your readers, saying, in effect, "You've just been reading my three central paragraphs. Once again, let me tell you what those three paragraphs were supporting." Then you tell them.

Clincher

A clincher is simply a finisher, a final sentence or two that leaves no doubt in the reader's mind that the essay has reached its end.

A SAMPLE FIVE-PARAGRAPH ESSAY

Now let's look at a "real" five-paragraph essay. As you read it, notice the points we've been discussing: the motivator, the blueprint, and so forth (an outline follows this essay, showing all these points).

Do you realize that newly born children are not even aware that parts of their bodies belong to them? I learned this fascinating fact in my psychology course from a book that says a baby "lies on his back, kicking his heels and watching the little fists flying past his face. But only very slowly does he come to know that they are attached to him and he can control them" (Mary Ann Spencer Pulaski, *Understanding Piaget,* p. 21). Children have a lot of learning to do before they can see the world—and themselves—through grown-up eyes. As children pass through this remarkable process of growing up, they often do some humorous things, especially in learning to speak, in discovering that all objects do not have human characteristics, and in trying to imitate others around them.

Not surprisingly, one area in which children are often humorous is in learning to speak. I remember one time I was talking to a friend on the phone while my little sister, Betsy, seemed to be playing inattentively on the floor nearby. After I hung up, Betsy asked me, "Why is the teacher going to give Janet an old tomato?" At first I couldn't figure out what Betsy was talking about. When I asked her what she meant, she said, "You said if Janet doesn't hand in her homework, the teacher is going to give her an old tomato." Finally I caught on. The word I had used was *ultimatum!*

Children also can be funny in the way they humanize the objects around them. According to my psychology book, "Up to

---

four or five years old, the child believes anything may be endowed with purpose and conscious activity. A ball may refuse to be thrown straight, or a 'naughty' chair may be responsible for bumping him" (Pulaski, *Understanding Piaget,* p. 45). I, myself, still can remember one vivid and scary afternoon when I was sure the sun was following me around, just waiting for the right moment to get me. I also can remember a time, not scary, when Betsy stood at the top of the stairs and yelled to her shoes at the bottom, "Shoes! Get up here!"

Another way in which children are sometimes funny is in their attempts to imitate what they see around them. All children look pretty silly when they dress up like their mothers and fathers and play "house." My psychology book tells of a more interesting example, though. The famous psychologist Jean Piaget wrote of the time his sixteen-month-old daughter quietly watched a visiting little boy throw a tantrum in trying to get out of his playpen. Piaget's daughter thought it would be fun to try the same thing: "The next day, she herself screamed in her playpen and tried to move it, stamping her foot lightly several times in succession. The imitation of the whole scene was most striking" (quoted in Pulaski, *Understanding Piaget,* p. 81).

Little children are funny creatures to watch, aren't they? But as we laugh, we have to admire, too, because the humorous mistakes are but temporary side trips that children take on the amazingly complicated journey to maturity—a long way from the beginning, when they lay in wonder, silently watching the strange, fingered spacecraft passing, back and forth, before their infant eyes.

Now let's look at an outline of that essay:

INTRODUCTION

Motivator	Children have many things to learn and adjust to as they grow up—including the awareness of the parts of their bodies.
Thesis	Children often do humorous things . . .
Blueprint	. . . in learning to speak, in discovering that all objects do not have humorous characteristics, and in attempting to imitate others.

FIRST CENTRAL PARAGRAPH

Topic sentence   Children are often humorous in learning to speak.
Specific support   Betsy mistook *ultimatum* for *old tomato*.

SECOND CENTRAL PARAGRAPH

Topic sentence   Children "humanize" the objects around them.
Specific support   Book says children blame balls and chairs as though the things were conscious.
Specific support   I thought the sun was out to get me.
Specific support   Betsy ordered her shoes to climb the stairs.

THIRD CENTRAL PARAGRAPH

Topic sentence   Children attempt to imitate what they see.
Specific support   They dress like their parents.
Specific support   Piaget's daughter imitated a tantrum a visiting child threw.

CONCLUSION

Reworded thesis   Children are funny creatures to watch.
Clincher   Reminder of the motivator that children have a lot of learning and adjusting to do.

PRELIMINARY DOCUMENTATION

Until now, you've been writing most of your papers based on your personal experience. Those papers can be interesting and important. At some time in your life, though, you need to learn to write about other topics—about the ideas and the words of other people. When you use the ideas and words of others, you need to let the reader know where. In other words, you need to learn about documentation.

You need to document any time you use the ideas or words of other people. However, we don't want to ask you to learn the fundamentals of the five-paragraph essay and the fundamentals of documentation all at once. On the other hand, we want you to be able to use the ideas and words of others now.

As a result, we've devised what we call a "preliminary system of documentation"—a temporary and easy way for you to acknowledge your sources. Later in the book, we devote two chapters to a more formal way of documenting your writing.

Here's our preliminary system:

- Put quotation marks around all words you take directly from a source.
- At the end of every sentence in which you use someone else's words or ideas, identify the source in parentheses. To identify the source, simply use the author's name (if there is one), the title of the book or article, and the

page number. Here are some examples of the documentation you could put after sentences when you use someone else's words or ideas:

(Dick Francis, *Forfeit,* p. 143)

(*The Columbia-Viking Desk Encyclopedia,* pp. 45–58)

(George Miller, "The Magical Number 7, Plus or Minus 2," p. 81).

Proper documentation serves two purposes:

- It tells your readers that you are using the ideas or words of others.
- It tells your readers where they can find your source.

Our preliminary system serves only the first purpose well, because your parenthetical information simply isn't complete. As a result, your instructor may ask you to keep your sources handy.

The sample essay in this chapter has examples of preliminary documentation. If you have any questions at all, please ask your instructor.

PRACTICAL WRITING

You don't find many five-paragraph essays in the everyday writing you read, but you sometimes see variations that come close. Let's look more closely at practical uses of the five-paragraph essay in school and at work.

Practical Writing in School

You can use the idea of the five-paragraph essay to help you organize much of your school writing. You may not end up with five paragraphs, of course, but you can often end up with an introduction with thesis and blueprint, central paragraphs with topic sentences, and a conclusion.

Let's continue with our example on the poetry of e. e. cummings. Here is a five-paragraph essay you might write for a freshman literature class:

SOCIETY AND THE INDIVIDUAL: FREEDOM IN THE POETRY OF E. E. CUMMINGS

A constant tension exists between the values of society and the values of the individuals who compose it. We saw that in our country in the 1920s after World War I had turned values upside down and emphasized the individual. We certainly saw it again in the 1960s with the hippies, flower children, and other more violent expressions. During both of those decades, the poetry of e. e. cummings was quite popular. And—no surprise—his poetry emphasized a break from traditional values and a move toward individual freedom. We can find that emphasis on freedom in the typographical layout of his poems, their frequent antigovernment content, and the celebration of the individual in his poetry on spring.

Perhaps the most obvious example of individual freedom is the freedom cummings himself took in the typographical layout of his poems. For example, consider the first line from one of his poems:

here's a little mouse)and

The poem begins without a capital letter! It has a closed parenthesis without an opening one! And it has no space after the closed parenthesis mark! This freedom from traditional typographical conventions is *typical* of cummings' poems—not just an occasional technique he used.

Another example of cummings' emphasis on the freedom of the individual is his scorn for governments that try to control that freedom. In one poem, a speaker delivers a clichéd political speech. This is the last line of the poem:

He spoke. And drank rapidly a glass of water.

The context of the poem makes it clear that the hypocritical speaker—praising the government—needs to wash the unclean words out of his mouth. Such antigovernment content is common in e. e. cummings' poetry.

Finally, we can see the emphasis on individual freedom in the delight cummings takes in the carefreeness of spring—a time when we like to "free" ourselves of "cares" and allow our emotions and passions to express themselves. One of my favorites has these first lines:

"sweet spring is your
time is my time is our
time for springtime is lovetime
and viva sweet love"

Beautiful lines, aren't they? You can *feel* the freedom and value of the individual coming through those lines.

So you can see that cummings' poetry broke from traditional values by moving toward individual freedom. We find it in the layout of his poems, their antigovernment content, and his celebration of the freedom that spring brings. Although his poems were especially popular during certain decades, the tension between society and the individual always exists. And that is why cummings has been able to speak not just for a generation or two but—at times in our lives—for all of us.

The five-paragraph essay is a really structured way to write, but it doesn't need to take the life or meaning out of what you have to say. That's why a highly structured five-paragraph essay can talk about one of our least structured writers—e. e. cummings—and still be effective.

You can easily find applications for the principles of the five-paragraph essay in virtually all of your college courses that require writing.

Practical Writing at Work

You should also find applications for the principles of the five-paragraph essay once you graduate. Again, that doesn't mean you will be certain that all your memos, letters, and reports are exactly five paragraphs long. It just means that the underlying structure—which is why we teach you the five-paragraph essay—can be extremely useful.

For example, busy readers usually prefer the main point up front—for the document as a whole and for the sections of a document. In other words, something resembling a thesis statement at the beginning of a document is helpful. And some form of topic sentence at the beginning of each section can be helpful, too.

And as long as a document has sections, why not name those sections up front, right after the main point? Naming the sections is (you guessed it) a blueprint. Business writers sometimes call it a "road map."

Let's look at an example of business writing that resembles our five-paragraph essay. Here's the situation: A manager writes a memo to her boss, asking permission to buy an expensive kind of printer and software that does fancy word processing. This is the memo:

Using the Principles of the Five-Paragraph Essay

From: Ed Malone
To: Janet Chambers
Subject: A proposal for a color printer and desktop publishing software

We need to improve the quality of the documents and proposals we're producing in our division. To add the polish and professional look we need, I recommend we buy a color printer plus additional purchases that will let our secretaries do desktop publishing. This memo will cover why we need the printer, why we need the additional purchases, and what our implementation plan will be.

First, I recommend we buy a color printer. The cost would be $3,400. The printer will give us two main benefits: It will add a color capability to both graphics work and desktop publishing. In fact, desktop publishing almost requires a color printer for a professional impact. The color printer is also fairly fast, so it will give us the crucial speed we need for rapid turnaround of final documents and proposals. It will make possible those last-minute additions and changes that often improve the final presentation.

Next, we'll need additional purchases to do desktop publishing on the printer. Here's specifically what we'll need:

two copies of graphics software
two training slots

The desktop publishing will give our documents a professional appearance, and it can easily combine text and graphics. That way the appearance of our documents will truly express the professional quality of our work.

Once we get a color printer and the additional purchases, here's what our implementation plan will be: We'll add the color printer to our network so it's widely available to the staff. We'll install the other hardware and software on the workstations belonging to the two secretaries. One secretary is ready to do desktop publishing as soon as we get her a mouse and a graphics board. She already has software, training, and experience publishing a proposal. The other secretary needs to take the training first. That training is offered 3 weeks from now. When he's trained, we should have an excellent start for desktop publishing.

I'll be glad to talk this over with you whenever you like.

The principles of the five-paragraph are all there, aren't they? Did you notice the main point and blueprint in the first paragraph? The topic sentences at the beginning of each major paragraph? The detailed support?

Now try to imagine that memo another way—*without* all those good techniques of organization. And imagine that you're the vice president getting it (and you're having a busy day!). You'd be much less likely to read it quickly, wouldn't you? And when you did read it, you'd probably have to struggle a bit, too.

So, the five-paragraph essay is a learning tool—and the principles it teaches can help you all your life.

EXERCISE

Outline this five-paragraph essay:

When a person thinks of that old-time, small-town doctor, he usually envisions a mannerly, dignified gentleman. However, this image did not fit my Uncle Rodney, a doctor in the small town of Bandon, Wyoming. Instead, Dr. Rodney was an obnoxious person because he had an annoying habit of speaking in crude, incoherent sentences; he had sloppy eating habits; and he was a messy smoker.

Probably Dr. Rodney's most irritating trait was his crude way of speaking. For example, I recall a particularly embarrassing moment during a family reunion at my mother-in-law's house when Dr. Rodney was asked to say a blessing before dinner. He managed a "Hump, bump, grump," or so it sounded, and almost immediately added "goddamnit" as he knocked over a bowl of grated corn he was grabbing. As a result, my mother-in-law—a very religious person—was mortified. On another occasion, Dr. Rodney's nurse said, "It's a good thing I can interpret what Dr. Rodney says and smooth over the rough feelings, or we would be out of patients."

Additionally, Dr. Rodney bothered many people with his messy eating habits. He shoveled food into his mouth at such an alarming rate that often he could not catch his breath. My brother-in-law once remarked, "When I see Uncle Rodney eat, I think of jackals devouring their kill." Furthermore, Dr. Rodney always finished his meal long before anyone else; then he would make a nauseating slurping sound by sucking air and saliva through the gaps between his top front teeth while he waited for everybody else to finish. Because of his atrocious eating habits, none of Dr. Rodney's neighbors invited him to dinner.

Dr. Rodney also was disliked because he was an inconsiderate smoker. Everywhere he went, he left a trail of ashes, a terrible stench, and wet, chewed-up cigar butts. After his death, the office cleaning lady confided that the townspeople used to bet on how many days would pass before anyone saw Dr. Rodney without a spot of tobacco juice on his shirt. Naturally, all the local children learned not to be downwind from him because no one could easily tolerate his odor of stale tobacco.

Clearly, Dr. Rodney was an obnoxious person whose talking, eating, and smoking habits alienated him from even his own family. He was indeed lucky that the town had only one doctor, or he might not have been employed.

INTRODUCTION

Motivator
Thesis Statement
Blueprint

FIRST CENTRAL PARAGRAPH

Topic sentence
   Specific support
   Specific support

SECOND CENTRAL PARAGRAPH

Topic sentence
   Specific support
   Specific support
   Specific support
   Specific support

THIRD CENTRAL PARAGRAPH

Topic sentence
   Specific support
   Specific support
   Specific support

CONCLUSION

Reworded thesis
Clincher

10 Alternative Techniques of Layout

This chapter offers some alternatives to the traditional layout of the five-paragraph essay. You certainly are not required to use them. You'll find that some instructors prefer these techniques; others don't.

The computer has allowed most of us to have more capability on our desks than most professional print shops had a couple decades ago. Today, we are increasingly concerned with the layout of our document, trying to help readers *see* its parts easily.

So, we offer three suggestions on layout for you to consider:

- headings
- short paragraphs
- indented lists (like this one)

Let's look more closely at these three techniques of layout.

HEADINGS

The word just above this sentence (*Headings*) is a heading—the name for the "title" of a section of writing. In fact, we like to think of a heading as a *label* for a section's content.

One advantage of a heading is that it adds some white space to your text, signaling your reader that you're moving to a new topic. That way, your layout visually reinforces your words.

Another advantage is that a heading gives the main idea of the section. In the model of the five-paragraph essay we just showed you, paragraphing showed new ideas. But sometimes paragraphs contain minor changes in thought. If you've used a heading to announce the topic of a section, you then can have paragraphs *within* that section. That way, the reader can follow all the minor shifts in organization, such as moving to a new item of specific support.

And the reader shouldn't get confused: the headings clearly show the various major sections of the paper.

You may wonder how to make headings. We suggest simply using initial capital letters and starting on the left margin. Here's a sample paper using headings:

A SAMPLE PAPER WITH HEADINGS

xxxxx xxxxxxxxxx xxxxxx xxx xxxxxxxxxx xxxx xxxxxx xxxxxxx xxxxxxx xxxxxxxxxxxxxx xxxxxx xxxxxxxxxxx xx xxxxxxxxxxx xxxxx xxxxxxxxxx xxxxxx xxxxxx xxx xxxxxxxxxx xxxx xxxxxx xxxxxxx xxxxxxx xxxxxxxxxxxxxx xxxxxx

This Is a Heading

xxx xxxxxxxxxx xxxx xxxxxx xxxxxxx xxxxxxx xxxxxxxxxxxxxx xxxxxx xxxxxxxxxxx xx xxxxxxxxxxx xxx xxxxxxxxxx xxxx xxxxxx xxxxxxx xxxxxxx xxxxxxxxxxxxxx xxxxxx xxxxxxxxxx xx xxxxxxxxxxx xxx

xxxxxxxxxx xxxx xxxxxx xxxxxxx xxxxxxx xxxx xxxxxx xxxxxxx xxxxxxx xxx xxxxxxxxxx xxxx xxxxxx xxxxxxx xxxxxxx xxxxxxxxxxxxxx xxxxxx xxxxxxxxxxx xx xxxxxxxxxxx xxx xxxxxxxxxx xxxx xxxxxx xxxxxxx xxxxxxx xxxxxxxxxxxxxx xxxxxx xxxxxxxxxx xx xxxxxxxxxxx

This Is Another Heading

xxx xxxxxxxxxx xxxx xxxxxx xxxxxxx xxxxxxx xxxxxxxxxxxxxx xxxxxx xxxxxx xxx xxxxxxxxxx xxxx xxxxxx xxxxxxx xxxxxxx xxxxxxxxxxxxxx xxxxxx xxxxxxxxxxx xx xxxxxxxxxx xxxxx xxxxxxxxxx xxxxx xxxxxxxxxx

xxx xxxxxxxxxx xxxx xxxxxx xxxxxxx xxxxxxx xxxxxxxxxxxxxx xxxxxx xxxxxxxxxxx xx xxxxxxxxxxx xx xxxxxxxxxx xxxxx xxxxxxxxxx xxxxxxxxxxxxxxxxxx xx xxx xxxxxxxxxx xxxx xxxxxx xxxxxxx xxxxxxx xxxxxxxxxxxxxx xxxxxx xxxxxxxxxx xx xxxxxxxxxx

---

You can have a single paragraph or several paragraphs under a heading.

Tips on Making Headings

These are some common standards for making headings:

- If you use a computer or newer typewriter, make all your headings **bold.** Don't use bold elsewhere in the paper (simply underline or use italics), or else you'll distract your reader's eyes from your headings.
- Put one more space above a heading than below it. That way your heading is visually part of the text it labels.
- Use at least two of each type of heading—never only one. Headings show subordinate ideas, so—just as with outlines—you need two or more.
- Don't put a heading all by itself as the last line on a page. Include at least two lines of the text after the heading. You may need to move the heading to the top of the next page.

SHORTER PARAGRAPHS

Once you provide headings, you can then use shorter paragraphs that show breaks in thought. For example, consider this paragraph from our sample five-paragraph essay in the last chapter:

Sample Paragraph Without Organizational Breaks

Children also can be funny in the way they "humanize" the objects around them. According to my psychology book, "Up to four or five years old, the child believes anything may be endowed with purpose and conscious activity. A ball may refuse to be thrown straight, or a 'naughty' chair may be responsible for bumping him" (Pulaski, *Understanding Piaget,* p. 45). I, myself, still can remember one vivid and scary afternoon when I was sure the sun was following me around, just waiting for the right moment to get me. I also can remember a time, not scary, when Betsy stood at the top of the stairs and yelled to her shoes at the bottom, "Shoes! Get up here!"

But if that portion of the essay had a heading (and the portion after had another heading), then we could show a small organizational break in this portion:

Sample Paragraph With Organizational Breaks

Discovering Objects Aren't Human

Children also can be funny in the way they "humanize" the objects around them. According to my psychology book, "Up to four or five years old, the child believes anything may be endowed with purpose and conscious activity. A ball may refuse to be thrown straight, or a 'naughty' chair may be responsible for bumping him" (Pulaski, *Understanding Piaget,* p. 45).

I, myself, still can remember one vivid and scary afternoon when I was sure the sun was following me around, just waiting for the right moment to get me. I also can remember a time, not scary, when Betsy stood at the top of the stairs and yelled to her shoes at the bottom, "Shoes! Get up here!"

The second paragraph signals a shift from one item of specific support (a statement by an authority) to another item of specific support (a quick example). Readers will know when the next topic sentence occurs because there will be a heading to help announce it.

INDENTED LISTS

Lists help *show* a series of items. That is, if you have two or three or more items in series in a sentence, consider breaking them out into an indented list. The term for the broken-out list is a "bulleted" or an "indented" list.

Tips on Making Indented Lists

To make an indented list (like this one):

- Use a bullet symbol (a hyphen will do fine, as will a lower-case letter *o*).
- Align the text in second (and following) lines with the text above—don't go all the way back to the left margin.
- Put the bullet symbol about one-half inch from the left margin.

- Space twice from the bullet symbol to the text.
- Double-space between bulleted items.

There is no standard way to capitalize or punctuate bulleted items. The system you see here (no capital letters or punctuation unless the items are full sentences) is very common. Just be consistent.

A SAMPLE FIVE-PARAGRAPH ESSAY WITH ALTERNATIVE LAYOUT

Now let's see what these alternative techniques of layout can do for a paper we saw in the last chapter.

HUMOROUS THINGS CHILDREN DO

Do you realize that newly born children are not even aware that parts of their bodies belong to them?

I learned this fascinating fact in my psychology course from a book that says a baby "lies on his back, kicking his heels and watching the little fists flying past his face. But only very slowly does he come to know that they are attached to him and he can control them" (Mary Ann Spencer Pulaski, *Understanding Piaget,* p. 21).

Children have a lot of learning to do before they can see the world—and themselves—through grown-up eyes. As children pass through this remarkable process of growing up, they often do some humorous things, especially:

- in learning to speak
- in discovering that all objects do not have human characteristics
- in trying to imitate others around them

Learning to Speak

Not surprisingly, one area in which children are often humorous is in learning to speak. I remember one time I was talking to a friend on the phone while my little sister, Betsy, seemed to be playing inattentively on the floor nearby. After I hung up, Betsy asked me, "Why is the teacher going to give Janet an old tomato?"

At first I couldn't figure out what Betsy was talking about. When I asked her what she meant, she said, "You said if Janet doesn't hand in her homework, the teacher is going to give her an old tomato." Finally I caught on. The word I had used was *ultimatum!*

Discovering Objects Aren't Human

Children also can be funny in the way they "humanize" the objects around them. According to my psychology book, "Up to four or five years old, the child believes anything may be endowed with purpose and conscious activity. A ball may refuse to be thrown straight, or a 'naughty' chair may be responsible for bumping him" (Pulaski, *Understanding Piaget*), p. 45.

I, myself, still can remember one vivid and scary afternoon when I was sure the sun was following me around, just waiting for the right moment to get me. I also can remember a time, not scary, when Betsy stood at the top of the stairs and yelled to her shoes at the bottom, "Shoes! Get up here!"

Imitating Others Around Them

Another way in which children are sometimes funny is in their attempts to imitate what they see around them. All children look pretty silly when they dress up like their mothers and play "house."

My psychology book tells of a more interesting example, though. The famous psychologist Jean Piaget wrote of the time his 16-month-old daughter quietly watched a visiting little boy throw a tantrum in trying to get out of his playpen. Piaget's daughter thought it would be fun to try the same thing: "The next day, she herself screamed in her playpen and tried to move it, stamping her foot lightly several times in succession. The imitation of the whole scene was most striking" (quoted in Pulaski, *Understanding Piaget,* p. 81).

Conclusion

Little children are funny creatures to watch, aren't they? But as we laugh, we have to admire, too, because the humorous mistakes are but temporary side trips that children take on the amazingly complicated journey to maturity—a long way from the beginning, when they lay in wonder, silently watching the strange, fingered spacecraft passing, back and forth, before their infant eyes.

It looks good, doesn't it? And for those of you who use computers, you can play around with the layout of your paper until you get it just right.

SINGLE SPACING AND DOUBLE SPACING

There used to be one way to space lines in school papers—double spaced. That has the advantage of giving your instructor room to make detailed comments.

Some instructors prefer single spacing because it can show more of the paper at once. Particularly if the paper has headings in it, the instructor can understand the organization more easily—more words and ideas are on each page.

EXERCISE

Ask your instructor which spacing to use.

From: Ed Malone
To: Janet Chambers
Subject: A proposal for a color printer and desktop
          publishing software

We need to improve the quality of the documents and proposals we're producing in our division. To add the polish and professional look we need, I recommend we buy a color printer plus additional purchases that will let our secretaries do desktop publishing. This memo will cover why we need the printer, why we need the additional purchases, and what our implementation plan will be.

First, I recommend we buy a color printer. The cost would be $3,400. The printer will give us two main benefits: It will add a color capability to both graphics work and desktop publishing. In fact, desktop publishing almost requires a color printer for a professional impact. The color printer is also fairly fast, so it will give us the crucial speed we need for rapid turnaround of final documents and proposals. It will make possible those last-minute additions and changes that often improve the final presentation.

Next, we'll need additional purchases to do desktop publishing on the printer. Here's specifically what we'll need:

two copies of graphics software
two training slots

The desktop publishing will give our documents a professional appearance, and it can easily combine text and graphics. That way the appearance of our documents will truly express the professional quality of our work.

Once we get a color printer and the additional purchases, here's what our implementation plan will be: We'll add the color printer to our network so it's widely available to the staff. We'll install the other hardware and software on the workstations belonging to the two secretaries. One secretary is ready to do desktop publishing as soon as we get her a mouse and a graphics board. She already has software, training, and experience publishing a proposal. The other secretary needs to take the training first. That training is offered 3 weeks from now. When he's trained, we should have an excellent start for desktop publishing.

I'll be glad to talk this over with you whenever you like.

Apply the three techniques of layout to a modified version of the paper we showed you in the last chapter:

Thesis Statement With Blueprint

The thesis statement with blueprint is an essential part of your five-paragraph essay. As the name suggests, it has two components:

- the main idea (thesis statement)
- the outline of your support (blueprint)

Let's look at each of these two components in more detail.

THESIS STATEMENT

The thesis statement is the main idea of your five-paragraph essay, the single idea your entire essay will support. Sound familiar? The *topic sentence* was the main idea of a one-paragraph essay. Now, the *thesis statement* is the main idea of anything larger than a one-paragraph essay—in this case, the main idea of the five-paragraph essay. Like the topic sentence, the thesis statement can have the form of *limited subject* is *precise opinion.* Here's the introduction to our sample five-paragraph essay—we've italicized the thesis:

Introduction With Thesis Statement

Do you realize that newly born children are not even aware that parts of their bodies belong to them? I learned this fascinating fact in my psychology course from a book that says a baby "lies on his back, kicking his heels and watching the little fists flying past his face. But only very slowly does he come to know that they are attached to him and he can control them" (Mary Ann Spencer Pulaski, *Understanding Piaget,* p. 21). Children have a lot of learning to do before they can see the world—and themselves—through grown-up eyes. *As children pass through this remarkable process of growing up, they often do some humorous things,* especially in learning to speak, in discovering that all objects do not have human characteristics, and in trying to imitate others around them.

The limited subject is *children as they grow up;* the precise opinion is *humorous.*

BLUEPRINT

What is a blueprint for an essay? As we mentioned in the last chapter, a blueprint is a summary of the main points you are about to present in the body of your paper. In other words, *the blueprint is a list of the ideas in your topic sentences.*

> ### Blueprint
>
> As the name blueprint suggests, the blueprint is like an architect's pattern for the structure she intends to build . . . only in this case, you are the architect, and the structure you intend to build is your essay.

Suppose you have this organization in mind for your five-paragraph essay:

> **Thesis statement**   Installing streetlights at least ten feet high is a good idea.
> **Topic sentence**   They can light up a wider area.
> **Topic sentence**   They are harder to vandalize.
> **Topic sentence**   They don't block people's view.

Now, to form a blueprint, simply list the basic ideas from the three topic sentences:

Because they light up a wider area, they are harder to vandalize, and they don't block people's view. . . .

Now let's combine the blueprint with the thesis statement to get the result this chapter covers—the thesis statement with blueprint:

Because they light up a wider area, they are harder to vandalize, and they don't block people's view, installing streetlights at least ten feet high is a good idea.

Finally, let's look at the introduction to the sample theme from the last chapter—we've italicized the blueprint:

Introduction With Thesis and Blueprint

Do you realize that newly born children are not even aware that parts of their bodies belong to them? I learned this fascinating fact in my psychology course from a book that says a baby "lies on his back, kicking his heels and watching the little fists flying past his face. But only very slowly does he come to know that they are attached to him and he can control them" (Mary Ann Spencer Pulaski, *Understanding Piaget,* p. 21). Children have a lot of learning to do before they can see the world—and themselves—through grown-up eyes. As children pass through this remarkable process of growing up, they often do some humorous things, *especially in learning to speak, in discovering that all objects do not have human characteristics, and in trying to imitate others around them.*

BLUEPRINTS ANSWERING "WHY?" "HOW?" AND "WHEN?"

The five-paragraph essay is really just an expanded Stage II paragraph, so you can use the same kind of support for both of them. Let's examine sample blueprints answering each of the questions "Why?" "How?" and "When?"

"WHY?" BLUEPRINT

If we ask "Why?" about a thesis statement, the answer will usually begin with *because.* Let's look an example: "Why do vegetable gardens take a lot of planning?"

Blueprint Answering "Why?"

Because the soil needs to be prepared, *because* the vegetables need to be planted at the right times, and *because* the fertilizing must take place on schedule, [then the thesis follows].

"HOW?" BLUEPRINT

A "How?" blueprint usually can begin with *by, with,* or *through.* Also, since "How?" blueprints are sometimes similar to "Why?" blueprints, they both can begin with *because.* For example: "How does Wanda distract you?"

Blueprints Answering "How?"

By singing, eating, and talking as I try to study,

With her singing, her eating, and her talking,

Through her singing, her eating, and her talking,

Because of her singing, her eating, and her talking,

"WHEN?" BLUEPRINT

Finally, you usually can begin a "When?" blueprint with, yes, the word *when*. "When is your roommate constantly sleepy?"

Blueprint Answering "When?"

When he gets up in the morning, sits in class, or studies in the evening,

DIFFERENT FORMS OF THE THESIS WITH BLUEPRINT

So far, we've shown you blueprints as part of the same sentence as the thesis, with the blueprint coming at the beginning of that thesis:

Thesis With Blueprint in the Same Sentence

Because they light up a wider area, they are harder to vandalize, and they don't block people's view, installing streetlights at least ten feet high is a good idea.

Actually, though, you can present the thesis with blueprint many different ways:

Different Forms of the Thesis With Blueprint

Installing streetlights at least ten feet high is a good idea because they light up a wider area, they are harder to vandalize, and they don't block people's view.

Installing streetlights at least ten feet high is a good idea: they light up a wider area, they are harder to vandalize, and they don't block people's view.

Installing streetlights at least ten feet high is a good idea. They light up a wider area. They are harder to vandalize. And they don't block people's view.

Please notice, though, that for each example, each item in the blueprint has the same structure. In the last example, each is an entire sentence.

This is a poor blueprint because the blueprint items do not have the same structure:

Poor Blueprint

Installing streetlights at least ten feet high is a good idea because they light up a wider area and they are harder to vandalize. Also, they don't block people's view.

A reader probably would be confused. Is the writer going to talk about two ideas or three? There seem to be three ideas (wider area, vandalizing, better view), but there are just two blueprint sentences following the thesis statement.

You can avoid confusing your reader by using the same structure—all sentences, all clauses, or all phrases—for each of your blueprint items. If you want more information, see the chapter on parallelism in Part Seven.

PRACTICAL WRITING

A blueprint works for much of your writing at school or work. Remember the five-paragraph essay on e. e. cummings' poetry? It included this thesis with blueprint:

A Thesis With Blueprint From a College Paper

We can find that emphasis on freedom in the typographical layout of his poems, their frequent antigovernment content, and the celebration of the individual in his poetry on spring.

Blueprints are also common in specialized journals. Here's a sample from a journal article on computers in *UNIX Review:*

A Blueprint on Problems With Computer Security

I've organized the problems into five categories:

- What can I do to mess up one of those system configuration files?
- You mean there's something special about setup programs?
- What's so important about physical security anyway?
- Are these manuals really useful for installing a system?
- That can't be a security breach! I've got a provably secure UNIX system!

The article then has sections on each of the blueprint items.

EXERCISES

A. Combine the thesis statement and ideas for topic sentences to produce a thesis with blueprint.
   1. **Thesis** There are important reasons for outdoor lighting for homes.
   Idea for topic sentence helps find doors and locks
   Idea for topic sentence helps prevent accidents
   Idea for topic sentence helps prevent crime
   Thesis with blueprint _____

   _____

   2. **Thesis** Electrical heating has advantages over natural gas.
   Idea for topic sentence cheaper
   Idea for topic sentence warmer

Idea for topic sentence more durable equipment
Thesis with blueprint _____
_____

3. **Thesis** Gloves have many uses.
Idea for topic sentence warmth
Idea for topic sentence decoration
Idea for topic sentence protection from injury
Thesis with blueprint _____
_____

4. **Thesis** American "hard-boiled" mysteries have many things in common.
Idea for topic sentence tough private eyes
Idea for topic sentence uncooperative police
Idea for topic sentence lying clients
Thesis with blueprint_____
_____

5. **Thesis** Mountain vacations are ideal for getting physically fit.
Idea for topic sentence hiking
Idea for topic sentence mountain climbing
Idea for topic sentence horseback riding
Thesis with blueprint _____
_____

B. Choose any one of the items from Exercise A and write a thesis statement with blueprint three different ways. See the last section of the chapter, "Different Forms of the Thesis With Blueprint," for some ideas.

C. Each item below gives a thesis statement. Invent three ideas for topic sentences. Then combine those ideas with the thesis statement to produce a thesis statement with blueprint.
1. **Thesis** A vacation home would be really useful for our family.
Topic sentence
Topic sentence_____
Topic sentence _____
Thesis with blueprint _____
2. **Thesis** Finding a part-time job is easy.
Topic sentence
Topic sentence_____
Topic sentence _____
Thesis with blueprint_____
3. **Thesis** Winter is a miserable season here.
Topic sentence
Topic sentence_____
Topic sentence_____
Thesis with blueprint_____

12 Central Paragraphs

A five-paragraph essay has three central paragraphs, and each one helps prove your thesis statement.

Essentially, then, central paragraphs are simply one-paragraph essays that support one item in your blueprint. In fact, each central paragraph is like a Stage I or Stage II paragraph.

Specific support in a central paragraph supports the paragraph's topic sentence, and the three topic sentences, taken together, support the thesis. Therefore, if each central paragraph supports its own topic sentence, and if the topic sentences are properly related to each other and to your thesis, then the central paragraphs should persuade the readers to accept your thesis statement.

Since we'll be talking about introductions and conclusions later, for the moment just consider a five-paragraph essay to look like this model.

> **Thesis Statement With Blueprint**
> **First Central Paragraph**
> **Second Central Paragraph**
> **Third Central Paragraph**
> **Thesis Statement With Blueprint**

This chapter deals with two differences between central paragraphs and the one-paragraph essay:

- omission of the reworded topic sentence
- additions to the topic sentence

OMISSION OF THE REWORDED TOPIC SENTENCE

Every Stage I and Stage II paragraph essay, a unit complete in itself, has three basic parts:

- a topic sentence
- specific support
- a reworded topic sentence

The reworded topic sentence provides a mark of finality to the argument.

A central paragraph, however, doesn't require this same mark of finality. Remember that a central paragraph doesn't present the entire argument of the essay. So you don't have to place a reworded topic sentence at the end of each central paragraph. After you've presented your last item of specific support, just go on to the next paragraph.

ADDITIONS TO THE TOPIC SENTENCE

Like a topic sentence for a one-paragraph essay, the topic sentence for a central paragraph presents the *main idea of the paragraph* in the basic form of *"limited subject* is *precise opinion."* However, the topic sentence for a central paragraph has two important additions:

- a *transition* from the preceding paragraph
- a *reminder* of the thesis

The first addition, the *transition,* provides coherence. Just as sentences within any paragraph must move smoothly from one to another, paragraphs within a theme must also flow together.

The second addition to the topic sentence, the *reminder of the thesis,* helps fit the central paragraph's main idea to the theme's main idea. The total argument will come together more easily if each central paragraph's idea (its topic sentence) connects to the theme's idea (the thesis statement). This addition, then, helps provide both coherence and unity.

Therefore, the topic sentence for a central paragraph should have these three parts:

- a transition
- a reminder of the thesis statement
- the main idea of the paragraph

EXAMPLES OF CENTRAL PARAGRAPHS

Let's look at some examples of central paragraphs. Here's the *first* central paragraph from the sample theme in Chapter 9. Can you find the three parts of the topic sentence?

First Central Paragraph

Not surprisingly, one area in which children are often humorous is in learning to speak. I remember one time I was talking to a friend on the phone while my little sister, Betsy, seemed to be playing inattentively on the floor nearby. After I hung up, Betsy asked me, "Why is the teacher going to give Janet an old tomato?" At first I couldn't figure out what Betsy was talking about. When I asked her what she meant, she said, "You said if Janet doesn't hand in her homework, the teacher is going to give her an old tomato." Finally, I caught on. The word I had used was *ultimatum!*

Here are the three parts:

Transition	"one area"
Reminder	"children are often humorous"
Main idea	"learning to speak"

Notice also the specific support for the topic sentence: a narrative example telling the brief story of Betsy's funny question. A central paragraph should have the same detailed support as a one-paragraph essay. Now let's look at the *second* central paragraph from the sample theme:

Second Central Paragraph

Children also can be funny in the way they "humanize" the objects around them. According to my psychology book, "Up to four or five years old, the child believes anything may be endowed with purpose and conscious activity. A ball may refuse to be thrown straight, or a 'naughty' chair may be responsible for bumping him" (Pulaski, *Understanding Piaget,* p. 45). I, myself, still can remember one vivid and scary afternoon when I was sure the sun was following me around, just waiting for the right moment to get me. I also can remember a time, not scary, when Betsy stood up at the top of the stairs and yelled to her shoes at the bottom, "Shoes! Get up here!"

Here are the three parts of the topic sentence:

Transition	"also"
Reminder	"children . . . can be funny"
Main idea	"the way they 'humanize' . . . objects"

This paragraph has a variety of support: a statement by an authority and two quick examples. Finally, let's look at the *third* central paragraph:

Third Central Paragraph

Another way in which children are sometimes funny is in their attempts to imitate what they see around them. All children look pretty silly when they dress up like their mothers and fathers and play "house." My psychology book tells of a more interesting example, though. The famous psychologist Jean Piaget wrote of the time his sixteen-month-old daughter quietly watched a visiting little boy throw a tantrum in trying to get out of his playpen. Piaget's daughter thought it would be fun to try the same thing: "The next day, she herself screamed in her playpen and tried to move it, stamping her foot lightly several times in succession. The imitation of the whole scene was most striking" (quoted in Pulaski, *Understanding Piaget,* p. 81).

Here are the three parts of the topic sentence:

Transition	"Another way"
Reminder	"children are sometimes funny"
Main idea	"their attempts to imitate what they see around them"

This paragraph has an interesting form of support: a narrative example stated by an authority—Piaget.

Because you must have space to develop your argument, you break it into parts—the arguments of the central paragraphs. Yet, like a jigsaw puzzle, a theme will never seem complete unless you connect the pieces. The additions to the topic sentence of each central paragraph help you fit the central paragraphs to each other and to your thesis statement.

EXERCISES

A. Let's say you're writing a five-paragraph essay with this thesis statement:
   Thesis Buying a computer requires special knowledge.

   For each topic sentence below, identify the transition, the reminder of the thesis, and the main idea.
   First topic sentence First, deciding how much computer memory to buy requires expertise.

   Transition _____

   Reminder _____

   Main idea _____

   Second topic sentence Also, deciding what size hard disk to use requires special knowledge.

   Transition _____

Reminder _____

Main Idea _____

Third topic sentence Finally, figuring out the type of monitor to purchase requires knowing about monitors in detail.

Transition _____

Reminder _____

Main Idea _____

B. Do the same thing for this thesis statement:
Thesis Driving a car requires constant attention.

First topic sentence For one thing, drivers must constantly look at the gauges on the dashboard.

Transition _____

Reminder _____

Main Idea _____

Second topic sentence As if that's not enough, drivers also must pay attention to the route they are traveling.

Transition _____

Reminder _____

Main Idea _____

Third topic sentence And drivers have to keep a sharp lookout for other traffic, including pedestrians.

Transition _____

Reminder _____

Main Idea _____

C. Do the same thing for this thesis statement:
Thesis Television meteorologists—more commonly known as TV weather forecasters—need special expertise.

First topic sentence Television forecasters, most importantly, have to understand weather data.

Transition _____

Reminder _____

Main Idea _____

Second topic sentence They also must know how to operate computer equipment to design their weather shows.

Transition _____

Reminder _____

Main Idea _____

Third topic sentence Further, they need to understand the proper behavior required on camera for giving forecasts in front of thousands of viewers.

Transition _____

Reminder _____

Main Idea _____

D. Here's a thesis statement and three main ideas for central paragraphs. Use these main ideas to write complete topic sentences—including transitions and reminders of the thesis.
Thesis Several outdoor sports help me keep physically fit.

Main idea jogging

Main Idea soccer

Main Idea basketball

First topic sentence _____

Transition _____

Reminder _____

Second topic sentence _____

Transition _____

Reminder _____

Third topic sentence _____

Transition _____

Reminder _____

E. Do the same with this thesis and three main ideas:
Thesis Some musical instruments are hard to play.

Main idea guitar

Main idea violin

Main idea trombone

First topic sentence _____

Transition _____

Reminder _____

Second topic sentence _____

Transition _____

Reminder _____

Third topic sentence _____

Transition _____

Reminder _____

F. For Exercises A through E, you've written topic sentences for a number of central paragraphs. Choose the one that interests you the most, and—inventing the support—write one central paragraph.

G. Recall for a minute the sample theme in Chapter 9 on the humorous things children do. In a way, the writer of that theme was an "expert" on children's funny behavior: She had been a child herself, and she had observed her sister (and undoubtedly many other children) growing up. She didn't depend in that theme on any expertise in psychology, only on the behavior of children she had observed. The expertise she did use—from the book on Piaget—was highly interesting, of course, but it wasn't an essential part of the thesis statement, nor was it the only support.

   You, too, are probably an "expert" in something. Perhaps you play golf well or understand how to tune an automobile engine or know every record the Beatles recorded. Choose something you know well and say something *significant* about it. Once you have something significant to say about your topic, turn that statement into a thesis statement with blueprint. Then, letting the thesis statement with blueprint serve as both the introduction and the conclusion, write the three central paragraphs of the five-paragraph essay (you'll write the full-length introduction and conclusion later as exercises for Chapters 13 and 14).

   Be sure to use the same kind of detailed support for each central paragraph that you would use for a one-paragraph essay, and be sure that each of your topic sentences contains a transition from the previous paragraph, a reminder of the thesis statement, and the main idea of the paragraph.

   If you use outside sources, use them only to find support, not to find a thesis. Otherwise, you'll merely be paraphrasing someone else. Also, be sure to place quotation marks around all words you borrow directly. At the end of every sentence containing borrowed words or ideas, acknowledge your source in parentheses (look again at Chapter 9 if you've forgotten the rules for the preliminary documentation system).

   If you have any questions about documentation, be sure to ask your instructor so there aren't any misunderstandings.

H. Think about the other courses you're taking and about some of the interesting ideas you are learning in those courses. From those ideas, devise a thesis statement with blueprint.

   Then, letting the thesis statement with blueprint serve as both the introduction and the conclusion, write the three central paragraphs of the five-paragraph essay (you'll write the full-length introduction and conclusion later as exercises for Chapters 13 and 14).

   Be sure to use the same kind of detailed support for each central paragraph that you would use for a one-paragraph essay, and be sure that each of your topic sentences contains a transition from the previous paragraph, a reminder of the thesis statement, and the main idea of the paragraph.

This exercise, in particular, will probably require some documentation. So be sure to place quotation marks around all words you borrow directly. At the end of every sentence containing borrowed words or ideas, acknowledge your source in parentheses (look again at Chapter 9 if you've forgotten the rules for the preliminary documentation system).

If you have any questions about documentation, be sure to ask your instructor so there aren't any misunderstandings.

I. Using your first job (or any job you've held) as a topic, devise a thesis statement. Perhaps your thesis could be about an important lesson you learned at work. Or what you learned not to do. Or how the job changed your attitude toward school, your friends, or your parents.

Let the thesis with blueprint serve as both the introduction and the conclusion. Then write the three central paragraphs of the five-paragraph essay (you'll write the full-length introduction and conclusion later as exercises for Chapters 13 and 14).

Also, be sure to follow the advice for support and documentation in Exercise G.

13 Introduction

Your introduction serves two important purposes:

- It gets your reader's attention.
- It tells your reader what your main idea is (and how you will develop it).

The part of your introduction that gets your reader's attention is called a *motivator*. The part that tells your reader what your main point is (and how you will develop it) is called the *thesis statement with blueprint*.

Since we've just discussed thesis statements with blueprints, we'll concentrate on motivators in this chapter.

Here's the introduction from our sample theme in Chapter 9. Can you find the motivator—the part that gets the reader's attention?

Introduction to a Five-Paragraph Essay

Do you realize that newly born children are not even aware that parts of their bodies belong to them? I learned this fascinating fact in my psychology course from a book that says a baby "lies on his back, kicking his heels and watching the little fists flying past his face. But only very slowly does he come to know that they are attached to him and he can control them" (Mary Ann Spencer Pulaski, *Understanding Piaget,* p. 21). Children have a lot of learning to do before they can see the world—and themselves—through grown-up eyes. As children pass through this remarkable process of growing up, they often do some humorous things, especially in learning to speak, in discovering that all objects do not have human characteristics, and in trying to imitate others around them.

The motivator is all but the last sentence, isn't it? The writer hopes to interest you by telling you something intriguing—that infants don't know that parts of their bodies belong to them. As you practice writing and look carefully at the writing of others, you'll find many good ways to motivate your reader. Here are three good ways—which we'll discuss in this chapter:

- the opposite opinion
- a brief story
- an interesting statement

THE OPPOSITE OPINION

A really easy way to begin your paper is to state the opinion your paper opposes and then make a transition to your thesis statement with blueprint. In other words, your introduction has this flow to it:

- what the opposition says
- transition
- what you say

Transitions With the Opposite Opinion

The transition is particularly important in this kind of introduction because you must move clearly from the position you oppose to the position you support.

Here's a sample introduction to an essay showing that smoking is not a pleasing habit:

> Some people think that smoking makes them appear sophisticated and mysterious, perhaps even seductive. They become Humphrey Bogart in *Casablanca* or Lauren Bacall in *To Have and Have Not.* Those people, however, are wrong. As far as I am concerned, smoking is really a disgusting habit—messy, irritating to others, and even harmful to nonsmokers.

Notice the strong transition ("Those people, however, are wrong"). And notice that the thesis statement and blueprint are obvious. Readers know clearly they have read the main idea of the paper and can anticipate how it will be developed.

Here is another introduction using the opposite opinion as the motivator:

> As I was walking down the hall yesterday, I overheard a professor complaining about computers: "Those things are going to ruin the writing of our students. A computer is just a fancied-up TV and arcade game disguised as an 'educational tool.' " But my experience with computers is entirely different. As word processors, for example, they can be immensely helpful with each stage of the writing process: prewriting, writing, and rewriting.

A BRIEF STORY

We all enjoy stories, so one of the most interesting ways to begin a paper is to tell your readers a brief story somehow related to your thesis statement. That way you've engaged their attention right from the start. By the time they've finished the story, sheer momentum carries them into the rest of your paper.

Here's a sample introduction that begins with a brief story:

> I walked into the living room, picked up a magazine, and settled back into my chair. When I opened the cover, I was confronted by a slender, elegant woman staring confidently into the distance and holding a cigarette in one hand. "Smoke cigarettes," she seemed to be saying, "and you, too, can be slender and elegant." I wanted so much to be like her. But I never took up smoking because—elegance and slenderness notwithstanding—I've always thought of it as a disgusting habit: messy, irritating to others, and even harmful to nonsmokers.

Notice that the introduction has a transition ("But I never took up . . .") between the motivator and thesis with blueprint.

Some introductions need a transition—like the one above, and all those that begin with opposite opinions—while others move smoothly from the motivator to the thesis with blueprint without any explicit transition words:

> I remember the first time I used a computer—or "word processor"—to do some writing. I was at a neighbor's house, so I just began a "letter" (one I wasn't planning to mail) to my friend. Instead of pausing frequently to think of things to say, I just wrote. The words seemed to come easily since I knew I could make changes later with no problem. Since then, I've used computers for most of my writing, and I've come to believe that they can be immensely helpful to us at each stage in the writing process: prewriting, writing, and rewriting.

AN INTERESTING STATEMENT

Another easy way to get your reader's attention is to begin with a statement that's interesting, either because the idea is intriguing or because, perhaps, the tone is angry. The introduction to the five-paragraph essay in Chapter 9 begins with an interesting statement, one that's intriguing: "Do you realize that newly born children are not even aware that parts of their bodies belong to them?"

The next example is a motivator that's interesting because the tone is angry (after all, if we're walking along and hear somebody yelling, we would probably stop because we're curious):

> I'm sick of smokers flicking ashes on my desk and throwing ashes on the rug. Long after these people have left, their messes remain, together with the

foul smoke they have exhaled from their tar-coated lungs. Let's face facts: smoking is a disgusting habit—messy, irritating, and even harmful to non-smokers.

The next example is only two sentences long, showing that an introduction can be effective even if it's fairly short:

Computers can *really* make a difference in how quickly and how easily you can get words on paper. In fact, computers—used as word processors—can be immensely helpful with each stage of the writing process: prewriting, writing, and rewriting.

The motivator for this introduction is interesting because the writer seems enthusiastic. If you convey your enthusiasm for your topic, your beginning will often be interesting, too.

When you are writing the introduction to your paper—whether you choose the opposite opinion, a brief story, or an interesting statement—be sure you fulfill the two important purposes of all introductions: interest your readers and tell them the main idea of your paper (and how you will develop it).

EXERCISES

A. In Exercise A for Chapter 11 ("Thesis Statement With Blueprint"), you wrote five thesis statements with blueprints. Choose one and write three introductions for it: one with the opposite opinion, one with a brief story, and one with an interesting statement.

B. For Exercises G, H, and I in Chapter 12 ("Central Paragraphs"), you wrote a thesis statement with blueprint followed by three central paragraphs. Now, using any of the three types of motivators we just discussed, write a full-length introduction for one of those exercises (G, H, or I). You may need to change the wording of the original thesis statement with blueprint for it to fit smoothly with your motivator, but don't change the essential meaning.

14 Conclusion

The conclusion, like the introduction, serves two purposes:

- It reminds the reader of the main point of your essay.
- It gives the reader a sense of finality.

The part that reminds the reader of the main point is the *reworded thesis statement*. The part that gives finality is the *clincher*. Let's look at the conclusion to the sample five-paragraph essay you saw in Chapter 9. Can you find the reworded thesis and the clincher?

Conclusion of a Five-Paragraph Essay

Little children are funny creatures to watch, aren't they? But as we laugh, we have to admire, too, because the humorous mistakes are but temporary side trips that children take on the amazingly complicated journey to maturity—a long way from the beginning, where they lay in wonder, silently watching the strange, fingered spacecraft passing, back and forth, before their infant eyes.

The reworded thesis is the first sentence; the clincher is the last one. You already know how to write a reworded thesis statement: it resembles the reworded topic sentence that you worked with on the one-paragraph essay. Therefore, this chapter concentrates on the clincher. We'll discuss two types:

- the reference to the motivator
- the interesting statement

THE REFERENCE TO THE MOTIVATOR

The simplest—and most common—clincher reminds the readers of the motivator you used in your introduction. This clincher has the advantage of bringing the paper full circle, an unmistakable signal that the paper is over.

The last chapter showed you three sample introductions with the thesis that smoking is disgusting. Let's look at those introductions again. Notice that each conclusion:

- begins with a reworded thesis statement
- finishes by referring to the motivator

Introduction to Essay 1 (Opposite Opinion)

Some people think that smoking makes them appear sophisticated and mysterious, perhaps even seductive. They become Humphrey Bogart in *Casablanca* or Lauren Bacall in *To Have and Have Not.* Those people, however, are wrong. As far as I am concerned, smoking is really a disgusting habit—messy, irritating to others, and even harmful to nonsmokers.

Conclusion to Essay 1

I am glad I never began such a disgusting habit, and I wish others had not started, either. I hope my sophisticated friends soon find out that Humphrey Bogart and Lauren Bacall were mysterious and appealing in spite of their habit, not because of it.

Introduction to Essay 2 (Brief Story)

I walked into the living room, picked up a magazine, and settled back into my chair. When I opened the cover, I was confronted by a slender, elegant woman staring confidently into the distance and holding a cigarette in one hand. "Smoke cigarettes," she seemed to be saying, "and you, too, can be slender and elegant." I wanted so much to be like her. But I never took up smoking because—elegance and slenderness notwithstanding—I've always thought of it as a disgusting habit: messy, irritating to others, and even harmful to nonsmokers.

Conclusion to Essay 2

I am glad I never began such a disgusting habit, and I wish others hadn't started, either. I no longer have the magazine with the elegant woman. But I don't miss her, the magazine—or smoking.

Introduction to Essay 3 (Interesting Statement)

I'm sick of smokers flicking ashes on my desk and throwing ashes on the rug. Long after these people have left, their messes remain, together with the foul smoke they have exhaled from their tar-coated lungs. Let's face facts: smoking is a disgusting habit—messy, irritating, and even harmful to nonsmokers.

Conclusion to Essay 3

I'm glad I never began such a disgusting habit. If other people hadn't started smoking, then neither their houses nor mine would be littered with smokers' messes and we would all be healthier.

AN INTERESTING STATEMENT

The last chapter showed you how to *begin* papers with interesting statements; an interesting statement is a good way to *end* a paper, too. Your statement might be interesting because of the information or because of the tone. Here's a conclusion that has an interesting statement because of the information:

I am glad I never began such a disgusting habit, and I wish others had not started, either. I hope my sophisticated friends soon find out that Humphrey Bogart, mysterious and appealing though he might have been, unfortunately died of cancer of the throat—possibly caused by smoking!

And here's a conclusion with an interesting—even angry—tone:

I am glad I never began such a disgusting habit, and I wish others had not started, either. Then the only smoking would take place at the fire-eater's show at the carnival—a spectacle that would give smoking the kind of dignity it deserves.

So, to finish your five-paragraph essay, simply reword the thesis statement and end with unmistakable finality: the clincher.

A Note of Caution

When you write your conclusion, be careful not to state any new, unsupported generalizations that your reader might question.

EXERCISES

A. Chapter 13 presents three introductions to a paper about computers. Using the *reference to the motivator* as a clincher, write a conclusion to each one.
B. Again, for the sample introductions in Chapter 13 on computers, choose one introduction and write a conclusion that has an *interesting statement* as your clincher.
C. For Exercise B in Chapter 13 you wrote an introduction to the three paragraphs you had written for Exercises G, H, or I in Chapter 12. Now finish your five-paragraph essay by writing the conclusion. Use either type of clincher.

CHECKLIST FOR THE FIVE-PARAGRAPH ESSAY

Introduction
_____   Does your introduction begin with a motivator?
_____   Does your introduction have a thesis statement with blueprint?
_____   Does your thesis statement have a limited subject?
_____   Does your thesis statement have a precise opinion?
_____   Are the items in your blueprint in the same order as your central paragraphs?
_____   Do the items in your blueprint all answer the same question: "Why?" "How?" or "When?"

Central Paragraphs
_____   Does each central paragraph begin with a topic sentence?
_____   Does each topic sentence have a transition from the previous paragraph?
_____   Does each topic sentence have a reminder of the thesis?
_____   Does each topic sentence state the main idea of the paragraph?
_____   Is your support specific enough to be convincing?
_____   Do all your items of support clearly support the topic sentence (unity)?
_____   Do you explain your support fully so the relation to the topic sentence is clear (coherence)?
_____   Does each item of support include a reminder of the opinion in the topic sentence (coherence)?
_____   Do you have transitions at the critical locations (coherence)?

Conclusion
_____   Does your conclusion have a reworded thesis statement?
_____   Does your conclusion end with a clincher?

Other
_____   Is your essay convincing?
_____   Is your essay interesting?
_____   Have you checked the spelling of the words you're unsure of?
_____   Is your paper neatly done so it's easy to read?

SECTION
TWO

BEYOND THE
MODEL ESSAY

PART

FOUR

More Patterns of Development

In Part Three you began your transition to the research paper by learning how to write longer papers and how to use a simple method of documentation. You'll continue that transition here, learning two new skills:

- First, you'll find out about four different ways to develop a paper: comparison and contrast, cause and effect, classification, and process.
- Second, you'll learn some easy ways to vary from the five-paragraph essay. Our sample essays in this part clearly grow out of the five-paragraph essay, but they all have differences from it.

Throughout Part Four, you'll apply the principles of the five-paragraph essay—but, as you'll see, those principles can easily apply to papers longer than five paragraphs. You'll continue to use:

- an introduction that tells the structure of your paper
- paragraphs that begin with topic sentences
- a conclusion that wraps things up

15 Comparison and Contrast

Comparison and contrast aren't new to you; they are extremely common ways of thinking. Whenever you examine how things are similar, you *compare* them. And when you look at their differences, you *contrast* them.

Sometimes you use comparison and contrast to talk about something new: by telling your readers how a thing is similar to or different from something they know, you can help them understand the new thing. For instance, to explain a rotary automobile engine, you'd probably compare and contrast it to the conventional automobile engine.

However, besides explaining something new, comparison and contrast also appear frequently in decision making: because A and B share some characteristics but differ in others, one is better and the other worse. You compare and contrast brands when you shop for groceries, stereos, automobiles, and so forth. When you chose the college you're attending, you probably compared and contrasted available schools, and you're likely to use comparison and contrast again when you choose your major. The list of examples could be endless.

The comparison-and-contrast theme, then, is really quite practical.

THESIS

Comparison and contrast lead logically to a thesis because you usually won't bother to compare and contrast unless you have some purpose in mind. You could, of course, stop once you note that A is like B or C is different from D. But your readers probably will want to know what the similarity or difference amounts to. You could write this for a thesis:

The rotary automobile engine is different from the conventional automobile engine.

However, once you've noted the difference, the readers will see that you've merely stated the obvious. Much more useful would be one of the following:

Although the mechanical structure of the rotary automobile engine is obviously different from that of the conventional automobile engine, the rotary engine offers little worthwhile improvement.

or

Although they both depend on internal combustion, the rotary automobile engine is a significant improvement over the conventional automobile engine.

Thus, comparison or contrast for its own sake is generally pointless, but both are useful to develop support for a thesis.

APPROACHES TO COMPARISON AND CONTRAST

As you may have noticed in the preceding sample thesis statements, there are two general approaches to the comparison-and-contrast paper. First, you can briefly note the difference between items but *concentrate on their similarity* (comparison).

Although the mechanical structure of the rotary automobile engine is obviously different from that of the conventional automobile engine, the rotary engine offers little worthwhile improvement.

Here the writer acknowledges that the engine types are different. Does the difference mean that the newer one—the rotary engine—is better? The writer says it isn't; the engines are really comparable. We can expect the theme to concentrate on the similarities of the engines.

For the second approach, you can briefly note the similarity between items but *concentrate on their differences* (contrast).

Although they both depend on internal combustion, the rotary automobile engine is a significant improvement over the conventional automobile engine.

Now the writer acknowledges one similarity—that the two engines have the same type of combustion—but he is concerned with showing that the rotary engine is better than the conventional engine.

Notice that with either similarity or difference you acknowledge the opposite. Why? You need to establish a reason for bringing the two items together. Noting that the items seem different gives you a reason for comparing them, and noting that the items appear to be similar establishes a reason for contrasting them. In both cases, the opposite can provide the motivator section of your theme's introduction.

At the same time, you must decide where in the essay you're going to discuss the similarities and differences. The thesis establishes your primary purpose, which you'll concentrate on; you'll obviously discuss that side in the central sections.

Yet, how will you deal with the opposite? You have two choices. If the opposite is well known, let the introduction handle it. But if the opposite is not generally understood, you may need to develop it in the body of the theme. In that case, cover it first in your central sections. Doing it this way leaves the primary idea in the position of emphasis—the end of the theme.

ORGANIZING YOUR CENTRAL PARAGRAPHS

When you've decided whether to concentrate on comparison or contrast, you still must decide *how* to do it. Suppose you want to contrast two brands of automobile to decide which to buy; you'll consider such subtopics as price, miles per gallon, and maintenance record. You must decide whether to devote the central paragraphs:

- to whole items (a paragraph for each of the cars)
- to their various elements (separate paragraphs for price, miles per gallon, and maintenance record)

The diagram shows the two most likely organizational types (we've used two items with three elements per item, but other combinations are certainly possible):

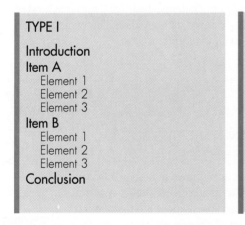

TYPE I

Introduction
Item A
   Element 1
   Element 2
   Element 3
Item B
   Element 1
   Element 2
   Element 3
Conclusion

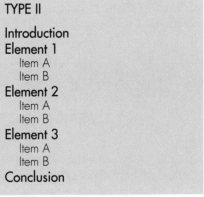

TYPE II

Introduction
Element 1
   Item A
   Item B
Element 2
   Item A
   Item B
Element 3
   Item A
   Item B
Conclusion

Which pattern is preferable? Well, notice that the Type I organization gives a sense of each item as a whole; however, the readers may have difficulty relating the elements. For example, suppose you compare a Ford and a Chrysler on the basis of seven elements. By the time the readers get to element five of the second car, the Chrysler, they've forgotten what they read about element five of the Ford. As a result, Type I organization is better for short papers dealing with only a few items and elements.

On the other hand, Type II organization disrupts the sense of the whole item as it builds the relationships of the elements. Still, Type II development can handle more items and more elements, so it's more useful than Type I for a longer comparison or contrast paper.

Order of Your Subtopics

Whether you choose the Type I or Type II organization for the central sections of your theme, make sure that you always cover the same subtopics in the same order. As with parallelism within a sentence (see Chapter 37), this symmetry will clearly show the relationships that are important for your ideas.

So which type is better? There's no absolute answer, but you'll see more papers using Type II organization, probably because people are more concerned with element-by-element similarities and differences.

TYPE I

To demonstrate the difference, we've included a Type I essay comparing kinds of school classes. Note how the writer, one of our students, deals first with one kind of class and its elements (teacher, students, results), then another. The essay is short enough that we as readers don't get lost in all the differences.

LEARNING OR NOT: ACTIVE AND PASSIVE CLASSES

Everyone who has gone to school knows that some classes are better, more interesting, livelier than others. We have all sat through classes where we learned little, except the facts and to be quiet. We also have been part of classes where we actively learned by being challenged by teachers and the subject to learn for ourselves.

Although classes often seem outwardly alike in having a teacher, in having some students, and in producing some results, the differences between passive and active classes are enormous.

Passive Classes

The passive kind of class usually has a teacher who lectures, puts outlines and terms on the chalkboard, and dispenses information to the students. Like my sophomore biology teacher, Mrs. Noguida, who rarely looked up from the orange notebook in which she had carefully typed all her lectures, teachers in a passive classroom simply dictate information and answers. They tell the students how to think and what to think. They pour facts into the students like water into a sieve. The students are forced, usually by the teacher's authority, to sit, listen, take notes, and regurgitate only what the teacher has said.

The only kinds of questions are about form: "What is the work in subpoint 3.a.(1)?" or "How do you spell *minuscule?*" The results in such a class are measured by multiple-choice or true-false questions, or questions that require memorized answers: "What is Newton's First Law?" "What are the three causes of the American Civil War?"

The results in such classes are also measured by how quickly the students forget the facts they had poured into them.

Active Classes

The other kind of class, the active kind, usually has a teacher who stimulates the students to learn for themselves by asking questions, by posing problems, and most of all by being a student, too.

Such a teacher might plan the outline of a course but doesn't force the class in only one direction. Instead, like Ms. Cerrillo, my junior history teacher, a teacher in an active class uses the discussion to lead to learning. Instead of lecturing on the causes of the Civil War, Ms. Cerrillo gave us a list of books and articles and said, "Find out what caused the Civil War." We had to search for ourselves, find some answers, then discuss what we found in class. From the discussions, we all learned more than just the facts; we learned the facts but we also learned how complex the causes were.

Students in active classes like that become more involved in their learning; they ask questions about why and how. The results in the active class are usually measured by essay answers, individual projects, and a change in attitude on the students' part. Learning becomes fun; although students may forget the facts just as quickly, their attitudes toward learning and their excitement in developing answers for themselves don't end with the last class.

We all remember having to learn that "4 × 9 = 36" and having to memorize dates like 1914–1918, 1776, and 1492. And those kinds of classes are important for laying some groundwork, but not much true learning takes place there. There is a difference between *knowing* a fact and *understanding* it. Despite their outward similarities, the passive kind of class is clearly inferior to the active one for helping students understand the world around them.

TYPE II

Here's a sample theme that compares two characters in literature. We've selected this theme because English instructors often ask students to write about literature; as you'll see, a theme comparing two fictional characters is fairly easy to organize. You'll also see how well the Type II organization works for comparing a large number of subtopic elements, even though there are only two items.

HOLMES AND DUPIN

Although Sir Arthur Conan Doyle created Sherlock Holmes in 1886, Holmes remains one of the most popular of detective characters. Moreover, Holmes' personality influenced the characterizations of other fictional detectives, both in Doyle's time and later. For example, Agatha Christie's Hercule Poirot is similar to Holmes.

Yet many readers of the Holmes stories don't realize that Holmes isn't entirely original. Holmes is very much like Chevalier C. Auguste Dupin, a character Edgar Allan Poe introduced in 1841. Of course, Holmes and Dupin have their differences; Holmes himself calls Dupin "a very inferior fellow" (Doyle, *A Study in Scarlet and The Sign of Four,* p. 25).

Nevertheless, pushing aside Holmes' criticism of Dupin, we can find numerous similarities between the two characters. Both in the conditions of their work and in personality, Holmes is nearly a copy of Dupin.

Conditions of Their Work

The conditions under which Dupin and Holmes work are alike. Both Dupin and Holmes are "consulting detectives," to use Holmes' name for the profession (Doyle, p. 23). This may not seem important, but we should notice that most other detective characters take cases on their own. Yet Dupin works on cases for Monsieur G———, Prefect of the Parisian police, and Holmes (at least when he first appears) works on cases that have stumped Scotland Yard detectives.

In addition, both characters dislike the policemen they work for, and for the same reason. In "The Purloined Letter," Dupin says that the police are "persevering, ingenious, cunning, and thoroughly versed in the knowledge which their duties seem chiefly to demand" but that they fail because they cannot adapt their methods "to the case and to the man" (Poe, *Great Tales and Poems of Edgar Allan Poe,* pp. 208–09). Similarly, Holmes says the Scotland Yard detectives are "both quick and energetic, but conventional—shockingly so" (Doyle, p. 28).

Still, Dupin and Holmes somehow control their scorn while they solve cases for the police. The "consulting detectives" have the satisfaction of solving puzzles, but they let the police steal the glory.

Their Personalities

Holmes' personality also matches Dupin's. Both characters are loners; they accept the company of the narrators of their stories, but of no one else. Poe writes in "The Murders in the Rue Morgue" that Dupin is "enamored of the night for her own sake"; in fact, Dupin and the narrator close the shutters of their house during the day and usually go out only at night (Poe, pp. 106–07). This love of darkness emphasizes Dupin's physical withdrawal from society. In Holmes' case, the withdrawal and gloominess lead to cocaine addiction; when Holmes isn't on a case, he withdraws from ordinary life as well as from society.

Of course, the detectives become active in society to solve cases, but each withdraws again when his case is over. At the opening of the second Dupin story, the narrator says that after his first case, Dupin "relapsed into his old habits of moody revery" (Poe, p. 144). And Holmes, at the end of *The Sign of Four,* calls for his cocaine so he, too, can withdraw.

Even when Dupin and Holmes actually enter society to solve puzzles, they remain mentally separate from other men. On a case, both Dupin and Holmes show energy unknown to most people. This energy involves them in society, but it doesn't mean that they actually join society. Instead, each stays separate by remaining unemotional; unlike ordinary men, they appear to be minds without feelings. In "The Murders in the Rue Morgue," the narrator describes the working Dupin as "frigid and abstract," with eyes "vacant in expression" (Poe, p. 107).

Doyle is more obvious about Holmes. In *The Sign of Four,* Holmes says that "detection is, or ought to be, an exact science and should be treated in the same cold and unemotional manner" (Doyle, p. 137). Like Dupin, then, Holmes prefers to have a mind free of emotions.

Holmes as Copy

Thus, the number of similarities between the two characters shows that the 1886 Holmes is a copy of the 1841 Dupin. They take their cases for the same reason and handle them with the same dislike for their police associates. Neither character can stand the world of normal men, choosing instead to withdraw into a secret shell. And even when they work with ordinary men, they remain aloof, emotionless.

These similarities are too numerous to be accidental. Clearly Doyle owes a large debt to Poe.

VARYING FROM THE MODEL ESSAY

There are two sample essays in this chapter, the one on active and passive classes and the one you just read on Holmes and Dupin. Both follow the general form of the five-paragraph essay rather closely. These, of course, are the main differences:

- They use *sections* instead of *paragraphs* (like most of the other sample essays in Part Four). Both samples have two central sections.
- They use headings to help readers see the organization. This is especially useful in longer papers—beyond the five-paragraph essay.

Similarities to the five-paragraph essay are these:

- They have a thesis statement and blueprint in the introduction.
- They begin each section with a topic sentence.

- They use detailed support throughout the sections.
- They conclude with a reminder of the thesis statement.

So, although there's a little variation from the five-paragraph essay, there's a lot of similarity, too.

EXERCISES

A. For each of the two topics below, first limit the topic and then write two thesis statements, one for each approach to a comparison-and-contrast paper. Here's an example to get you started:

Topic automobiles

Limited topic the bodies of sports cars

Acknowledge the difference and concentrate on the similarity.

Although there are many different designs for the bodies of sports cars, most of them have a great deal in common.

Acknowledge the similarity and concentrate on the difference.

Although the bodies of sports cars have a great deal in common, there are some important differences.

1. **Topic** women's [or men's] clothing

   Limited topic_____

   Acknowledge the difference and concentrate on the similarity.

   _____

   _____

   Acknowledge the similarity and concentrate on the difference.

   _____

   _____

2. **Topic** college living arrangements

   Limited topic_____

   Acknowledge the difference and concentrate on the similarity.

   _____

   _____

   Acknowledge the similarity and concentrate on the difference.

   _____

   _____

B. Choose one of the thesis statements you developed for Exercise A and outline the central sections for a theme to support the thesis. Make your outline conform to either the Type I or the Type II organization: for each central section you will need to show a topic item with subtopic elements (Type I) or a topic element with subtopic items (Type II).

C. Here are some possible topics for comparison-and-contrast papers:

buildings	television
animals	sports
ethnic groups	science
books	a current event

First, limit the topic; then, write a thesis that concentrates on comparison or contrast. Organize your support with the Type I or Type II pattern, and then write the essay. If you wish to vary from the model, do so. And if you use outside sources for support, be sure to document them (you can use the preliminary system we showed you in Chapter 9, as the second sample theme in the chapter does).

D. Think about the other courses you're taking. Choose a topic and write a comparison and contrast paper. And if you use outside sources for support, be sure to document them (you can use the preliminary system, as the second sample theme in the chapter does).

CHAPTER

16 Cause and Effect

Remember the "Why?" subtopic sentences you studied in Chapter 8? Maybe you didn't realize it at the time, but you were studying one kind of cause-and-effect paper. We'll examine cause-effect papers more closely in this chapter.

A *cause* is a reason something happens; an *effect,* then, is whatever results. As a simple example, we might say, "Because the television set is unplugged, it doesn't work." The *cause* is that the set is unplugged; the *effect* is that the set doesn't work.

Kinds of Cause-Effect Papers

You can write three kinds of cause-effect papers:

- You can state that the effect is true and examine the *cause* in detail.
- You can state that the cause is true and examine the *effect* in detail.
- Or you can try to show that the *entire cause-effect statement* is true.

EXAMINING THE CAUSES

Sometimes the controversial part of a cause-effect statement is the cause, so your paper naturally will examine that part in detail. Let's say you've decided to write about this thesis: "The aggravated assault rate here at Gila Monster Maximum Security Prison has decreased dramatically because of the warden's innovations."

The effect—that the aggravated assault rate has dropped—shouldn't be controversial, so take care of that part quickly with a statistic or two in your introduction: "In the last year, the aggravated assault rate at Gila Monster Maximum Security Prison has plummeted from nineteen per month to only four per month." After dispensing with the effect, spend the rest of your paper telling us about the warden's policies and why they work.

How? Write a section about each of the warden's important policies. Your outline might look something like this:

Thesis	Because of the warden's innovations, the aggravated assault rate at Gila Monster Maximum Security Prison has decreased dramatically.
Topic sentence	The warden's new leather-craft shop allows inmates a constructive way to spend their time.
Topic sentence	The warden has started an intramural sports program that permits the prisoners a physical outlet for their pent-up emotions.
Topic sentence	The new coed visiting areas allow the inmates the chance to discuss relevant social issues with members of the opposite sex.

Did you notice that the thesis begins with *because?* That word clearly established that the essay will examine cause and effect. Another way of saying it is this: if you want to write a cause-and-effect paper, you must have the word *because* somewhere in the thesis statement.

Of course, you don't need to have exactly three central sections. Two especially well-developed sections or four or five shorter ones also could work.

EXAMINING THE EFFECTS

Sometimes the cause is fairly straightforward, but the effect needs elaboration. What if your thesis is that "Because Napoleon's wars killed many young men who otherwise could have worked a lifetime, Europe's standard of living dropped markedly"? Not many people would doubt that the wars killed many young men who could have done a lot of work, but people still might doubt that the standard of living actually dropped. You need to state the cause as a fact and then elaborate upon the effect.

You then could begin the theme by mentioning in the introduction (perhaps using the "striking statement" motivator) how many young men were slaughtered. Then you could develop the theme by discussing the effect ("Europe's standard of living dropped markedly") in three or four European countries. Here's a possible outline:

Thesis	Because Napoleon's wars killed many young men who otherwise could have worked a lifetime, Europe's standard of living dropped markedly.
Topic sentence	After Napoleon's wars, Russia had a lower standard of living.
Topic sentence	Austria also had a lower standard of living.
Topic sentence	Even Napoleon's home, France, had a lower standard of living.

Sometimes you have to deal with ideas that require a little more complexity. The cause may be a general assertion, but the effects are real and often complicated. In this sample paper by one of our students, though it deals with technical matters and borrowed ideas, you will find a thesis with blueprint and three central ideas.

THE SEARCH FOR EXTRATERRESTRIAL LIFE

When the first hominid stood upright, we speculate that it must have looked up to the heavens in wonder, for we find ourselves doing so today. As we look at the nighttime sky with all its stars and spaces, we can't help wondering about life out there.

Perhaps the curiosity, the need to know, which motivated our ancestors to explore this planet, to go into the most forbidding jungles, or to sail the most hazardous seas, also motivates us. We think that what happened here on Earth might have happened elsewhere in the cosmos, and we follow our interest to press farther into the universe, searching for life.

Because of our enduring quest to know the unknown, our search for extraterrestrial life, a search that already has taken people to the moon, will grow in the years ahead. Whether in the form of space probes, radio and radar signals in outer space, or interstellar travel, the human race will continue to look up to the heavens looking for life beyond this Earth.

Space Probes

"The search for extraterrestrial life," according to Isaac Asimov, "took its first flying leap in 1969 when man walked on the moon" (*Extraterrestrial Civilization,* p. 183). This great step proved that we were not destined to spend the rest of our existence earthbound.

Subsequent successful moon landings demonstrated our race's ability to traverse space to the moon and return safely. More distant planets also were out there to be explored. Viking I and II, for example, were sent to Mars in 1975 to test the planet for the possibility for life. Landing in 1976, they found Martian soil not unlike Earth's "but richer in iron and less rich in aluminum" (Asimov, p. 59). The bad news was the absence of carbon, which is essential for life as we know it.

Consequently, the search for life beyond Earth turned to other planets and other means—long-distance radio and interstellar travel.

Radio and Radar Signals

Attempts at interstellar communications have been going on for many years, but they take a long time. Because radio waves travel at the speed of light, it would take over a hundred years for a question to be asked and answered from a near star only fifty light-years away. And when we send out radio signals, we have no way of knowing if anyone is even listening.

But despite the long delays, astronomers have been sending radio signals for almost twenty years using "single or arrayed radio techniques, sensitive radio detectors, advanced computers for processing received information, and the imagination and skill of dedicated scientists" (Carl Sagan, "The Quest for Extraterrestrial Life," *Smithsonian,* May 1978, p. 39). They listen for meaningful sounds from outer space because scientists theorize that any civilization akin to ours would learn to use radio signals most readily. The largest listening dish in the world—in the Russian Caucasus—is devoted to this search for intelligent life beyond our planet (Sagan, p. 43).

Interstellar Travel

An even more dramatic attempt to find life in space will come with interstellar travel. However, the barriers to interstellar exploration are enormous, both technically and humanly. For example, according to NASA, an interstellar spacecraft would need a totally efficient fuel, one that hasn't been developed yet. It may even have to wait for the discovery of antimatter. Almost certainly such a fuel would require metal alloys to withstand heat beyond anything we now know (NASA, *Interstellar Communications,* 1963, pp. 144–50).

Both these problems likely will be overcome; human intelligence and the quest for knowing probably will meet those challenges as we have in the past.

The real barrier to interstellar travel, however, is that same human being. We do not know if humans can endure the extreme durations of space travel. Not only would travelers be confined to cramped quarters with limited exercise and have little variety to see, but also the crew might well suffer mentally from the confinement.

Furthermore, if Einstein's theory of relativity is correct, the phenomenon of "time delation" will mean that the Earth from which travelers leave will be far different from the one to which they return. "Time delation" means that the rate at which time seems to progress slows with increased speed; this phenomenon would mean that a traveler hurtling through space would live what seemed to him or her a normal lifetime, while 5,000 years elapsed on Earth (Asimov, pp. 231–32). Thus, a traveler searching for life on other stars would return to an Earth that had no family, or friends, perhaps not even the nation that sent out the explorer.

Continuing the Search

Despite the barriers (and the limited success), the search for extraterrestrial life will continue. The chances seem too great that somewhere in the estimated 280 billion planetary systems in our galaxy (Asimov, p. 109), intelligent creatures also have developed.

With the technological advances we already have made, united with the never-ending quest to explore the unknown, our search for extraterrestrial life in the great expanse of space will go on. It must, just as it was inevitable that the first hominids would look up to the heavens so long ago.

EXAMINING THE ENTIRE CAUSE-EFFECT STATEMENT

Sometimes cause-effect papers examine the entire statement instead of only half of it. Perhaps both cause and effect are controversial, or perhaps neither is controversial but the fact that they have a cause-effect relationship is.

Let's look first at a cause-effect statement in which both parts are controversial and need elaboration. What if we say that "Because Colorado land developers have no long-term stake in the development they sell, customers often end up with property they cannot inhabit"? We'll have to convince readers of two ideas: that the developers do not have any long-term interests in development and that the new landowners can't live on their property. Both parts need support.

One simple way to organize the support is to write a section on the cause and a section on the effect. We could show in the first central section that Colorado developers don't have any long-term interests in the land; in the next section, then, we could show that the new owners often can't use their property.

However, we probably could write a better paper by examining both parts of the cause-effect statement in the same section. How? We could use examples. We'll make each central section a narrative example of the entire cause-effect statement.

One section might be about Pyrite Acres, a development bulldozed out of the desert at the base of the Sangre de Cristo mountains. The developer, after selling the last site, disappeared into Arizona with all the money. He had not found time to tell the new owners that the underground water supply was so low it could last for only another year or two. Then—if our thesis is really valid—we should be able to present a section on each of two or three similar situations with other developers. Extended examples can be effective any time both the cause and effect need support.

Extended examples can help in another case—one in which both the cause and the effect are fairly straightforward, but their relationship is not.

Consider this statement: "Because many mountain climbers are elated after a difficult climb, they are in danger from carelessness after the difficulty is past." We can accept easily that climbers are elated after a difficult ascent; we also can accept that climbers who are careless afterward are in danger. We probably would like to see support for the idea that the elation from a difficult climb produces that carelessness.

The following sample theme uses extended examples to provide such support.

THE MATTERHORN EFFECT

Only a little over a century ago, some people in Europe thought that the Matterhorn—that awesome, beautiful pinnacle— was the highest mountain in the world. Many climbers from many nations had raced to climb it, but none had succeeded. Then in 1865, an Englishman, Edward Whymper, and six others reached the summit, but only Whymper and two others lived to tell about it. The rest, careless from elation and fatigue, died when one climber slipped on a relatively easy part of the descent and carried three others over a 4,000-foot cliff.

That carelessness, a mental letdown that climbers tend to experience after succeeding at something hard, is called the "Matterhorn effect." I've seen it myself.

The Matterhorn Effect—and Me

I remember how pleased I was when I first climbed Borderline, a hard route up a 150-foot spire in the Garden of the Gods, Colorado. Only six others had ever climbed it. My forearms were so cramped from exertion that I could barely pull the rope up as my climbing partner, Leonard Coyne, seconded the route.

After reaching the top, Leonard mentioned that he knew the descent route was fairly hard, though the previous climbers had disdained using a rope for it. Filled with overconfidence, I simply tossed the rope to the ground below. *We* had just done the tough ascent, so surely *we* did not need a rope either. Then I started down the nearly vertical face.

Suddenly Leonard yelled, "Your handhold is loose! Grab my leg!" There I was—unroped, 150 feet above the ground, and apprehensively holding a couple of loose flakes of rock—when my *foothold* broke. I still don't know what kept me on the rock, but apparently as my foothold gave way, my foot slipped into a barely visible toehold.

I didn't fall, but if I hadn't been overconfident from the hard ascent, I would never have ventured into that dangerous position without a rope.

The Matterhorn Effect—and Leonard

I've seen the Matterhorn effect almost claim Leonard, too. Last summer, he, Gary Campbell, and I had just finished climbing the northwest face of Half Dome, a magnificent 2,000-foot vertical cliff in Yosemite, California. We'd been climbing, eating, and sleeping on the face for three days, and finally we were on top—well, almost. Actually we were about 30 feet from the top, but that part was really easy. We untied, coiled the ropes, and stowed our climbing hardware. Leonard slung on one of the packs—a rather unwieldy thing with a sleeping bag tied precariously to the outside—and started up the last 30 feet. As he began to haul himself onto a five-foot shelf, the pack shifted on his back, almost jerking him off the rock.

Two thousand feet above the ground, he balanced—like a turtle about to flip on its back—for what seemed like a minute before he rolled slowly forward onto the shelf. Three days of numbing fatigue and the elation of doing such a hard climb had caused us all to have a mental letdown; we had put away the ropes too soon. That letdown almost cost Leonard his life.

The point is clear to me: the Matterhorn effect is real for anybody who has just done something hard, but especially for climbers. I've seen it in myself too many times and too many times in others. But—so far, at least—I've been fortunate not to learn about it in the way Edward Whymper and his companions did.

Each extended example in this sample theme presents the entire cause-effect relationship. The cause (the author's elation and fatigue on Borderline and Leonard's on Half Dome) seems to lead quite naturally to the effect (the near-accidents).

PITFALLS OF THE CAUSE-EFFECT THEME

Be careful not to choose a subject that is too general for your paper. In a theme, you could never hope to convince disbelievers of this thesis: "Because the United States wanted to ensure the freedom of South Vietnam, it went to war against North Vietnam." You'd need to write a book, or a substantial chapter in one, to support that statement.

You also must be careful that your cause-effect statement presents the important cause and not just a secondary one. We'd be foolish to blame a field-goal kicker for losing an important game just because he missed a 32-yard attempt during the last five seconds. The team may have lost in part because of that missed attempt, but what about the quarterback who threw an interception during the first quarter, the defensive lineman who missed a key tackle, or the coach who canceled practice last Wednesday? Be sure, in other words, that your cause is really the main cause.

VARYING FROM THE MODEL ESSAY

As you saw in the preceding chapter, one of our purposes in Part Four is to help you learn how to vary from the model essay. How does our sample about the Matterhorn effect differ from the model five-paragraph essay you learned in Part Three? Before we discuss the differences, look back at that sample and underline the thesis, blueprint, and topic sentences. Then read on.

You probably underlined this sentence as the thesis: "That carelessness, a mental letdown that climbers tend to experience after succeeding at something hard, is called the 'Matterhorn effect.' " It doesn't exactly state the main idea of the paper (that the Matterhorn effect is real), but certainly it implies it. Readers expect the rest of the paper to convince them that the Matterhorn effect exists.

Did you find a blueprint? The last sentence of the introduction—"I've seen it myself"—is not really a blueprint of the topic ideas for each paragraph, but it certainly *implies* the development. We know we are about to read some examples.

The topic sentence for the first central section also is implied, not by any one sentence but by the heading for the entire section. A stated topic sentence isn't nearly as important as unified support and coherence. As long as you *could* write a topic sentence for a section—the section, in other words, is unified—and as long as the readers have no doubt what they are reading and why, a topic sentence isn't always necessary.

EXERCISES

A. Use these topics to answer the items below:

parents	a country in the news
dentists	a person in the news
a hobby	education in the home
religion	advertising

1. Write a cause-effect thesis with a cause that is controversial but an effect that isn't. Then write three proposed topic sentences to show how you could develop your thesis.

   Thesis _____

   _____

   Topic sentence _____

   _____

   Topic sentence _____

   _____

   Topic sentence _____

   _____

2. Write a cause-effect thesis with an effect that is controversial but a cause that isn't. Again, write the topic sentences you'd use.

   Thesis _____

   _____

   Topic sentence _____

   _____

   Topic sentence _____

   _____

   Topic sentence _____

   _____

3. Write a cause-effect thesis that has both a controversial cause and a controversial effect. Write the proposed topic sentences.

   Thesis _____

   _____

   Topic sentence _____

   _____

   Topic sentence _____

   _____

Topic sentence _____

_____

B. Find your own support and write a cause-effect theme using this thesis: "Because they often try to dupe me, I object to many food advertisements." Choose some other kind of advertisement if you like, but attach the advertisements to your paper when you hand it in. If you wish to vary from the model theme, do so.

C. Choose something that had a significant effect on you and write a cause-effect paper. If you use outside sources for support, be sure to document them. You can use the preliminary system you learned in Chapter 9.

D. Choose one of the topics in Exercise A (not necessarily one you outlined) and write the paper. If you use outside sources for support, be sure to document them. You can use the preliminary system you learned in Chapter 9.

E. Think about one of your other courses and write a cause-effect paper based on something you've learned in that course. If you use outside sources for support, be sure to document them. You can use the preliminary system you learned in Chapter 9.

17 Classification

Often we find ourselves with a long list of items we'd like to talk about but with no simple way to discuss them. We know we could handle the items if we put them into three or four groups. This process of grouping a long list into categories is *classification.*

Consider this example. At the end of classes on Friday, you look for a way to tackle all the studying you need to do over the weekend. Some of the work is so simple that you can do it right away before you go to a movie. You want to save some of the assignments for Sunday so the lessons will be fresh in your mind on Monday morning. And there are a couple of small research projects that would be good for a library session on Saturday.

To cope with the amount of studying you have to do, you classify the assignments under these headings:

things to study Friday
things to study Saturday
things to study Sunday

Now you've reduced a long list to three groups, but the important idea is that the groups all answer the same question: When is a good time to do this work? In other words, you've classified according to *one* characteristic related to all the items in the list.

If you classify on the basis of a different characteristic related to the items, you'll get a different listing. For example, as usual you don't study as hard over the weekend as you planned to on Friday afternoon; late Sunday night you find yourself with most of the work still to be done. Perhaps you make a new list, like this:

put off until next weekend

put off until final exams

put off forever

Now the groupings are based on how long you can avoid doing the work, so this listing will not be identical with the one you made on Friday afternoon.

Classifying

Dozens of times each week we organize items by classification. We classify when we sort laundry into piles for machine wash, hand wash, or dry clean; or when we sort the machine wash into piles for hot water, warm water, or cold water. We think of automobiles in groupings by size (subcompact, compact, intermediate, and so on), by cost (under $15,000, $15,000–$20,000, and so on), or by expected use (individual, family, or commercial).

Because classification is such a common way of thinking, it is also a popular type of essay development. The groupings automatically provide us with the essay's *organization* and help us see what we want to say about the groups, our *thesis*.

ORGANIZATION

Since it breaks a topic into packages, classification results in a simple pattern that matches the model for the multiparagraph essay. Each category forms a central section:

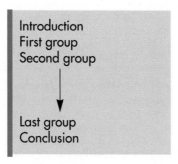

Introduction
First group
Second group

Last group
Conclusion

You'll see an essay using a pattern similar to this one later in the chapter.

Yet, easy as the pattern of development is, you need to avoid its three potential pitfalls. You can tumble into any one of them if you're not careful when you classify.

The first problem is limiting the subject you intend to classify. A subject that is too broad could contain hundreds of items. You could put these hundreds into two or three groups, but the groups probably wouldn't be useful since each would still include a long list of items. On the other hand, you could classify hundreds of items into a large number of groups (say, fifteen), but then you'd have to write an essay with fifteen central paragraphs. In either case, you might as well not classify. Instead, limit the subject until it includes a workable number of items. For example, you choose "Ethnic Groups" as your subject. The world has too many ethnic groups for you to work with. You limit yourself to "Major Ethnic Groups in the United States," but the number of items still seems endless. Limiting the subject to "Major Ethnic Groups in Iowa City" should solve the problem.

The second and most common problem is related to unity. Remember that to classify is to group on the basis of *one* characteristic related to each item. If more than one kind of grouping shows up in your essay, you've failed to maintain unity; and readers who are troubled by the groupings themselves probably will not be convinced by your argument. Consider this list of categories for types of car:

American
Italian
Japanese
Luxury
German

"Luxury" is not a country of origin. The grouping is unacceptable.

Finally, you need to realize that many classifications that work well for grouping items actually have minor flaws. For instance, we often put motorized passenger vehicles that run on land into three convenient groups: cars, trucks, and buses. Yet this classification does not cover the special vehicle that looks like a large station wagon (a car) but is built on a truck chassis (a truck) and can carry nine adults (a small bus).

There's no simple rule for dealing with this problem; however, there is a reasonable procedure to follow when you find an exception to your classes:

- First, judge the importance of the exception. If the exception destroys the point you are trying to make (the thesis of your argument), then rethink your groupings.
- And if a single exception brings to mind dozens more, then again you must regroup.
- Finally, if the exception remains a minor flaw, you may want to simply acknowledge the complication somewhere in your paper.

Or you may be able to exclude the exception by the way you word your subject. For example, if you write about "Religions on My Campus," you'll have to deal with all of them, including that of the single student who has made an idol of the oak tree on the campus mall; but if you write about "Major Religions on My Campus," you eliminate the minor exceptions to your categories.

THESIS

Classification leads logically to one of two types of thesis. The classification may itself be the thesis. Or the classification may be only the means of organizing the argument that persuades the readers to accept the thesis. The first is easier to write, but the second generally makes a better essay.

If your classification reveals striking groupings, the classification itself may be the thesis. Such a thesis takes the general form of "There are (*number of groups*) for (*topic*)." For example, "There are three types of teacher," or "There are two types of politician." Not very interesting, really. Still, sometimes the groupings themselves reveal your stand on the topic. Then the "there are" thesis may work. Consider this example:

> Today there are two types of politician: the dishonest and the half-honest.

Implicit in these classes is the thesis that no politician today is completely honest.

Often, however, the "there are" thesis is not satisfying by itself. The readers yawn and mutter, "So what?" What they are really asking is why the writer bothered to classify items. Consider this thesis:

> There are four types of door locks available for home use.

If your readers happen to be interested in locks, the thesis may work. Probably more interesting would be an essay that uses the types of door locks to make a more important point, such as this:

> Although there are four types of door locks available for home use, an expert burglar can fool any of them.

Now the thesis is that the locks are not foolproof; the writer will develop the essay with a central section for each type of lock, but she'll be showing in each case that the locks will not stop a determined burglar.

When you develop a subject by classification, you'll have to judge the value of your classification. Will the readers care that you've identified groups? Or do the groups merely help reveal something more important?

Here's a sample essay in which the classification serves as an organizational stepping-stone to get to the thesis idea:

THE WAISTLAND OF TV ADVERTISEMENTS

Like thousands of Americans, my compulsive drive to eat
keeps me continually on a diet. When I told a friend that I eat if

---

I'm happy, sad, or just sort of blah, he said I need to occupy my mind. He suggested that when I'm hungry I should watch television. This solution seemed particularly appropriate, for I enjoy television when I'm happy, when I'm sad, and when my mind is too dull to feel much of anything. My friend was right about the television shows; even the worst of them draws my attention away from food.

But my friend forgot about the advertisements. Whether commercials for food in restaurants or for food to take home, these television advertisements represent cruel and all-too-usual punishment for the dieter.

Ads for Restaurants

Numerous restaurant ads provide seemingly continuous reminders of a world of eating enjoyment, all of it forbidden on my 1,200-calorie diet. There are so many restaurant ads that I can turn from channel to channel during commercial time and usually be assaulted with only one laundry detergent ad, one pet food ad, but four ads for restaurants.

After a week on my diet, I'm jealous of the kitten in the Cat Chow commercial; imagine what the barrage of restaurant ads does to me. There are commercials for steak (with salad, potato, and toast), pizza (thick or thin crust, with dozens of toppings to choose from), fish or clams, chicken (with fixin's), hamburgers (with or without cheese, decorated with catsup and mustard, sprinkled with chopped onions and lettuce, topped with a pickle, stuffed in a lightly toasted bun), roast beef or ham sandwiches (for a change from the hamburger habit), and tacos or burritos (as well as related Mexican foods that I've never heard of but begin to crave anyway when I see them on TV).

Need I go on? Probably by now even your stomach has started to rumble, and you've had more for supper than my spoonful of cottage cheese on half a small peach (made more appetizing by a scrap of wilting lettuce for decoration).

Ads for Take-Home Food

Less numerous than restaurant ads but more enticing are the commercials for the foods I can buy to take home.

When I've been starved for carbohydrates for a few days, the convenience of the take-home foods appeals to the remnants of my ability to reason. You see, if my willpower wavers and I go to a restaurant—even a quick-order place—someone who knows I'm dieting may catch me, but it's easy to dart into a grocery store, ice-cream parlor, or doughnut shop and dash home without being seen.

Besides, the TV ads for foods to take home are so inviting. For example, you may remember seeing the advertisement for one of the doughnut shops in town. As the TV camera pans slowly across a counter laden with bakery goodies, I begin to drool. The commercial's sound track broadcasts a man calling to his wife to run to the TV to see the panorama of food laid out before his— and my—impressionable eyes.

He says that the sight of the doughnuts will "drive him crazy," and his voice sounds as though he's already slightly deranged because of what he sees. He proclaims the scene "heavenly," but I know it's a dieter's hell.

I've always assumed he demands that his wife give him her car keys so he can rush to the doughnut shop; I say "assumed" because I've never stayed at my TV set long enough to hear the end of the commercial. I'm on my way out the door to beat that crazy fool to the best of the doughnuts.

Just Deserts

You're reading the ravings of a dieter too often distracted by hunger and too long provoked by TV commercials for food.

Yes, I confess—stop the torture—the ads are obviously effective. I salivate right on cue for all the food advertisers. But in my few remaining rational moments, I can still judge those advertisements for restaurants and take-home foods: To the dieter, they're cruel. They play on the dieter's weakness, the compulsion to eat.

But I'll have my revenge, in my own limited way. My friend has invited me to his apartment tomorrow to watch TV, as he puts it, "to relieve the depression" of my latest diet. I'll sit calmly in his favorite chair; I'll stare innocently at his television. But when the first commercial for food comes on, I'm going to cut the plug off his set.

While he's paralyzed by shock, I'll go into his kitchen to make myself a sandwich.

Behind the writer's humorous mask is a pattern of development dependent upon classification. Because he recognizes that there are too many different food ads to deal with individually, the writer has classified them into two groups—foods to eat in restaurants and foods to eat at home.

Are you bothered by the fact that some of the foods he classifies as restaurant foods could be taken home? Probably not, because the inconsistency will not damage his thesis. And besides, for him the classification may well be valid; some types of foods he consistently eats at restaurants (though he could take them home), and some types he buys for his pantry.

What we should recognize is this: classifications are arbitrary, but they do allow us a reasonable means to organize material. All in all, the classification in this essay is reasonable. It allows the writer to package his support material so that he can get to his thesis.

VARYING FROM THE MODEL ESSAY

Did you notice the minor differences in the sample essay for this chapter? For one, the thesis is not a simple statement of *"limited subject* is *precise opinion,"* but we could still tell that the writer would need to show that the food ads are numerous and that they are "cruel."

You may have noticed that the first central section is the Stage I type, whereas the second central section, which uses subtopic ideas, is a Stage II type.

Finally, in the conclusion no single sentence fully restates the thesis; nevertheless, the first five sentences of the conclusion as a whole do remind us of the thesis.

As you can see, the general pattern of the multiparagraph essay remains, even though there are deviations from the model.

EXERCISES

A. Circle the class in each list below that breaks the unity of the classification.

1. **Topic**   computers
   Classes   spreadsheets
                 word processing
                 keyboard
                 database management

2. **Topic**   art
   Classes   portraits
                 Van Gogh
                 landscapes
                 still lifes

3. **Topic**   sports
   Classes   football
                 basketball

soccer

tennis racquet

4. **Topic**   medical profession

   Classes   ambulance attendant

   emergency room

   physician

   medical technologist

B. Each subject below is too broad to classify easily. First limit the subject and then name at least three classes.

Example

Topic   music

Limited topic classical music

Classes   early Renaissance

late Renaissance   OR   solo

Eighteenth Century   small group

Romantic   symphonic

Early Modern

1. **Topic** environment

   Limited topic_____

   Classes _____

   _____

   _____

   _____

2. **Topic** politics

   Limited topic_____

   Classes _____

   _____

   _____

   _____

3. **Topic** entertainment

   Limited topic_____

   Classes _____

   _____

   _____

   _____

4. **Topic**   travel

   Limited topic_____

   Classes _____

   _____

   _____

   _____

C. Choose one of the limited topics from Exercise B and write an essay that you organize by classification. Remember that you can make your writing more interesting if
   you use classification to develop a thesis other than the classification itself.
D. Use classification to develop an essay about one of the following topics. You'll need
   to limit the topic before you attempt to classify it, just as you did in Exercise B.

   electronic devices
   wars
   high school
   acquaintances
   furniture

   If you use outside sources for support, be sure to document them with the preliminary
   system you learned in Chapter 9.

18 Process

There are two kinds of processes. The first is simply how we do something. For example, a description of this kind of process could be:

- a recipe that tells us how to cook something
- a computer manual that tells us how to do something on a computer
- the Internal Revenue Service instructions that tell us how to prepare our tax forms (well, sort of . . .)

And so forth.

Scientists and engineers will tell you there is another kind of process description: how some*thing* does something. For example:

- How does an automobile engine work?
- Or a telescope?
- Or even photosynthesis?

Describing either kind of process (how some*one* or some*thing* does something) can be a real challenge. You'll find, though, that the structure we've presented throughout the book works nicely to help you meet this challenge.

DESCRIBING HOW SOME*ONE* DOES SOMETHING (INSTRUCTIONS)

Let's look first at instructions—telling people how to do something.

Here are some terrible instructions (real ones—"real" bad ones, that is):

Attributes may be assigned to the elements of a document either directly or indirectly; these two ways of assigning attributes are referred to as direct-formatting" and "styles." Direct formatting has a direct effect on document layout. Assigning a style tells the word processor to look on a style sheet to acquire direct formatting.

Would you like to try following those instructions?

Here are some suggestions for preparing instructions that could have made those instructions you just read easier to follow:

1. *Organize the instructions into a step-by-step procedure.* If you truly understand the instructions you are about to give, this should be easy to do. And steps are much easier for the reader to follow than continuous narrative. We are using steps right now.
2. *Start each step with a verb (as in this sentence).* Instructions tell people what to do, what action to take. Verbs are action words. So starting each step with the specific action gets right to what the reader needs to know. Virtually all good computer manuals (and there are many good ones) start each step with a verb.
3. *Use a layout that clearly shows the steps.* Headings, bulleted paragraphs, and numbered paragraphs are all easy techniques to let the reader see the steps in the process you're describing.
4. *Test your instructions on somebody else.* Try to choose somebody who is typical of the people you really plan to instruct. It's amazing how easy it is to leave out steps when you're writing. Early computer manuals gained their deservedly terrible reputation because they didn't test the instructions adequately. Now the top-notch computer companies test their manuals extensively before publishing them.

Now let's look at an sample essay—it applies the first three of those steps:

GETTING READY TO PAINT A ROOM

Painters will tell you that the hardest parts of painting are getting ready and cleaning up—the painting itself is pretty easy. And painters will also tell you that getting ready can make cleaning up lots easier and prevent disasters, too. So if you have to paint something (and nearly everyone has to paint a room at some time or other—at home, in a dorm, in a first apartment), you can make the painting simpler if you follow these steps to get ready.

Protect Furnishings in the Room

Clearly, the best time to paint a room is when it's empty. If you're in that fortunate situation, skip to the next step.

But if your room isn't empty, your first step is to protect what's there:

1. *Move the furniture.* Get it away from the walls and into the center of the room, stacking wherever possible to use as little floor space as you can.
2. *Use drop cloths.* Cover all furniture and the floor. The best drop cloths have fabric on the top and plastic on the bottom. Drop cloths that are all plastic don't absorb spilled paint, so they stay messy. On the other hand, drop cloths that are all fabric can leak through to what's underneath.

Remove Electrical Covers

The next step is to remove cover plates for wall switches and outlets. The covers are usually held in place with one or two screws, so remove the screws and place them in a plastic bag.

Use Drafting Tape

Tape over anything you want to stay free of paint—windows, woodwork, door hinges, doorknobs, etc. You'll want to use a sharp knife to cut the tape precisely rather than just tearing it. Also, check the stickiness of the tape—some is so sticky that it can remove the paint underneath it, the paint you want to save! "Drafting tape" is only slightly sticky, so use that.

Profit from Your Preparations

These few steps can be time consuming, but anyone who has tried skipping them can tell you a cautionary tale with the moral of "haste makes waste." And the time you spend preparing is saved many times over during the next two stages of the painting process: putting the paint on the wall and (especially) cleaning up!

Simple and efficient, isn't it? Notice the obvious organization that echoes the clear structure you learned for the five-paragraph essay: The brief introduction tells what's coming; each step begins with the main point (in a heading).

DESCRIBING HOW SOME*THING* DOES SOMETHING

The second kind of process paper tells how some*thing* works. Describing this kind of process uses basically the same guidelines as for writing instructions:

- Organize the process into steps.
- Use an appealing layout on the page.

Essentially, you divide whatever you're describing into parts—and then describe each one. For example, if you decide to tell, in broad terms, how a computer works, you'd no doubt divide it into at least these parts:

- the central processor
- the memory
- the hard drive
- the keyboard (or other input device, such as a mouse)
- the viewing device (such as the monitor)

Although this kind of description couldn't go into any real detail, it could certainly be valuable, a good overview of the main parts and how they work together.

So, your paper would probably begin by setting out your subject (describing the computer). Then you'd probably give a blueprint, naming the parts (such as the central processor). Then you'd have a section on each of those parts.

VARYING FROM THE MODEL ESSAY

The five-paragraph essay you learned earlier in this book is highly organized—and so are descriptions of processes. The sample in this chapter (on painting a room) differed from the model because it didn't start with a blueprint and didn't always use topic sentences—it depended on the headings to convey the topic ideas. Those are all common techniques in process papers.

However, by now in the course, you've no doubt seen that a clear structure is important, but you needn't follow it to the letter. Just be sure you and your reader know where you are in the paper at all times. The models here help you do that. They help you get started and often serve as the actual structure for what you write.

You're now ready to begin the next section of the book: writing research papers!

EXERCISES

A. Let's say you're going to give instructions on how to get ready for class or work in the morning. Without writing the paper, simply list the various steps, in order, that you think someone should follow (or that you actually do follow).

B. Now let's say you're going to describe how something simple—a mercury thermometer—operates. Or choose something other than a thermometer. Go to an encyclopedia (or other source) if necessary, and do a little research. Then outline how that "something" works.

C. Now, write the paper for Exercise A. Be sure to follow the conventions on documentation we discuss in Chapter 9.

D. And now write the paper for Exercise B. Be sure to follow the conventions on documentation we discuss in Chapter 9.

E. Everyone knows something other people don't know but might be interested in. Perhaps you're good at golf, computers, or gardening. Choose something you know how to do and write a clear, concise set of instructions that tells your readers how to do it. You might try out these instructions on a friend before you hand in your paper. It's amazing how easily people (including all of us, of course) can go wrong unless the instructions are absolutely unambiguous.

   One caution: most instructors prefer you don't just write the instructions for cooking something—a recipe, in other words. That can get pretty boring. Be sure to choose something that doesn't simply paraphrase from a book—something you already know about!

F. You can probably get some good ideas for a description of a process from other courses. For example, in astronomy you've probably learned how the universe may have developed (a *large* process!). In geology, perhaps you've learned how mountains or canyons developed. In sociology, you might have learned how one culture meshes with another. In journalism, you might have learned how to write a good lead.

   Think of a good process and write about it. Choose either how some*one* does something or how some*thing* does something. Be sure to follow the conventions on documentation we discuss in Chapter 9.

The Research Paper

You've probably been having nightmares about the research paper ever since we first mentioned it. Actually, you already know most of the skills involved. You know the fundamentals of organization and support, and you may have looked at the punctuation and expression chapters. You've even used some outside sources and a simple method of documentation. The only new skills you need to learn are efficient ways to find your support in the library, organize it, use it in the paper, and document it. You'll find these new skills demand more time and patience than you needed for your earlier papers, but they are not difficult to learn.

19 Overview of the Research Paper

Sooner or later the longer paper comes to us all, usually because it's assigned, or perhaps because we find ourselves interested in a subject. But regardless of the reason, we're all faced with the same problem: How do we say anything intelligent for five or ten pages or more?

Either we write about a subject we know intimately, or we go to some other source—an interview with an eyewitness, perhaps, or a book in the library. When we must use sources outside our own minds or experience, we rely on research.

Unlike some of the earlier exercises and paragraphs in this book, the research paper has *no invented evidence.* You must find the specific support for your research paper by consulting real sources, not imaginary ones.

By now you may be worried because of stories you've heard about research papers. A research paper can be long, and it can be a lot of work. It can be particularly troublesome if you put it off until the last minute. The process of research and writing requires a number of careful steps. You'll find it hard to compress all of them into a long night's work—or even a day or two.

What a Research Paper Is and Isn't

It's not:

- a rehash of encyclopedia articles
- a string of quotations, one after another, like sausages
- a mass of invented support
- a mystical kind of writing that's more difficult than the kinds you've been doing

> It is:
>
> - an organized statement (with limited subject and precise opinion) about a topic, using support from sources outside your own experience
> - a paper that credits sources with thorough documentation
> - a normal requirement in many college courses and professional jobs
> - the next step in your development as a writer

THE SHAPE OF THE RESEARCH PAPER

Like the writing you did for Part Four, the research paper is an expanded form of the five-paragraph essay. Of course it's longer, but the basic structure is still the same. The chart on the next page shows the relationship between a five-paragraph essay and a longer research paper.

Not every paragraph must have exactly three items of specific support, nor must every main idea have exactly three paragraphs of support. Some may have more and some less. Whatever the number, the support paragraphs help persuade your readers to accept one of the major topic sentences in the same way specific support helps persuade them to accept the topic sentences in a five-paragraph essay. And the major topic sentences in the research paper help convince your readers of the thesis. By now you've learned that a model is simply a guide, a handy way to begin thinking about your paper. Treat this model the same way.

THE RESEARCH PAPER'S PURPOSE

Why write a long paper? A research paper could be used:

- to explore a particular problem (leading to a thesis identifying the major cause of the British defeat at Singapore in World War II, for example)
- to inform readers about a development (with a thesis about the effects of an increase in the minimum wage)
- to trace the history of a situation (developing a thesis identifying why America became involved in the Panama Canal)
- to present the solution to a problem (with a thesis on how Americans can deal with lethal crimes among the nation's youth)

Research papers are a means of presenting a large amount of information about a particular topic, information gathered from outside the writer's own knowledge and experience. And the purposes of these papers can be as varied as are the reasons for presenting large amounts of information.

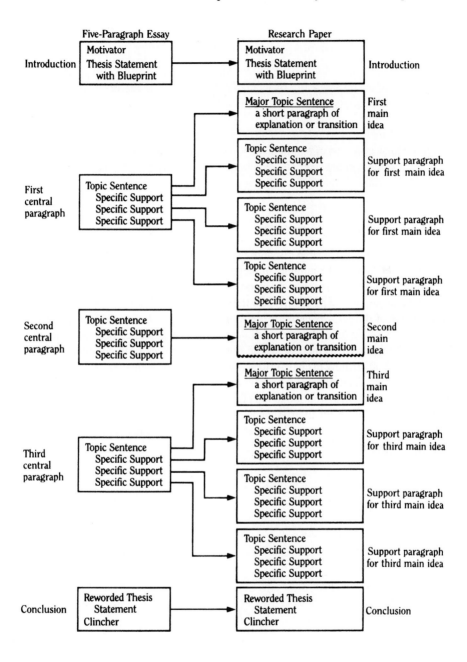

Practical Applications for Research Papers

A research paper is not just a classroom exercise. It has many practical uses. Businesses use research reports as marketing studies and reports to stockholders. The military services call them staff studies and intelligence reports. Inspectors and auditors call them reports of findings. Doctors call them case studies. Professors sometimes call them monographs. Whatever the names, reports that present large amounts of information from research or investigations of some sort are likely to remain part of your life beyond the classroom.

A SAMPLE RESEARCH PAPER

To see what is possible in a research paper of about 1,500 words, look at the sample paper that follows. Comments on pages facing the paper highlight points you'll learn more about in subsequent chapters.

For the most part the page layout in the sample paper follows the guidance in the third edition of the *MLA Handbook for Writers of Research Papers.* In a few places, however, we've departed from the MLA page format guidance because it restricts layout techniques. Nevertheless, we've noted those places in the comments facing the pages so you'll know the MLA rules if your instructor wants your paper to adhere strictly to the MLA guidance. Of course, we've also explained why we departed from the MLA format to help you judge the effect of the alterations.

Some instructors want their students to submit outlines with their final papers. Chapter 22, which discusses outlining, shows a formal sentence outline for this sample research paper.

A   The MLA research paper format, which your instructor may want you to use, does not include a title page, but many instructors have requested that we include a sample.

If you want to follow the MLA format completely, your paper will begin with the first page of the body (that is, without a title page and without an abstract). You'll provide identifying information at the top of the first page of the body, flush left with the paper's left margin, one inch from the top edge of the paper, and with all identification elements double-spaced. Provide the following: full name, instructor's name, course title, and date. After this information you will double-space to find the line on which to type your paper's title.

A

HOSTAGES OF TESTING

by

Jennifer James

for
English 111
Professor Wilson
15 April 1990

B   The MLA research paper format does not call for an abstract. Again, numerous instructors have requested that we include a sample. For this reason the sample paper includes an *informative abstract,* providing it after the title page and before the paper's body, much like an executive summary. Chapter 22 discusses informative and descriptive abstracts.

B

James ii

ABSTRACT

Minimum competency tests are of questionable value for students; they hold at risk the quality of education of all students—not just those who fail one or more times—making them hostages to the testing system. The tests were a response to a need for simple measures of quality to restore public confidence in American education. What resulted were standardized examinations of development of minimal skills—primarily in reading, writing, and mathematics—that were linked to serious consequences. Unfortunately, the tests lead to three major drawbacks in education: class time lost to coaching, narrowing or trivialization in the curriculum, and deflection of the curriculum away from areas of value. Thus, even though minimum competency test scores have increased, these improvements are a natural result of the high stakes connected to the tests. With the tests defining both curriculum content and teacher success or failure, true education is at risk, even though there is no evidence connecting the tests to success in life.

C

The MLA page format, which your instructor may want you to use, calls for your last name and the page number one-half inch from the top of each page and flush with the right margin. You'll see this style illustrated on page 2 and subsequent pages of the sample paper. MLA guidance calls for this information on page 1 as well, but we've deleted it. Traditionally, the first page of a document bears no page marking.

MLA guidance directs you to type the title of the paper and double-space to begin the first line of text in the body of your paper. The result is a solid-looking mass of type that doesn't provide visual separation for the paper's title. We've added extra space after the title, setting it off for readers to see. Using white space in this way is a simple design technique that enhances the appearance of a paper.

D

The thesis statement for this paper is in two sentences: "Despite their appeal to the public, minimum competency tests are of questionable value for the students. They hold at risk the quality of education of all students—not just those who fail one or more times—making them hostages to the testing system." The second sentence could stand on its own as the thesis, of course, but readers get the full meaning of the thesis statement from the two sentences in combination.

E

This paper puts the blueprint in a separate paragraph with bullets to mark the blueprint items. The blueprint also would work if it were part of the previous paragraph and had no bullets. However, the layout here leaves no doubt about what is to follow. This type of overt organizational device is particularly important in business and technical writing—and it can add to other types of writing as well.

F

Marked here is a first-level (or major) heading. In Chapter 10 you saw what a single level of headings could do to help readers grasp the information in a short paper. A longer paper may need more levels—this one has two.

The heading at the beginning of the first block of "body" text provides a benefit for the introduction as well. Commonly the first paragraph of a short research paper is a single paragraph—beginning with a motivator and ending with the thesis statement with blueprint. The sample paper has the necessary parts, but they are divided into three paragraphs for easier reading—instead of being one long paragraph. The heading at the *end* of the introduction keeps readers from confusing introductory and body paragraphs.

MLA page format does not address headings. However, MLA guidance does call for consistent double-spacing throughout the research paper. Presumably, then, it would allow no extra space before or after headings within the body of the paper. As you can see, we advise using extra space before and after headings.

That spacing is an important design technique. The white space signals to readers that you're moving to a new topic and sets off the heading, focusing on the title it provides for the following material. In this way, layout reinforces your words.

G

Documenting borrowed material is one of the new skills you'll learn in studying the research paper. Notice that the information from the Madaus article has an introduction ("George Madaus provides. . . .") so that readers can tell where the borrowed material begins. The parenthetical reference at the end of the borrowing—"(614)"—marks where the borrowing ends and tells specifically which part of the Madaus article the writer drew upon.

HOSTAGES OF TESTING

C

Many school systems today use standardized tests for final examinations. Typically teachers drill their students on lists of names, dates, and places that may be on the test. Some teachers even tell their students that if they see certain questions, they should provide certain answers. This type of preparation is called "teaching to the test," although "cramming to the test" would seem more appropriate. The problem is a typical result when schools use standardized tests for large numbers of students and the stakes are high for students and teachers.

When school systems use minimum competency tests to determine whether students will reach high school graduation, testing becomes even more serious. Across the United States, thousands of students are subject to minimum competency tests, yet those tests lead to a number of problems, among them "teaching to the test." Despite their appeal to the public, minimum competency tests are of questionable value for the students. They hold at risk the quality of education of all students—not just those who fail one or more times—making them hostages to the testing system.

D

Why the minimum competency tests interfere with learning becomes clear from a discussion of:
- why the tests were adopted
- what minimum competency tests are
- problems the tests generate for the classroom
- how the testing holds students at risk

E

WHY MINIMUM COMPETENCY TESTS WERE ADOPTED

F

Minimum competency tests should be viewed against the background that led to their creation. George Madaus provides an overview of the events that led to competency testing. In the 1960s and early 1970s, the public became convinced that the quality of education in the United States was inadequate. Employers claimed high school diplomas were meaningless.

G

Notice also that the parenthetical reference—the page number in parentheses—comes before the period that ends the sentence.

You'll learn more about presenting and documenting borrowed material in Chapters 23 through 25.

See the parenthetical reference at the end of the first sentence? Where did the summary begin? Your obligation to your readers is to be sure they always know where borrowed material begins and ends. No problem here: Clearly the borrowed material begins at the start of the paragraph. However, if you think readers may question where your borrowed material begins, introduce the borrowing by mentioning the source's author or title.

The second sentence of the paragraph ("What the public wanted. . . .") is the writer's own. Readers can tell that because the first sentence ends with a parenthetical reference and the third sentence begins with an introduction to another borrowing.

The parenthetical reference at the end of the first sentence—"(Salganik 608)"—provides both the name of the author of the source and the page number for the borrowing. This is a "standard" parenthetical reference. All the other parenthetical references in the sample paper have only page numbers. Why? When an introduction to a borrowing identifies the source in the Works Cited listing, the parenthetical reference needs only the page designation. You'll learn more about parenthetical references and this streamlining technique in Chapter 24.

Quotations that require four or fewer lines of typing in your paper will be incorporated into the flow of your paper but set off with quotation marks to designate the exact words from your source. Longer quotations, like this one, are indented as a block. Notice that the indented quotation does *not* begin and end with quotation marks; the block indentation functions in the place of quotation marks to set off the exact words of the source from your own words.

Notice also that the parenthetical reference—"(608)"—comes *after* the ending punctuation for the quotation. For long, indented quotations, space twice after the ending punctuation of the quotation, provide the parenthetical reference, and put *no* punctuation after the closing parenthesis of the reference. Note: this is the style *only* for quotations set off with block indentation.

James 2

News of declines in Scholastic Aptitude Test scores convinced many that schools were not doing their jobs. And, of course, education costs continued to rise (614). The public wanted proof that youth were being prepared for life and that tax dollars were not being wasted.

Attempts in the 1960s to develop detailed activity plans and report progress to parents proved too complex for most parents (Salganik 608). What the public wanted was simplicity—scores they could understand and proof that money spent on education brought improvement. As Laura Salganik notes:

> in the new climate of uncertainty about the adequacy of the schools (and thus about the competence of educators), testing introduced a welcome simplicity to the task of restoring both educational quality and public confidence in the schools. Few people were willing to argue with the use of tests as a means of ensuring quality control.   (608)

To policy makers, standardized testing appeared to offer accurate, unbiased assessment tools. As Andrew Strenio explains, standardized tests appear to be "objective," because they are scored by machine rather than by a person, and to many that equates to "scientific" (63–65, 192–94). To policy makers and school administrators, the standardized tests appeared to offer a convenient, cost-effective way of improving education and especially of pleasing the public. And if the goal is to demonstrate that students graduate from high school with at least minimal skills, what better way to show it than to administer a minimum competency test?

WHAT MINIMUM COMPETENCY TESTS ARE

Minimum competency tests are standardized examinations, almost always multiple choice, developed to ensure that students have developed minimal proficiencies. In most states the tests are on reading, writing, and math, with a few adding other skills. Usually the tests are connected to some serious consequence,

J   This short quotation is incorporated into the flow of the student writer's work. Notice that the quoted material, which is set off with quotation marks, does not begin with a capital letter. That is, the first portion of the quotation is itself not a full sentence, although it is set into the student's writing so that there is a complete sentence structure. You can, and should, trim the material you quote to fit it into your own writing as support for your points. The quotations should fit into the grammar and sense of your own writing. Of course, it's *not* acceptable to edit the original material in such a way that you misrepresent what its author said or wrote—for example, by leaving out *not* or *never.* Chapter 23 explains techniques for dealing with quotations: omitting words, adding words, adding emphasis, verifying quotation accuracy, altering initial capitalization, and altering final punctuation.

Notice also that the parenthetical reference here—"(8)"—follows the quotation marks but precedes the ending punctuation for the sentence. This technique applies to quotations incorporated into the flow of your paragraphs, but not to long, indented quotations.

K   "Time Lost to Coaching" and the two headings that follow are second-level (or minor) headings. The heading style this simple research paper employs is one good way to make headings in a typed paper. As Chapter 22 illustrates, if your computer or word processor permits changes in type sizes, faces, and styles, you can make fancier headings. The important point is that a major heading should stand out more on the page than a minor heading does.

If you compare the heading levels in this paper with its formal sentence outline (in Chapter 22), you'll see that the writer has employed first-level headings for each major block (Roman numeral outline level) of the body plus the conclusion. She has provided second-level headings only for the sub-blocks (capital letter outline level) within one major block. Why? This major block on the problems that the testing generates has three clearly defined subordinate sections; the second-level headings help readers grasp that material. The other major blocks, especially the one on what minimum competency tests are, do not have this same type of separation within the blocks—so minor headings would not be functional. Don't feel you have to provide a subheading for every division of your final outline. But do use headings to focus attention on the contents of your paper where such focus is appropriate.

James 3

such as promotion to a higher grade; the most common connection is to high school graduation. Karen Klein reports that by 1984, 40 states had some type of minimum competency testing program, about half of them a requirement for graduation (565).

PROBLEMS THE TESTS GENERATE FOR THE CLASSROOM

The American Association of School Administrators noted the most serious drawback of the minimum competency movement: "its almost total reliance on testing. Testing alone cannot guarantee that students will become more competent" (8). What the testing does, however, is create serious problems for the educational process in the classroom. Critics of minimum competency testing point out these problems: time lost in coaching students, narrowing of the material taught, and deflection in the curriculum overall.

Time Lost to Coaching

When a test has serious consequences for either students or teachers, significant classroom time goes into preparing the students—time taken away from other studies. This is "teaching to the test." For example, George Madaus reports that the Department of Education in New Jersey admitted providing local districts with the previous year's test and that some teachers coached students for weeks or even months (616). For students who fail a minimum competency test, the loss of normal class time can be greater. Michael Henry reports that 33 to 50 percent of Maryland's students fail the citizenship competency test at least once. As a result, a student who has not passed by the end of the junior year can have been taken out of 15 weeks of normal classroom work in world geography, world history, and U.S. history (11).

Narrowing of the Curriculum

Teachers also report that the tests lead to narrowing, or

L   Just as headings allowed the writer to divide the introduction into three paragraphs without risk of confusing readers about the paper's organization, headings allow the writer to break a long paragraph into two at this point. Clearly both paragraphs have to do with "Deflection in the Curriculum."

James 4

trivialization, of the curriculum. Michael Henry charges that the Maryland competency test has reduced the concept of citizenship to "an exercise in trivia": "The test requires a commitment to memory of hundreds of details—information probably forgotten before the last test booklet has been packed and shipped back to the state board of education" (11). The problem results because test makers have difficulty designing multiple-choice questions that go beyond identification of correct rules or facts or of simple computations. Thus, composition becomes rules of grammar and punctuation, not actual writing. As Gerald Bracey notes, "It is difficult to present science as an ongoing process of discovery, as a detective story, when test items converge on the recall of a single right answer" (686).

Deflection in the Curriculum

The third major effect of minimum competency testing is deflection in the curriculum. Deflection results when emphasis is placed on preparing students for the test material rather than on other curriculum areas of equal or greater merit. Most competency tests focus on reading, writing, and math; that leaves the arts and social sciences, for instance, without emphasis. It even ignores courses such as shop and home economics that are designed to prepare students for later life.

Charles Suhor cites a survey of the effects of testing in Florida in 1977. Results showed that because of the focus on basic skills, there had been reduced emphasis on literature, language, and composition (639). Gerald Bracey provides a particularly apt example: The Virginia math competency test assessed recognition of parallel lines, but not of perpendicular lines. One version of the test, however, included a question on perpendicular lines, and student performance on that question dropped significantly (685). The conclusion is simple: if the test covers an item, it receives classroom attention, yet other areas— even closely related ones—may be ignored.

M   Tables and figures often will not fit exactly where you'd like them to go in your final paper. For that reason, it's best to prepare them so they can "float" freely within the paper—that is, so you do not have to place them in only one particular place. Refer to a table (or figure) by number—as with "(see Table 1)." Then place the table (or figure) where you'd like it to go if it will fit there. If it won't fit, you can place it intact at the top of the next page (or on a separate page for a very large table or figure).

N   Prepare a table as the sample paper shows it. Give the table a number and a title; show the source, if necessary, at the end of the table, set off by a short line dividing it from the table contents. You may want to put tables and figures within boxes to separate the graphics from your text; many computer word processing programs provide such a capability. Illustrated here is a technique of setting the table off with single lines above and below—a layout technique you can achieve with only a standard typewriter.

The MLA format for a table differs somewhat from what you see here. If you need to follow MLA guidance exactly, make these changes: Type the table designator and title on separate lines as shown, but place them flush left at the left margin of your paper. Double-space *throughout* the table. Use a full ruled line (margin to margin) in place of italic type to set off column headings. Do not set the table off from your text with lines or a box, and do not provide extra space above or below the table.

James 5

HOW MINIMUM COMPETENCY TESTING HOLDS STUDENTS AT RISK

These problems are likely to result to some degree from any standardized testing. Without doubt, however, they become more acute when the stakes are high, as they are with minimum competency testing. How, then, can these tests be defended? Advocates and the public seem to be convinced by increases in scores. James Popham provides figures of improvement associated with competency testing (see Table 1). Gerald Bracey

TABLE 1

TEST SCORE IMPROVEMENTS FOR LOCALITIES USING COMPETENCY TESTS

Locale	Subjects	Grade	Period	Percent Improvement
Alabama	Reading, Writing, Math	11	1983–85	4–8
Connecticut	Reading, Writing, Math	9	1980–84	6–16
Detroit	Reading, Writing, Math	12	1981–86	19
Maryland	Reading, Writing, Math	9	1980–86	13–25
	Citizenship	9	1983–86	23
New Jersey	Reading, Math	9	1977–85	16–19
	Reading, Math	10	1982–85	8–11

Source: James W. Popham, "The Merits of Measurement-Driven Instruction," *Phi Delta Kappan* 68 (1987): 682.

argues against a simple interpretation of such data. He points out that when students are threatened with failure and teachers with loss of jobs, "it is something less than miraculous to find that test scores rise" (686).

A vocal advocate of minimum competency testing, James Popham accepts that the tests affect teaching and wants to push things further. He advocates using tests with serious consequences to drive curriculum, to determine what teachers

O

The introduction to the paper does not need a heading to announce where it starts (although it benefits from the heading for the beginning of the paper's body, which also marks where the introduction ends). The conclusion, however, needs a heading to separate it from the body of the paper.

Would "Conclusion" work as the heading? Yes, but not well. "Conclusion" would mark the move from the paper's body to its conclusion. But good headings should be more than mere place marks. They're also titles that lead readers into the substance of the material that follows.

James 6

will teach. This, he feels, will overcome mediocre teaching in the classroom (680–81). However, there is another way to look at what he is asking for. So teachers will teach certain things in certain ways, their students should be held at risk; then outsiders can be assured the teachers are doing what is required of them. This is a hostage situation.

Finally, any analysis of the value of minimum competency testing should consider research about the effect of minimum competency testing on earnings after high school graduation, especially since the tests were adopted partially because of employer complaints about student quality. Karen Klein cites two studies of the relationship of math and reading scores of students not attending college to their earning after leaving high school. Those studies showed scores and earnings were totally unrelated. However, she points out that other research shows people between 16 and 21 are twice as likely to be unemployed if they have no diploma. And as Klein notes, for most students who are going to college, the minimum competency tests are just a "formality" (566). So who actually benefits from the tests?

MINIMUM COMPETENCY TESTS DO NOT PROMOTE LEARNING

The minimum competency tests, it seems, provide simple statistics that appear to "prove" the usefulness of the tests. Yet, looking behind those statistics to see what the impact is on the classroom and on the preparation of students for life shows the results are very different. The tests indeed appear to force students to learn bits of information, and—not surprisingly—overall improvement on retaining bits of information improves as a result. But do those bits equate to learning? Many educators say no. At the same time, the cost to all students is severe. Time that could be spent on developing thinking and reasoning is spent on memorization. Vital subjects are reduced to bare minimums that can be tested easily, so that the minimum level

James 7

for competency becomes the maximum level for teaching. Courses and activities that do not lead to test preparation begin to be ignored. In this way, the quality of education of American students is held hostage by the minimum competency testing process.

P

The Works Cited page begins on a separate page from the text of the research paper. Chapter 25 explains in detail the styles for Works Cited entries.

If you need to follow MLA page layout guidance exactly, begin the section title—"Works Cited"—one inch from the top of the paper and double-space to get to the line for the first entry. That is, do not provide additional space between the section title and the beginning of the entries. We've shown extra space for the same reason we set off the paper's title, the headings, and the table—to let white space signal breaks and to highlight the material set off.

James 8

WORKS CITED

American Association of School Administrators. *The Competency Movement: Problems and Solutions.* By Shirley Boes Neill. AASA Critical Issues Report. Sacramento: Education News Service, 1978.

Bracey, Gerald W. "Measurement-Driven Instruction: Catchy Phrase, Dangerous Practice." *Phi Delta Kappan* 68 (1987): 683–86.

Henry, Michael. "A True Test or a Trivia Game?" *Newsweek* 22 June. 1987: 10–11.

Klein, Karen. "Minimum Competency Testing: Shaping and Reflecting Curricula." *Phi Delta Kappan* 65 (1984): 565–67.

Madaus, George F. "Test Scores as Administrative Mechanisms in Educational Policy." *Phi Delta Kappan* 66 (1985): 611–17.

Popham, James W. "The Merits of Measurement-Driven Instruction." *Phi Delta Kappan* 68 (1987): 679–82.

Salganik, Laura Hersh. "Why Testing Reforms Are So Popular and How They Are Changing Education." *Phi Delta Kappan* 66 (1985): 607–10.

Strenio, Andrew J., Jr. *The Testing Trap.* New York: Ransom, 1981.

Suhor, Charles. "Objective Tests and Writing Samples: How Do They Affect Instruction in Composition?" *Phi Delta Kappan* 66 (1985): 635–39.

PREVIEWING THE RESEARCH PAPER PROCESS

You already know what a good thesis looks like—a precise opinion about a limited topic. Research papers, too, require a good thesis, but because the research paper is longer and uses other people's ideas, we might call the thesis a thoughtful assertion about the limited topic. That means the research thesis is more than just an opinion: it's opinion supported by facts, ideas, and words of other authorities. To help you devise a good thesis, we'll preview the research process here.

Although you might be an intuitive writer and settle immediately on the exact thesis statement you'll use in writing your paper, that would be very unusual. If you're an ordinary mortal like most of us, this will be more common: You pick a topic, narrow it enough to make the scale of research reasonable, and move slowly toward the final thesis statement as your research goes along. For example, the writer of the sample paper began with *testing,* narrowed that to *minimum competency testing* after beginning her research, and finally settled on *the negative impact of minimum competency testing on the quality of education* as the basis for her thesis statement.

In the next six chapters we'll go into more detail, but here's the research paper procedure we recommend to start you on your way:

- *Select a general topic* that interests you.
- *Do some preliminary reading* in handy, reliable sources to find out whether your topic and your ideas about it seem to be based on accurate assumptions and whether reliable, relevant sources appear to be available. If you're unhappy about your topic at this point, choose something else.
- *Develop a working thesis statement* to set a reasonable scope for research. As you find sources and think about what you've learned, constantly refine your working thesis by checking to see whether the subject is precise. Keep your mind open so that you can refine the working thesis when necessary.
- *Find supporting sources* that deal with your topic. You needn't limit your search to library sources, although the time available to work on your paper may prevent you from conducting interviews or tests. For this reason, most of our discussion about research papers focuses on library resources. Be sure to evaluate your sources for relevance and reliability rather than blindly trusting what you read and hear. And be sure to keep accurate records about your sources; you'll need information about them when you document your paper.
- *Gather supporting facts and opinions* from your sources. You won't be able to remember every detail, and you'll need some sort of system to match information with sources so you'll be able to document what you borrow. (We'll discuss two very different ways of accomplishing these objectives.)
- *Organize your thoughts and support.* You should develop working outlines as you conduct your research; they help you see where you're going with your investigation—especially where you need more material. Before you draft your paper, however, you'll need to develop some sort of final outline to guide your writing. Moreover, many instructors require their students

to submit formal outlines either before they begin writing or with the final paper.

- *Write a first draft.* The writing step is much like you've done for shorter papers, but you'll also be incorporating borrowed material from your research. As you write, you can insert the appropriate parenthetical references in the text for part of the documentation process. You'll also write and organize Works Cited entries for the listing that ends your research paper.
- *Revise the draft*—as many times as necessary to get the paper right.
- *Prepare the final version of your paper to hand in.*

POSSIBLE TOPICS

Now we'll look at some topics that may stir your imagination. Any of these broad topics could lead to a good narrow topic and thesis, or they may suggest similar topics that interest you. All, however, need to be narrowed carefully. Moreover, you'll do yourself and your readers a real favor if you stay away from some kinds of topics. Avoid writing about contemporary politics or religion—such topics often are too personal to write a research paper about. Thus, they are frequently ineffective from the beginning.

Remember, the topics that follow all need deliberate limiting. And, of course, before you can develop a thesis, each needs a thoughtful assertion—a precise opinion—made about it.

Acid Rain	Endangered Species	Panama Canal
Adoption	Environmental Legislation	Pollution
AIDS Research	Espionage	Prison Overcrowding
Airline Deregulation	Flemish Painting	Rain Forests
Auto Safety	Gambling	Refugees
Ballet	Hazardous Wastes	Reunification of Germany
Bicycling	Hospices	Savings and Loan Banks
Cable Television	Insulation	Speech Disorders
Censorship	International Terrorism	Strip-mining
Changes in Europe	Iraq's Invasion of Kuwait	Tax Reform
Chemical Fertilizers	Islamic Movement	Teen Alcoholism
Child Abuse	Junk Bonds	Trojan War
Child Custody	Learning Disorders	Urban Transportation
Commercial Satellites	Midwives	Vegetarianism
Digital Technology	Minoans	Volcanoes
Drugs in Sport	Missing Children	Worker Productivity
Drug Testing	Organ Donation	Yoga

CHAPTER

20 | Finding Support

Sometimes when you have to write a research paper you won't know much about the subject, so you won't know what you want to say until you've studied the subject enough to narrow it to a manageable size, to a thesis. For example, from the broad subject of *pollution,* you might narrow to *pollution from plastics* and even further to the narrower thesis that *Fast food restaurants are the primary source of polluting plastics in North America.*

WHERE TO BEGIN

One way both to narrow your topic and to get a lead on information you need is to do some preliminary research in general reference tools such as encyclopedias. Even here, keep an informal record of your research by listing briefly the title and headings or subjects you looked under. This step is especially important if later you want to return to pick up the bit of information you remember reading but neglected to write down.

You may be in for some surprises as you continue working on your subject; what you find may take you in unexpected directions. Despite your initial belief, you might find, for example, that two of the fast-food chains have stopped using plastics and are active in research to prevent their products from contributing to pollution. When such a change happens, you must revise your thesis. In this case, you might say something like, "Although many people think fast-food chains are destructive polluters, they are actually working hard to prevent pollution caused by their products."

Once you have a working thesis, you're ready to begin the more formal research process. The problem is to know where to begin among all the resources available.

You may want to conduct a survey or series of experiments. Your research could involve audio or video tapes or viewing a series of television programs. Or perhaps you'll want to interview participants in a relatively recent event of some importance— or business executives involved in an ongoing project. Finding sources for a research paper can include any search for information relevant to a topic and thesis.

Most college research paper projects, however, involve library research and are usually limited to the books and articles that are readily available in the college library. The limitation is the time you have available to conduct your research and prepare your paper. For this very practical reason, our discussion of sources focuses on the college library. Fortunately, though, the things you're learning about conducting research and writing a research paper apply just as well to other types of research you might conduct if you had more time available.

College libraries today provide a mixture of online data bases, CD-ROM disks, and shelved books and periodicals. Research tools, in particular, probably are automated in your school's library, though some of the most useful reference guides may be on CD-ROM or in book form, depending on your library's holdings. In addition, your library may well have one or more online information services, providing automated access to reference works and periodical articles. All of this means that no book such as this one can predict exactly what your college library holds. Fortunately, though, we can discuss what you're most likely to find and point out what you should look for. Still, knowing what resources you have available will require a little exploration on your own.

BOOKS

THE CATALOG

Traditionally, the primary guide to a library's book collection has been called the "card catalog," because all the library's books were listed on index cards filed in long, narrow drawers. Today your library probably doesn't have such cards, but it will have a catalog of some sort, perhaps on microfilm, but most likely in a computer file. Whatever the form and name, it will provide essentially the same information as did the traditional card catalog. Since most college libraries now have computerized catalogs, let's deal with those first.

THE COMPUTERIZED CATALOG

To begin using your library's computerized catalog of books, you'll need to follow the directions either near the computer or on the screen. The directions can lead you in several ways to find books you need for your research. Generally, those directions tell you to enter an author's name, a book's title, or the subject you're interested in. Here's a sample first screen from one library:

```
What type of search do you wish to do?
    1.  TIL = Title, journal title, series title, etc.
    2.  AUT = Author, illustrator, editor, organization, etc.
    3.  A-T = Combination of author and title.
    4.  SUB = Subject heading assigned by library.
    5.  NUM = Call number, ISBN, ISSN, etc.
    6.  KEY = One word taken from a title, author or subject.
Enter number or code, then press CARRIAGE RETURN.
```

You can see that this list also includes the combination of author and title, the call number (the number the library files the book under in the book stacks), or a key word search. If you're looking for books by one author, naturally you'd try an author search. If you know a book's title, you can ask the computer to get the call number you need.

But the computer can help you in other ways by searching the index for you. You could ask for a subject or a key word search. Let's say you decide to ask for a key word search for *pollution*. Here's what you'd get:

LIB *TIL KEYWORD SEARCH

Your Title Keyword: POLLUTION

Matches 385 titles

	No. of citations in entire catalog	Your Lib
1 2nd Soviet-Swedish Symposium on the Pollution of the Baltic>	1	1
2 Acid rain and emissions trading: implementing a market appr>	1	1
3 Aerophysics of air pollution /	1	1
4 Against pollution and hunger; [proceedings]	1	1
5 Air pollution.	9	9
6 AIR POLLUTION-1970	5	5
7 Air pollution and acid rain: the biological impact /	1	1
8 Air pollution, acid rain, and the future of forests/	1	1
9 Air pollution and athletic performance /	1	1
10 Air pollution, the automobile, and public health /	1	1
11 Air pollution control /	4	4

Type a number to see more information -OR-
FOR - move forward in this list   CAT - begin a new search
CMD - see additional commands

With 385 titles that include your key word, you might have more information than you can use. So, let's go back to the computer to look at a subject search for *pollution*. This search lists all titles that the library has filed under that subject. With this search you get 86 entries:

	No. of citations in entire catalog	Your Lib
1 Pollution.	91	86
2 Pollution Abstracts Periodicals.	1	
3 Pollution Addresses, Essays, Lectures.	2	2
4 Pollution Bibliography.	4	4
5 Pollution Bibliography Periodicals.	1	1
6 Pollution British Columbia Congresses.	1	1
7 Pollution Congresses.	13	13
8 Pollution Control Equipment.	3	3
9 Pollution Control Equipment Handbooks, Manuals, etc.	1	1
10 Pollution Control Equipment Linings.	1	1
11 Pollution Control Equipment Maintenance and Repair.	1	1

If you then ask for a listing of number 4 above, "Pollution Bibliography," you see a short title list of the four entries cataloged under that subject heading:

		matches	4 citations
			(All in this library)
Ref # Author	Title		Date
1 Burk, Janet L.	Environmental concerns: a bibliogr >		1975
2 Kiraldi, Louis, 1911-	Pollution: a selected bibliography >		1971
3 McDonald, Rita.	Guide to literature on environmenta >		1970
4 Rehfus, Ruth.	Mercury contamination in the natura >		1970

If we want to see more about a source on air pollution, different keystrokes give a short entry for one of the books identified in our earlier search. This short entry gives the author, title, and call number and indicates that the book is in the library—all important bits of information.

AUTHOR: Lynn, David A.
TITLE: Air pollution, threat and response / David A. Lynn.
IMPRINT: Reading, Mass.: Addison-Wesley Pub. Co., c1976.

	Loan	Cpy	
Location	Type	#	Status
BKSTAX	BOOK	1	In Library

Call Number: TD 883 .L96

But just being in the library isn't quite enough (either for you or for the book); you need more information. One more keystroke gives a full entry, one that tells how big the book is, whether it has a more detailed bibliography, and another subject ("air pollution") you might search for.

AUTHOR: Lynn, David A.
TITLE: Air pollution, threat and response / David A. Lynn.
IMPRINT: Reading, Mass.: Addison-Wesley Pub. Co., c1976.
PHYSICAL FEATURES: x, 388 p.: ill.; 24 cm.
NOTES: CALL NO.: TD 883 .L96 * Includes index. * Bibliography: p. 349-364.
SUBJECTS: Air—Pollution.
CALL NUMBER: TD 883 .L96 *TD 883 .L96

Without leaving the computer terminal, then, you can get a list of the books the library has on your subject, their call numbers, and other detailed information about them. Unlike the card catalog, this computer catalog even tells whether the book is available for checkout.

THE CARD CATALOG

Your library may have the traditional card catalog. Cards come in three kinds: author, title, and subject. If you know a book's author or title, look for one of those. But as you look for support for your research paper, you may know only a general subject, say *architecture.* Then you can look at cards filed under that heading.

The information on the card catalog cards, like that in the computerized catalog, will save you time. All three kinds of cards start as author cards. A title card has the title typed across the top so it can be alphabetized by title easily, and a subject card has the subject typed on top so it can be alphabetized by subject. Beyond that top line, however, the contents of the cards are the same.

If you were trying to find out something about building styles of ancient civilizations, you could look for books on architecture, specifically on the history of architecture. In the card catalog under the subject heading "Architecture—History" you might find this card:

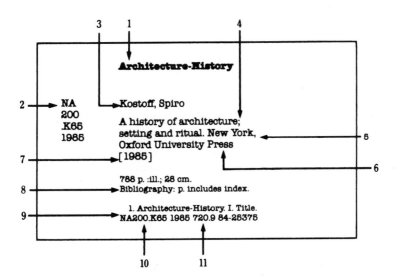

1. Subject heading. A title card would have the book's title instead. The basic author card would have nothing in this position.
2. Call number. The library where we found this card uses the Library of Congress classification system for filing its books. If it had used the Dewey decimal classification system, "720.9" would have appeared in this position.

3. Author's name.
4. Title.
5. Place of publication.
6. Publisher.
7. Publication date.
8. Notes on special contents. The book is illustrated, has a bibliography, and is indexed. Information about the number of pages may prove useful in evaluating the potential value of the book. The bibliography is especially important, for it can lead to other related books.
9. Recommended subject headings.
10. Recommended Library of Congress number.
11. Recommended Dewey decimal number.

Besides finding this card under "Architecture—History," you would find it under the author's name and the book's title. Depending on how a library files its cards, the three card types may be integrated in the same catalog or filed separately.

PERIODICALS

Your library's book catalog, whatever its form, is only one way to find the support material you need for your research. Periodicals—popular magazines, professional journals, and newspapers—are also basic sources, sometimes the most important ones. Even the most recent book is at least a year out of date by the time it appears, and the information in it may be several years old. If you're writing about the Battle of Hastings in 1066, books could be your principal sources. But if your topic requires last-minute, up-to-date information, you'll need to use some periodicals.

How do you find what you need? You could leaf through some recent magazines in hope of finding an article that will help. But even looking at the table of contents in each issue of a single magazine or journal would take more time than you can afford. You need access to reference tools that will help you find the right articles the way the book catalog helps you find the right books. For periodicals, however, there are many catalogs. The most useful one (if your library has one) probably will be the computerized periodical index.

COMPUTERIZED INDEX

The samples of computer screens we'll look at next are adapted from a college library in a large city; the library belongs to a consortium of college libraries in the metropolitan area. The book and periodical catalogs for these libraries are interrelated so that a student can search the data bases for all the college libraries in the consortium at once—greatly increasing the number of research sources available. Here's the base screen for the computer system at one of the schools:

```
LIBRARY DATA BASE SELECTION MENU
On this terminal, you may search the data bases below. Choose a data base by entering
its four-letter label. You may change data bases at any time by typing CHO (CHOOSE)
and the four-letter label.


CATS      Consortium Libraries Catalog
GENL      Periodical Indexes (multisubject)
PAPR      Newspaper Index (U.S. newspapers only)
ERIC      ERIC (Educational Resources Information Center)
ABII      ABI/Inform (Business & Management Index)


          Select a data base label from above
```

Choosing *CATS* would allow us to search the combined computerized book catalogs for the college libraries in the consortium. *PAPR* would allow us to search
among abstracts for thousands of newspaper articles in major newspapers across the
United States. *ERIC* would give us access to a specialized index for sources in the
education field. And *ABII* would put us in a specialized index for business and management. We'll choose *GENL,* which takes us to a number of aggregated general
indexes for magazines and journals.

```
                                                        Periodical Indexes
                                                             Introduction

            INTRODUCTION TO PERIODICAL INDEXES (GENL)


GENL is the online version of several well-known indexes to periodical literature. All
indexes are searched simultaneously.

BP              Business Periodicals Index        From July 1982-
GS              General Science Index             From May 1984-
HU              Humanities Index                  From February 1984-
IL              Index to Legal Periodicals        From August 1981-
RG              Readers' Guide                    From January 1983-
SS              Social Sciences Index             From February 1983-

From any citation, you may type HOL and press <RETURN> to determine if the periodical
is held by a consortium library.
To search by:      Title      T=              Author      A=
                   Subject    S=              Key Word    K=

                        Enter search command
```

As this screen indicates, we can search for a title, an author, a subject, or a key word.
Let's try a key word search for *pollution.*

```
Search Request: K=POLLUTION                          Periodical Indexes
Search Results: 15531 Entries Found                      Key Word Index

          DATE    TITLE:                              AUTHOR:
  1       1994    After oil damage, Carolinas look to fe   Jensen, Charles      RG
  2       1994    Agreement will shield corporation fro                         GS
  3       1994    Air pollution and federal law changes                         GS
  4       1994    Appeals Court questions federal guid     Lookabill, Richard   BP
  5       1994    Barge in oil disaster had been conde     Bottoms, Evelyn R    RG
  6       1994    Big oil spill fouls beaches on Atlantic                       RG
  7       1994    Boat in oil dumping incident operated    Donaldson, James     RG

  STArt over          Type number to display record        <F8> FORward page
  HELp                MARk
  OTHer options
```

This search yields 15,531 articles—far more that we want to consider looking at one by one. So let's narrow the search by looking for *pollution and air,* which limits "pollution" to "air pollution."

```
Search Request: K=POLLUTION AND AIR                  Periodical Indexes
Search Results: 5041 Entries Found                       Key Word Index

          DATE    TITLE:                              AUTHOR:
  1       1994    Agreement will shield corporation fro                         GS
  2       1994    Air pollution and federal law changes                         GS
  3       1994    Cutting pollution from semis             Robertson, Charles   GS
  4       1994    Denver officials charge several firms                         BP
  5       1994    Detroit starts to listen to protests fro Stockland, Peter     BP
  6       1994    Detroit views air pollution as everybo                        BP
  7       1994    Federal court decision may force clea    Eggen, Steven        BP

  STArt over          Type number to display record        <F8> FORward page
  HELp                MARk
  OTHer options
```

Searching for *air and pollution* cuts the number of articles available to 5,041, but that's still too many to try to look at. Let's try looking for articles for a particular year; we search next for *(pollution and air) and 1994,* with the following results:

```
Search Request: K=(POLLUTION AND AIR) AND 1994          Periodical Indexes
Search Results: 42 Entries Found                          Key Word Index

          DATE      TITLE:                            AUTHOR:
   1      1994      Agreement will shield corporation fro              GS
   2      1994      Air pollution and federal law changes              GS
   3      1994      Cutting pollution from semis        Robertson, Charles    GS
   4      1994      Denver officials charge several firms               BP
   5      1994      Detroit starts to listen to protests fro  Stockland, Peter   BP
   6      1994      Detroit views air pollution as everybo             BP
   7      1994      Federal court decision may force clea   Eggen, Steven     BP

   STArt over        Type number to display record        <F8> FORward page
   HELp              MARk
   OTHer options
```

This time our search limits the number of articles to 42. Since not all will be easily available, this is a good time to see just what the articles are and whether they are available. Let's look at information about the third article in the list above.

```
Search Request: K=(POLLUTION AND AIR) AND 1994          Periodical Indexes
3 of 42 Entries Found                                        Long View

AUTHOR (S):              Robertson, Charles.

TITLE:                   Cutting pollution from semis.

SOURCE:                  Life With Health v. 3 (Jan./Feb. '94) p. 16-8

SPECIAL FEATURES:        p. 16-8

SUBJECT DESCRIPTORS:     Air pollution—Control.
                         Trucks.
                         Oil fuel.

STArt over        HOLdings          MARk          <F6> NEXt record
HELp              BRIef view                      <F5> PREvious record
OTHer options     INDex
```

Now we see the authors, the article title, and information about the periodical that contains the article. We also see a list of subjects under which the article is indexed; a list such as this may help in our own search by suggesting subjects we might want to search for.

One other piece of information is important to us at this point: Does our library, or another nearby library, hold this article? Asking for *HOLdings* gives another screen that tells us which libraries in the consortium have the particular issue of the magazine with this article and where they hold it (on the shelf, in microform, or on CD-ROM). When we check for this article, we find that our own library holds the issue on microfilm.

Database Searches

When you search an electronic database, whether online or on CD-ROM, take a few minutes to see how the system allows you to search. Most search systems employ limiting terms from Boolean logic (and often are called "Boolean queries"). The Boolean operators are *and, or,* and *not.* (Some search systems change *and* and *not* to *with* and *without.*)

If we search a group of articles with two terms linked by *and,* the system finds all articles that contain both terms. If we connect the search terms with *or,* the system finds all the articles that contain either term. And if we use *not,* the system finds all the articles for the first term but deletes those that also contain the second term.

Here's a sample: We searched a CD-ROM collection about countries of the world for articles with references to Menachem Begin, prime minister of Israel from 1977 to 1983. We didn't want to use his first and last names as search terms since many references would have only his last name. Unfortunately, his last name is also an English verb, as in "Egypt will *begin* building. . . ." So we decided to use as our search terms *Begin* and *Israel* (search systems usually disregard case, so capitals or lowercase letters give the same results).

A search for *Begin* yielded 564 articles, while *Israel* gave 401. *Begin or Israel* gave 861 articles (less than the sum of *Begin* plus *Israel* since some articles would have both). *Begin and Israel* yielded 99 articles.

Our search system also allowed searches for two terms (with an *and* relationship) within a given word range. We selected a 50-word range, figuring this would give us articles about Menachem Begin that mentioned *Begin* in context with *Israel* (thereby excluding instances such as "Egypt will begin building. . . ."). A search of *Begin [50] Israel* yielded 28 articles. Why 28 articles for *Begin [50] Israel* when *Begin and Israel* yielded 99? The 99 articles include a number with references such as "Israel will begin building. . . ." Thus, the most useful search for our purposes proved to be *Begin [50] Israel.*

COMMON INDEXES

If your library doesn't have an automated search capability for common periodical indexes, you'll need to look for indexes in book or CD-ROM form. Among the more common reference tools, you may find these in your library:

- *Annual Bibliography of English Language and Literature.* Indexes articles and books about authors and literature written in English.

- *Biography Index.* An index to biographical material on living and historical figures.

- *Book Review Digest.* A summary of book reviews for modern literature; useful for finding out how a book was received.

- *Business Periodicals Digest.* As the title indicates, an index of business and economics articles.

- *Education Index.* For articles dealing with education research and development.

- *MLA International Bibliography.* Published annually by the Modern Language Association; covers scholarly journals and books about language and literature in English and other languages.

- *New York Times Index.* A key, comprehensive index to all news events in the *New York Times;* a basic tool, good for almost any topic including books reviewed in the *New York Review of Books.*

- *PAIS (Public Affairs Information Services) International in Print.* In January 1991, the *PAIS Bulletin* merged with the *PAIS Foreign Language Index* to become *PAIS International.* It indexes some 1,300 periodicals of general interest as well as some books.

- *Readers' Guide to Periodical Literature.* Indexes some 200 magazines and journals considered to contain articles of general (or "popular") interest: *Time, Newsweek, U.S. News and World Report, Jet, Good Housekeeping, Popular Mechanics,* and the like.

- *Social Sciences, Humanities, and General Sciences Indexes.* A family of indexes covering scholarly and professional journals on these subjects. (The *International Index,* published 1907–65, became the *Social Sciences and Humanities Index,* which split in 1974 into the *Social Sciences Index* and the *Humanities Index;* the *General Sciences Index* joined the family in 1978.)

Even if your library has an automated search capability for periodical articles, you still may want to look for some of these indexes. For example, the automated data base we searched in our sample earlier in this chapter included five of the indexes above. Yet, if our topic concerned language or literature, we'd still want to look at the *Annual Bibliography of English Language and Literature* and the *MLA International Bibliography.*

Other good sources of help are subject bibliographies. While the indexes above are generally for an academic or business field, there also are published bibliographies for very limited subjects, such as Vincent van Gogh, the Arab–Israeli wars, novels in early America, of the refugee problem. Consult an experienced librarian for help finding a bibliography for your particular subject.

ABSTRACTS

Another kind of reference tool, an abstract, may help your research. There are hundreds of abstracts to cover thousands of topics. Consider consulting the collections of specialized abstracts for your field: *Biological Abstracts, Chemical Abstracts, Historical Abstracts,* or *Psychological Abstracts,* for example.

An abstract summarizes the contents of a technical or scholarly article, and the summary is much longer than the brief comment you may find in a general index. In addition to summarizing the contents of the article, the abstract provides bibliographic information you'll need to find the work the abstract covers. You'll have to check your library's list of periodical holdings to see if the journal and issue are available.

Remember that an abstract is not an article, but a summary only. Like a metal detector, it can tell you that something is there, but not how valuable it is. To use the article you must read it. As a general rule, don't cite abstracts in your parenthetical references or Works Cited listing. Go to the original.

INFORMATION SERVICES AND CD-ROMS

There are some 20 online information services that offer full-text search and retrieval of articles from a wide variety of print sources. Among the leading systems are DIALOG, Data-Star, and NEXIS. DIALOG, for example, has over 450 full-text databases providing access to some 2,600 sources, including magazine, journal, and newspaper articles; newswires; reference books (including many common and specialized indexes and abstract collections); newsletters; government documents; and conference reports and papers. You'll want to see what information services your library makes available and what they contain.

Your library also may offer access into the Internet, the prototype of the so-called "information superhighway." The Internet can give you access to a multitude of university and research institute, corporate, and government information data banks.

Moreover, a number of online information services are available for home use: America Online, Prodigy, and CompuServe are among these. Most offer at least connection to an online multimedia encyclopedia and a number of online news services. In addition, either through one of these information services or through a network service provider, you can connect your home computer to the Internet. In addition to giving you access to research institute and government data banks, it can attach you to automated library services, allowing you to search your library's book and periodical computerized catalogs from your home.

CD-ROM disks are high-volume storage devices. Each disk can store the equivalent of hundreds of books. CD-ROMs offer large compilations of reference sources you may find useful. You'll want to find out what CD-ROMs your library has to offer and where you can use them.

In addition, many CD-ROMs are being offered for sale for home use. Several multimedia encyclopedias are available on CD-ROM, as are collections of text, pictures, and even sound and video segments for specialized topics. And, for instance, *Time* magazine has issued a disk with the text of over 20,000 *Time* articles, including the full text of the magazines from 1989 through 1992 as well as important articles going back as far as 1923. Thus, a CD-ROM drive and a modem for your home computer can give you access to volumes of research material that a few years ago would have been available only in a well-endowed library.

EVALUATING YOUR SOURCES

Some sources are more valuable than others. Understanding the differences between *primary sources* and *secondary sources* can help you evaluate the material you find and determine how to use it in supporting your own points.

PRIMARY SOURCES

A primary source is an original source of basic facts or opinions on your subject: eyewitness accounts, official investigations, newspaper articles of the time. If you conduct original research—personal interviews, for example—the material you gather falls in the primary source category.

The following is an excerpt from page 443 of Volume 1 of the *Personal Memoirs of U.S. Grant* (published by Charles L. Webster & Company of New York in 1885); here Ulysses S. Grant is explaining why he risked operations against Vicksburg without first setting up a protected logistics base:

> Marching across this country in the face of an enemy was impossible; navigating it proved equally impracticable. The strategical way according to the rule, therefore, would have been to go back to Memphis; establish that as a base of supplies; fortify it so that the storehouses could be held by a small garrison, and move from there along the line of railroad, repairing as we advanced, to the Yallabusha, or to Jackson, Mississippi. At this time the North had become very much discouraged. Many strong Union men believed that the war must prove a failure. The elections of 1862 had gone against the party which was for the prosecution of the war to save the Union if it took the last man and last dollar. Voluntary enlistments had ceased throughout the greater part of the North, and the draft had been resorted to to fill up our ranks. It was my judgment at the time that to make a backward movement as long as that from Vicksburg to Memphis, would be interpreted, by many of those yet full of hope for the preservation of the Union, as a defeat, and that the draft would be resisted, desertions ensue and the power to capture and punish deserters lost. There was nothing left to be done but to *go forward to a decisive victory.* This was in my mind from the moment I took command in person at Young's Point.

If you're writing a paper about the Battle of Vicksburg, or perhaps about General Grant's strategic planning of Civil War campaigns, then Grant's own words showing his thoughts about the Vicksburg campaign are particularly important. Other writers might tell you what Grant probably was thinking, but Grant on Grant's thinking provides one of the best sources. Primary sources are not always easy to find, but they're worth looking for.

SECONDARY SOURCES

A secondary source is secondhand, removed at least one step from primary sources. It uses primary sources or other secondary sources as its basis. Thus a 1991 article about Grant's Vicksburg campaign would be a secondary source, drawing perhaps from Grant's *Memoirs* but also from the writing of other people who were at Vicksburg and from other books and articles analyzing the Vicksburg operations.

Compare these two lists:

Primary Source	**Secondary Source**
• The Panama Canal Treaty printed in the *Congressional Record*	• An article about the Panama Canal Treaty in *Time*
• Shakespeare's Sonnet 73	• A critical analysis of Shakespeare's sonnets
• The transcript of a trial	• An article in *Newsweek* about that trial
• An 1865 newspaper article about Lincoln's assassination	• A 1990 book about Lincoln's assassination

The distinction isn't always clear-cut. The last primary source might have been considered a secondary source in 1865, if the writer wasn't present at the assassination. Today we'd call it a primary source because a journalist in 1865 had greater opportunities for investigating true primary sources (such as eyewitnesses) and also could capture the feelings of the time.

Secondary sources select, filter, evaluate, and analyze material from primary sources (as well as other secondary sources). That is both their value and their weakness. Primary sources are more likely to provide "unfiltered truth," but primary sources generally lack the scope provided by secondary sources, which draw on multiple primary and secondary sources. That is, secondary sources are valuable because their writers already have done a lot of work for you, but at the same time you have to be cautious and guard against the biases of the writers who selected and filtered truth for you.

So which source type should you look for? Both. Try to find as many primary sources as you can. If you're writing about a topic for which witnesses are available near you, try to arrange an interview. And look into old newspaper files if they're available.

But look for secondary sources, too. Each type of source—primary and secondary—has its own strengths and weaknesses. And each type can help you evaluate the other. Details from primary sources can help you determine the validity of the conclusions in secondary sources; secondary sources, on the other hand, can help you understand the primary sources by telling you what to look for.

No matter what type of source you find, you need to decide whether it is *relevant* (of value for your treatment of your topic) and *reliable*.

RELEVANT MATERIAL

What you find about a potential source in a catalog, index, or abstract can suggest that a source will have information important for your thesis, but you'll have to get the work in hand before you can be sure. Here are things to check:

In a book
• the table of contents

- the index
- the preface, foreword, or author's introduction (if the book has these)

In an article
- skim the headings (if the article has them) and starts of paragraphs

Let's consider the third item under books for a moment. Students often overlook prefaces, forewords, and introductions, but these can be valuable indicators of relevance. Frequently they discuss the range of material in a book and the author's intentions in writing it. Scope and intentions also can help you judge the source's reliability.

RELIABLE MATERIAL

You always have to ask yourself, "Can I trust what I'm reading?" Just because something is printed doesn't make it so.

How do you know when to be suspicious? You always should be a little wary, but be especially so if the tone of a source—the personality an author projects—raises questions. Forewords and the like can be particularly important for evaluating an author's objectivity.

For example, consider the problem with sources about the battle of the Alamo, when a group of Texans stood up against a larger, better armed Mexican force. Most of us know stories about the battle and its heroes—and that's part of the problem with source reliability. The event is surrounded with numerous legends, a scarcity of eye-witness reports, self-serving accounts from some individuals associated with the event, and numerous secondary source evaluations that treat the people and related events from various perspectives.

In one book about the Alamo, for example, we find a foreword in which the book's author touts the noble motives of the Texans and the glory they deserve. In the foreword to another book we find an author commenting on the difficulty of gathering trustworthy material about the event. Do these forewords prove anything about the books? No, but we could be more comfortable at the outset about the objectivity of the author of the second book. Of course, we still would have to evaluate the reliability of the information as we read.

Date of publication can be helpful in evaluating the reliability of information. It's not as simple, though, as believing that newer sources are more reliable than older ones. But, for example, a book or article published shortly after the Soviet reactor failure at Chernobyl is less likely to be accurate about the long-term effects of that disaster than one written in 1990. (And one in 2050 will have a greater advantage on this same point.) So don't exclude older sources, but look for recent ones when the data you want is recent.

Finally, as you widen your research, you'll find that the best help in evaluating the reliability of sources comes from the data in other sources. Look for overlapping information—and be skeptical about information that varies significantly from the norm. The exceptions could be extremely reliable and important, of course, but they merit careful examination.

EXERCISES

A. Answer the following questions about the materials available in your college library:

1. Is the catalog of books automated?
2. Does the library have automated access to one or more periodical indexes? To an index for newspaper articles?
3. Are reference tools available on CD-ROM? What about reference materials such as encyclopedias or collections of articles? List three of the CD-ROMs that look like they could be useful for your research project.
4. What online information services does your library provide? Can you get into the Internet from your library?

B. In 1992, *Time* magazine ran an article about a 5,300-year-old body found in the Alps between Austria and Italy in late 1991. The body has been dubbed the "Iceman."

1. What is the title of the *Time* article?
2. What is the full date of the *Time* issue that includes the article?
3. On what page does the article begin?
4. What events, according to *Time*, destroyed much of the archaeological value of the site where the body was found?
5. How did you go about finding this article?

C. Other magazines and journals also included articles about the Iceman. Find three periodical articles about him. With each article title, provide the name of the reference tool where you found the article listed.

D. In December 1989, the *New York Times* reported that deposed Romanian (or Rumanian) leader Nicolaę Ceau escu had been held captive in a moving armored vehicle for several days prior to his trial and execution. Use library resources to answer the following:

1. How many days was he imprisoned in the moving armored car?
2. Who was held prisoner with him?
3. What issue of the *New York Times* carried the article?
4. In what section and on what page did the article appear?
5. What library reference tool did you use to answer these questions?

E. In 1993 and 1994, the Western world was trying to restore peace to the former Yugoslavia. Use library reference tools to do the following:

1. List three different periodical articles on the subject. Use at least two different reference tools to find these articles. With each article title, provide the name of the reference tool where you found the article listed.

2. List the name, date, and page number of a national newspaper article that treated the subject. Also name the reference tool in which you found the listing.

3. List the name, date, and page number of a local newspaper article that treated the subject. How did you find this article?

F. In 1989, *Defense and Foreign Affairs* published an article by Carleton A. Conant about Libyan chemical weapon developments.

1. What was the name of the article?

2. Which national government was alleging that the Libyans were developing a chemical weapon manufacturing capability?

3. In what issue did the article appear, and on what pages?

4. What reference tool did you use to find the article?

21 Taking and Organizing Notes

Let's review for a moment. You settle on a general topic and narrow it as much as you reasonably can. Your preliminary reading helps you focus the topic and at the same time reassures you that sources appear to be available for you to draw on for support material. For example, let's say you're interested in those prehistoric people who left their homes on the Asian continent and for some reason found their way to the American continent and developed new lives here. You realize that *prehistoric Indians* is too large a topic, so you reduce it to *prehistoric Indians in North America,* to *the new way of life in America.* That, you decide, is still too broad, but it's a place to start with your preliminary reading. This preliminary exploration of the topic leads you to a new, interesting idea: contrary to the popular belief you've heard for years that the prehistoric Indians wandered across the American continent struggling to survive, there is relatively recent evidence that the prehistoric Indians adapted well and produced sophisticated cultures.

Using the computerized listings of books and periodicals from your library's reference section, you find that available sources appear to be adequate to support your research. You have in hand a list of books and periodical articles that look promising. Now what? Here's where the work begins.

You obviously can't remember every fact or idea you find as you read those sources. You could keep all the books and magazines piled up around you and then flip through them to find a bit of support when you need it. But that's the hard way. Therefore, most researchers develop some systematic way to organize their research reading. This organization is not the same as ordering ideas and their support for writing your paper. The organization here involves keeping track of the research information you find as you work through your potential sources.

This chapter shows you two methods for noting specific ideas and facts and keeping them organized. The most commonly taught system for keeping track of research information involves taking notes on note cards. This system, which we'll call "the traditional system," has proved its value to thousands of researchers. The second system we'll call "the copying machine system" because it relies heavily on a stack of coins and a copying machine. It offers a shortcut in the notetaking process by eliminating the need to write down notes.

THE TRADITIONAL SYSTEM

Both the traditional and the copying machine systems involve keeping track of *two* kinds of information. The first kind is information about the sources you use; the second kind is the information you find in those sources.

The traditional system employs two sets of index cards—one set for each kind of information. Some researchers prefer two sizes of index cards (for example, 3 x 5 cards for sources and 4 x 6 or 5 x 8 cards for notes from the sources); others use the same size cards for both kinds of information. No matter what size of index cards you choose, here's the traditional notetaking process.

BIBLIOGRAPHY CARDS

For Books

Pick the most likely looking book and check the table of contents or index to see which parts of the book apply. (It's just not sensible to read the entire book if only Chapter 2 deals with prehistoric American Indians.)

If the book has nothing useful, put it aside to return to the library as soon as you can. Someone else may need it.

When you find a book that has information you think you might use, make out a *bibliography card.* Record only one book on each card and be careful to include all the necessary data about the book. Chapter 25, "Works Cited," explains in detail the information you'll need and shows the various formats for presenting that information for your final paper. For now, be sure your bibliography card has all the following items that apply to the book you're recording:

- author(s) or group responsible
- title and subtitle of book (and volume title if part of a multivolume set)
- title of part of the book (if you're using only a piece of the book, such as an essay in a collection)
- translator(s)
- editor(s)
- edition (don't worry about the number of "printings," but do note the edition if the book is other than the first edition)
- volume number and number of volumes in a multivolume set
- series (if the work is part of a series, such as "Studies in Anthropology, No. 5")
- place of publication (the first one listed if there are several)
- publisher

- date of publication (latest copyright date, not date of printing)
- inclusive page numbers of a part of the book (if you're using only a piece of the book, such as an essay in a collection)

You can save yourself time later by putting all the items in correct bibliographic format for your paper's Works Cited pages (Chapter 25 shows formats). Here's a sample bibliography card with the necessary information in the form required for its Works Cited entry:

Note these things about the bibliography card:

A. Always include the *library call number* for books; it will save you time if you have to go back to recheck a quotation or find information you forgot to copy down.
B. Include all the applicable information (author, title, etc.) from the list above.
C. Add your own *bibliography code.* We use the first two letters of the first author's last name. But you may use any consistent system—numbering, small letters, Roman numerals. The coding system will save you time as you take notes and as you write drafts of your paper.
D. *Optional.* As a reminder, add a brief note about what the book contains.

With your first bibliography card, you've begun to compile your paper's working bibliography. As you consult the books and articles you've found, prepare a separate card for each one.

For Articles in Periodicals

For magazines, journals, and newspapers, be sure your bibliography card has all the following items that apply to the article you're recording:

- author(s) (articles may be unsigned, and sometimes you'll find only initials for the author)
- title of article
- type of article (for letters to the editor and reviews)
- name of periodical
- series number (such as "old" or "new")
- newspaper edition (if the newspaper publishes more than one edition per day)
- volume and/or issue number(s)
- date of publication
- inclusive page numbers for the article

Also note whether the periodical is paginated continuously throughout a volume or independently by issue. For example, if issue 2 of a volume ends with page 563 and issue 3 of the same volume begins with page 564, the publication paginates continuously throughout a volume. If each issue starts with page 1, then the issues are paginated independently. This distinction won't matter for your research, but it will help you decide which format to use when you write your entries for the Works Cited pages of your final paper.

For Other Source Types

Besides books and articles in periodicals, your sources may include speeches; lectures; class handouts; reference works, such as encyclopedias or *Who's Who;* computer software; material from computer or information services; CD-ROM disks; unpublished theses, dissertations, or letters; interviews; films, filmstrips, slide programs, or videocassettes; radio or television programs; records or tapes; or legal records or documents. The bits of information you'll need to record now so you can document these varied source types later differ greatly from type to type. Check the Works Cited formats in Chapter 25 to see what data you need to keep track of.

NOTE CARDS

When you come across a fact or idea you think you can use, make a *note card.* Put only one fact or idea on each card. When you are ready to use the information for your draft, you can move the information more freely if you have only one idea on each card.

Now read the following passage from page 244 of the Struever and Holton book about the archaeological diggings at the Koster farm near Kampsville, Illinois. ("Horizon 11" is the designation for a level of human occupation dating to about 6400 B.C.)

> Traditionally, archaeologists have assumed that Archaic people went through a long, slow, gradual process in learning how to cope with their environment and how to extract a decent living from it. They thought it took the aborigines several thousand years, from

Paleo-Indian times (circa 12,000–8000 B.C.) to 2500 B.C., to learn about various foods in eastern North America and how to exploit them.

This is simply not true. The Koster people knew their food resources intimately and did a superb job of feeding their communities. During the occupation of Horizon 11, Early Archaic people had developed a highly selective exploitation pattern of subsistence. They were not just taking foods randomly from the landscape. Rather, they calculated how to provide the community with the most nutritious foods possible while expending the least effort. In addition to deer and smaller mammals, they ate large quantities of fish, freshwater mussels, and nuts. Fish and nuts—in addition to being available each year, and easy to take in large quantities—are highly complementary components of a nutritious diet. Nuts contain fat for high energy, which many freshwater fish lack. The kind of input-output analysis which was taking place was worthy of the most sophisticated culture.

Quotation Note Cards

Here's a sample note card for a *quotation* of an important portion of that passage:

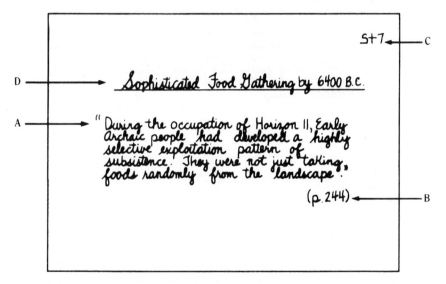

What to include on a quotation note card:

A. Put *quotation marks* around quoted material.
B. Put the *page number* (here, p. 244) in parentheses. If you are using a book that is part of a multivolume set but that doesn't have a separate title, include the volume number and then the page number like this: (3:172).
C. The *code number* shows that this is the seventh card made from the Struever and Holton book. Using the bibliography code (St) from the bibliography card makes it unnecessary to put complete bibliographic information on each note card, and the number added (to make St7) provides a code that distinguishes this note card from others from the same book. In Chapter 22 we'll

show you another way to use the code number. For now, keep all note cards from the same work together.

D.   *Optional.* Use key word headings that might help you later to arrange the facts and ideas and to make sure you have enough support.

Summary Note Cards

If you had *summarized* the entire passage, condensing the original material into a shorter version in your own words, the card would look like this:

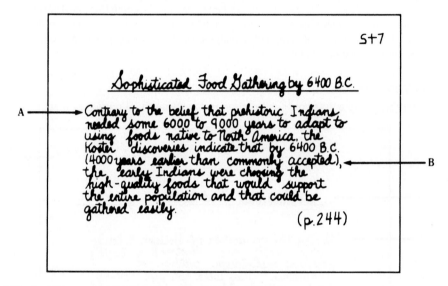

What's different about a summary note card?

A.   *No quotation marks.* Of course, even though you don't borrow the exact words, you do borrow the idea, and you must give credit for it (more about this in Chapter 23).

B.   *Your own words but the author's ideas.* More important than reducing the length of the original, with a summary you mentally "process" the material, capturing the idea or facts and making yourself more knowledgeable about your topic. Notice that the comment in parentheses within the summary above is an *interpretation* of the evidence in the original, demonstrating that the writer of the note card has processed the passage.

Paraphrase Note Cards

A *paraphrase,* too, is a retelling of the original in your own words. But a paraphrase is different from a summary: the paraphrase tends to follow the sentence-by-sentence pattern of the original more closely and also is about the same length as the original. Use paraphrase note cards sparingly. If you're going to take notes that closely follow the original, why not quote instead? Then you'll have the exact words in case you decide to quote all or part of the passage in your paper. Still, a paraphrase

is useful when the original is technical or complex or when it isn't worded well—
then the paraphrase can help simplify or "interpret" the original. If we paraphrase the
two sentences quoted in the sample quotation note card on page 203, the paraphrase
would look like this:

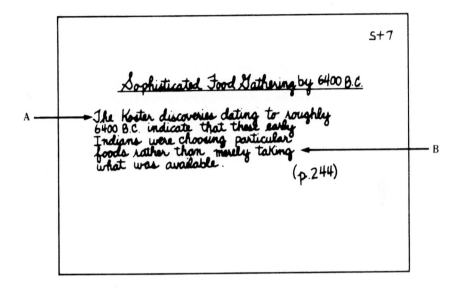

What's special about the paraphrase note card?

A. *Your own words,* so there are no quotation marks. Of course, a paraphrase (or
a summary) could include *some* exact words from the original, and those
words would go in quotation marks. Yet, the paraphrase as a whole is not a
quotation. But it is a borrowing that requires your giving credit for it (more
on that in Chapter 23).

B. *An interpretation of the original,* especially complex or technical wording.
"During the occupation of Horizon 11" has become "dating roughly to 6400
B.C.," and "highly selective exploitation pattern of subsistence" has been sim-
plified to "choosing particular foods."

PLAGIARISM

Research papers use borrowed material, but academic integrity requires that the
writer of the paper properly credit the borrowing. Failure to credit your sources is
dishonest, a form of cheating called *plagiarism.* Plagiarism is presenting someone
else's words or ideas as if they were your own. The word *plagiarism* comes from the
Latin for "kidnapping," which raises an interesting comparison. If you plagiarize—
by failing to give proper credit for material you take from your sources—you're per-
forming an act of "academic kidnapping," and your act will be scorned and punished
if you are caught.

On the other hand, borrowing material is perfectly acceptable because you give credit for words and ideas to the original writer. In fact, one mark of accomplished writers is their ability to integrate borrowed material smoothly into their own writing—to introduce the borrowed material, to incorporate the borrowing into the flow of their ideas, and to give proper credit when and where it is due. Never, however, would accomplished writers present the borrowings as if they were their own.

Students who intend to steal material from others and present it as if it were their own generally know exactly what they're doing. But what about the majority who have no intention of cheating? Can they plagiarize? Well, they certainly can create circumstances that appear to prove wrongdoing; that is, extreme clumsiness at presenting borrowed material can look exactly like intentional cheating.

So how—exactly—can you avoid being accused of wrongdoing? Here are the errors you want to avoid:

- Presenting someone else's idea but not documenting it (so the idea seems to be yours).
- Presenting someone else's words without documenting them (so they seem to be part of your writing).
- Quoting someone else's words—perhaps even documenting them—but failing to use quotation marks to identify what is borrowed (making the words seem to be your own).

If you're careful to keep track of your sources' words and ideas when you take notes, and if you're also careful when you work the material into your paper, you're not likely to be guilty of any of those errors.

Most of the problems with taking notes come with paraphrases and summaries. If you're putting the original into your own words and you want to retain wording from the original, you must use quotation marks. What if a student writes something like this?

> For many years archaeologists have assumed that the prehistoric Indians needed several thousand years to discover how to exploit the various foods in eastern North America, but the Koster Indians had learned to be highly selective in their food choices rather than just taking foods randomly from the landscape (Struever and Holton 244).

This looks like a paraphrase or summary, right? It looks like one, but it's an unacknowledged, loose quotation. The writer has borrowed key words when he seems to be borrowing only ideas. Even giving the source credit through the parenthetical documentation at the end of the passage doesn't solve the problem. The passage should look like this:

> For many years "archaeologists have assumed" that the prehistoric Indians needed "several thousand years" to discover "how to exploit" the "various foods in eastern North America," but the Koster Indians had learned to be "highly selective" in their food choices rather than "just taking foods randomly from the landscape" (Struever and Holton 244).

Of course, that passage looks peculiar. No thought has been given to choosing portions of the original for a quotation—rather, the use of key words from the original appears to be accidental.

You can mix quotation with summary and paraphrase, but be selective in the quotation part. And keep this rule in mind: *Whenever you use another author's words, put them in quotation marks.* Failure to do so is dishonest.

Electronic Notetaking

When you take notes from electronic sources—online articles or CD-ROM, for example—the medium provides a shortcut. Most computerized sources allow you to take notes directly into your own data file. You can summarize or paraphrase as you read, or you can copy directly from the original into your electronic notes. For quoting, copying electronically from the original means you can get the material down exactly as written without risk of misquoting.

But wait! This shortcut also provides a quick trip to plagiarism unless you're careful!

When you copy material from the original directly into your own data file, nothing automatically puts quotation marks around what you borrowed. You have to remember to take care of that step. Make it your practice to always mark the direct borrowings with quotation marks as you copy them. Failure to do so as you copy the material electronically could lead to serious problems later.

THE COPY MACHINE SYSTEM

As you can see, the traditional system requires considerable writing, and that can slow you down, interrupting your train of thought during research. The copy machine system offers an alternative.

- Use a copy machine to make a copy when you find a portion of a book or an article that looks worthwhile.
- Write the complete bibliographic information on the copy (just as you would on a bibliography card in the traditional system).
- Use a *highlighting* pen to mark anything you want to be able to refer to later (the equivalent of writing down quotations in the traditional system). Please do not highlight material in library copies of books and periodicals.

WHICH SYSTEM SHOULD YOU USE?

The traditional system takes time but offers two distinct advantages:

- As you take notes, you are actively involved with the material, so you will understand it better than if you had only glanced through it.

- Note cards offer flexibility: you can rearrange them to match your outline or even place them in the rough draft to save time during the writing stage.

At the same time, though, the traditional system can be tedious. Nevertheless, for many researchers the benefits of the painstaking process outweigh the cost.

For others, the pain of notetaking outweighs the benefits. If you are one of these, consider the copy machine system. You won't be able to shuffle note cards. Moreover, you'll still have to spend time processing the material you've highlighted on the copies—turning the original material from your sources into quotations, summaries, and paraphrases to integrate with your own writing. However, you'll do that processing as you write the draft of your paper, so you'll choose the form for presentation to fit your needs as you write. That offers flexibility not possible with the traditional system.

Choose the system that fits your personality. Either system can work well. What won't work is having no system at all: random reading combined with mistaken confidence in your ability to remember details from research when the time comes to write your paper.

EXERCISES

A. The passage below is from page 141 of *The Native Americans: An Illustrated History.* The passage concerns the Spanish invasion of the Pueblos of the Rio Grande Valley (in what is now New Mexico) in the early 1500s. The authors of the book are David Hurst Thomas, et al. The book was edited by Betty and Jan Ballantine. It was published in 1993 by Turner Publishing, Inc., of Atlanta, Georgia. In the library it has call number E77.N352 1993.

So much regional variety initially made resistance to the Spanish difficult, for the Pueblos did not traditionally cooperate easily with each other, much less with their often unfriendly, more nomadic neighbors. Coronado, gullible as all the Spanish were to tales of vast wealth waiting to be picked up, believed extravagant reports of a fabulously rich multistoried city near today's Arizona-New Mexico border. The place, called Cibola, did actually exist—after its own fashion. It was a town of Zuñi pueblos. Coronado and several hundred Spaniards, accompanied by their native Mexican servants, marched north to Zuñi. They found neither a city, nor gold, nor a population in any way disposed to welcome them. So they stormed Zuñi, ravaged the town, and having destroyed what was there, continued east to occupy a similar town near today's Albuquerque.

1. Make a bibliography card for the book.
2. Select a significant point from the passage and prepare a note card quoting directly from it.
3. Now prepare another note card paraphrasing the lines you quoted in Exercise A2.
4. Prepare a note card summarizing the entire paragraph; use no more that two sentences of your own words for the summary.
5. A final check:

- Did you put a bibliography code on the bibliography card?
- Did you use that code on the note cards?
- Is the library call number on the bibliography card?
- Did you use quotation marks where needed?

B. In the periodicals in the library, you find an article in *Native Peoples* about the Lacandón Maya Indians, who live today in the rain forest of the Mexican state of Chiapas. *Native Peoples* is a quarterly journal that paginates each issue independently. The article, by Joyce Gregory, is entitled "Lacandón Maya: Living Legacy in Chiapas." It appears on pages 38 to 46 of the Spring 1994 issue of *Native Peoples;* this issue is volume 7, number 3 of the journal. The following passage is from pages 38 and 39; page 38 ends with "Spanish conquistadors," while page 39 begins with "subdued resistance."

    The Lacandónes are descended from Maya survivors who fled into the rain forest during the Spanish conquest of Yucatan and Guatemala. Unlike the Aztecs, whose empire was crushed by the advancing Spaniards and their allies in 1521, the Maya had no single ruler or capital at the time of the Spanish invasion. Consequently, the period of Maya conquest stretched over nearly two hundred years, as Spanish conquistadors subdued resistance that erupted sporadically throughout Mexico's Yucatan peninsula and Guatemala's Petén region. Not until 1697 did Spanish soldiers and missionaries successfully storm the last functioning ceremonial center, Tayasal (now Flores), in Lake Petén Itzá. But on entering the island-city, they found that the Maya defenders, like earlier holdouts in other strongholds, had disappeared into the rain forest.

    Anthropologists believe that small family groups of Maya continued to live an unobtrusive life in the forest, hunting, fishing, and raising corn and other vegetables in small *milpas,* right up to the present century. They shunned contact with the larger society, but were known to loggers, itinerant *chicleros* extracting sap from chicosapote trees, and traders who bartered modern conveniences for Lacandón tobacco.

1. Make a bibliography card for the article.
2. Select a significant point from the passage and prepare a note card quoting directly from it.
3. Now prepare another note card paraphrasing the lines you quoted in Exercise B2.
4. Prepare a note card summarizing the entire passage; use no more than three sentences of your own words for the summary.
5. A final check:

- Did you put a bibliography code on the bibliography card?
- Did you use that number on the note cards?
- Did you use quotation marks where needed?

22 Organizing Your Thoughts and Support

In the last chapter we discussed organizing your research material so you know which supporting ideas and facts are from which sources. Now we need to look at organization in a different way—this time ordering ideas and their support so you can write your paper.

OUTLINING

Of course, you don't need to wait until you've finished taking notes to begin organizing that new knowledge. You'll do well to develop an outline early and revise and expand it as you learn more. A working outline helps you discover gaps in your support, suggesting areas for continued research. In other words, you need to work back and forth between notetaking and outlining—each influences the other.

A WORKING OUTLINE

How do you begin organizing support material? By thinking. Jot down the *key* ideas you've discovered about your topic—just the key words. Now look for patterns:

- Do certain ideas seem to fall logically into clusters? Look for points that fit into groups with other points.
- Do you see a pattern of thought that relates those clusters of ideas to each other? Would chronological order work? How about cause and effect or one of the other patterns of development you studied in Part Four?

Once you recognize the basic arrangement that will work to bring order to the ideas and supporting facts for your topic, fill in a simple working outline.

Basic Working Outline

Introduction—working thesis
 I. First major topic:
  A. Support idea:
  B. Support idea:
  C. Support idea:
 II. Second major topic:
  A. Support idea:
  B. Support idea:
  C. Support idea:
 III. Third major topic:
  A. Support idea:
  B. Support idea:
  C. Support idea:
Conclusion—restated working thesis

Does the working outline form look familiar? It should. It's the same basic pattern you've been working with from the beginning of this book, expanded to handle more ideas than you needed for shorter papers. Of course, you may not need exactly three major topics with three support ideas for each. This is just a model.

An outline reduces a large quantity of information to its bare skeleton—just the main ideas and key support. It's a tool to show logically and clearly the relationships among the main points of your paper.

As you conduct your research, the working outline can help you see gaps in your support. Moreover, trying to fit the pieces together as you go along can help you discover new areas you may want to examine—new directions for your research.

A FINAL OUTLINE

When you've worked out fully the major ideas, supporting ideas, *and* specific support for your paper, you'll have its complete skeletal organization. That skeleton provides the framework for your writing. It ensures that you follow a logical structure as you write.

Outline Numbering and Lettering Scheme

 I.
 II.
  A.
  B.
   1.
   2.

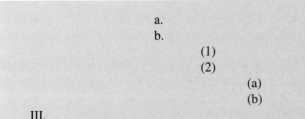

III.

- If you have a *I*, there should be a *II*; if you have an *A*, there should be a *B*; and so on.
- Normally you should not need to go beyond the fourth level—the *a* and *b*.

The final outline you prepare to guide your writing could be a topic outline or a sentence outline.

A *topic outline* lists key points as ideas but does not show complete thoughts. Each entry begins with a capital letter, but the entry has no punctuation at the end since it isn't a complete sentence.

Partial Topic Outline

Here's a topic outline for the first major idea of the sample research paper in Chapter 19:

I. Why minimum competency tests were adopted
  A. Public perception of inadequacy in education
    1. Employers' view of high school diplomas
    2. Decline in SAT scores
    3. Perception of costs versus quality
  B. Standardized testing of minimum skills as simple proof
    1. Failure of complex reporting to parents
    2. Seemingly scientific basis of standardized tests
    3. Appeal to decision makers

The key points of a topic outline are adequate for someone familiar with the material summarized in the topic entries. Thus, a topic outline can work well as a guide for writing. It may be all you need to prepare before you begin writing the first draft of your research paper.

However, because the entries in the topic outline don't provide complete thoughts, the outline usually doesn't communicate well to anyone besides the person who wrote it. In particular, the unity and coherence of the points within the topic blocks may not be obvious in a topic outline.

For this reason, many instructors require their students to submit sentence outlines for their research papers—either before writing a draft or with the final paper. A sentence outline more clearly demonstrates the links among points within the out-line—so unity and coherence become more clear. As a practical matter, the sentence outline is the outline type that someone besides the writer—such as an instructor—can read and understand.

In a *sentence outline,* each entry begins with a capital letter and ends with the punctuation appropriate for the sentence. Following is the sentence outline for the sample research paper in Chapter 19. It's formatted to be handed in with the research paper; for that reason its pagination begins with the page number following the Works Cited page of the sample paper. If your instructor wants the outline to come at the beginning, use the same format but change the page numbers to lowercase Roman numerals (i, ii, etc.—*James i,* for example).

James 9

Thesis: Minimum competency tests are of questionable value for students; they hold at risk the quality of education of all students—not just those who fail one or more times—making them hostages to the testing system.

I. Minimum competency tests should be viewed against the background that led to their creation: the need for simple measures of quality that would restore public confidence in American education and the standardized tests of minimum skills that resulted.
   A. In the 1960s and early 1970s, the American public felt that the quality of education was inadequate.
      1. Employers claimed high school diplomas were meaningless.
      2. The public interpreted the decline of Scholastic Aptitude Test scores as proof that secondary schools were failing.
      3. Meanwhile education costs rose, prompting calls for proof that tax dollars were buying quality in education.
   B. The public desire for simple, easy-to-understand proof of quality led to standardized tests of minimum skills.
      1. After complex reporting to parents failed to restore public confidence in education, testing appealed for its simplicity.
      2. Standardized tests offer apparently scientific, unbiased measures of quality.
      3. Standardized tests offered decision makers a convenient, cost-effective way to both improve education and satisfy public demands.
II. The tests that resulted measure development of minimal skills, or minimum competency.
   A. Minimum competency tests are standardized examinations of development of minimal skills, primarily in reading, writing, and math.

    B. Usually the tests are connected to serious consequences, such as promotion to a higher grade or graduation from high school.

    C. By 1984, 40 states had adopted some type of minimum competency testing, about half connected to high school graduation.

III. Standardized testing of minimum competencies leads to three major drawbacks of mass testing: class time lost to coaching, narrowing of the curriculum, and deflection in the overall curriculum.

    A. Minimum competency tests result in significant amounts of time being devoted to coaching students for the test—time taken from other classroom activities.

        1. The New Jersey Department of Education admitted providing local districts with testing materials used for extensive coaching.

        2. Maryland's citizenship competency test can lead to a student's being taken out of regular social science classes for up to 15 weeks for remedial coaching.

    B. Minimum competency tests lead to narrowing, or trivialization, of the curriculum.

        1. Maryland's citizenship competency test reduces citizenship to a trivia test.

        2. Multiple-choice questions reduce writing to rules of grammar and punctuation.

        3. Testing science competency reduces science from a process of investigation to identification of basic facts.

    C. Minimum competency tests lead to deflection in the overall curriculum.

        1. Deflection results from emphasis on tested material rather than on other curriculum areas not tested.

        2. A survey of testing in Florida in 1977 showed that emphasis on basic skills deflected from literature, language, and composition.

James 11

   3. Virginia's math competency testing of recognition
      of parallel lines resulted in reduced student ability
      to recognize perpendicular lines.
IV. The effects of minimum competency testing that are used
    as justification by advocates hold the educations of
    students at risk.
    A. Improvements in test scores are an overly simplistic
       measure of success.
       1. Minimum competency test scores for a number of
          states show improvements.
       2. Improvements in scores can be interpreted as a
          natural reaction to the high stakes connected to
          the tests.
    B. Use of minimum competency tests to both determine
       curriculum and judge whether teachers comply holds
       students hostage.
       1. Minimum competency testing can determine what
          and how teachers teach.
       2. High-stakes testing to judge whether teachers are
          teaching as they are directed places students at
          risk.
    C. Minimum competency tests have no demonstrated
       connection to success in life.
       1. For students not attending college, two studies
          comparing test scores and earnings show no
          connection.
       2. Research shows a significant connection between
          unemployment and lack of a high school diploma.
       3. For most students attending college, tests of
          minimum competency are meaningless.

Conclusion: Although minimum competency testing appears to
offer simple, satisfying statistical evidence of the usefulness of
the tests, behind this evidence are serious impacts that hold
hostage the quality of education of American students.

OUTLINING AND THE COMPUTER

Computer programs can be a big help with outlining. With some programs, in fact, the outline on the computer serves as a direct step toward establishing headings within the paper that you write on the computer.

There are several computer programs whose primary purpose is to assist with organizing thinking. Their output, as you might expect, is an outline. These programs are intended to assist with brainstorming and to convert the disorganized results of brainstorming into the organized pattern of an outline. The programs allow rapid clustering of points and easy movement of blocks of material among the various subordination levels that make up the outline.

Some of the programs permit users to "hide" (save in a hidden mode) notes, paragraphs, and even graphics under an entry in the outline. With this type of capability you can write a rough version of a piece of your paper as you think about it while you're organizing your material. You then tuck it away behind its outline point. As you write your paper, you reveal the hidden text and incorporate it into your draft.

Many computer word processing programs have some of these same features for outlining. They have built-in formats that set up the standard letter-number system of an outline, and they allow you to move material easily from one level of subordination to another within the outline. If the word processing program operates with a split-screen or windows mode, you can review the outline on screen as you write the paper's draft in another part of the screen. Some word processing programs even are set up to convert parts of an outline into particular levels of headings in the text of a document.

HEADINGS FOR LARGE PAPERS

Just as the points in an outline guide you through the research paper, headings—which equate to major points in an outline for a paper—guide readers through the material they read. In Chapter 10 we showed you a good way to make headings—using initial capital letters and starting on the left margin. But because research papers can get fairly long, you may need more than one type of heading (to show more levels of subordination).

Here are two types we suggest:

Two Heading Styles

XXXXXXXX XXXXX XXXXXXXXX XXXX XXXXXXXX XXXX

XXXXX XXXXXX XXXXX XXXX XXXXXXXXX XXXX XXXXXXX

```
                    THIS IS A MAJOR HEADING


        XXXXXXXX XXXXX XXXXXXXXX XXXX XXXXXXXX

XXXXXXXX XXXXX XXXXX XXXX XXXXXXXXX XXXX


This Is a Minor Heading

        XXXXXXXX XXXXX XXXXXXXXX XXXX XXXXXXXX XXXX

XXXXXXXXXX XXXXX XXXX XXXXXXXXX XXXX


This Is Another Minor Heading

        XXXXXXXX XXXXX XXXXXXXXX XXXX XXXXXXXX XXXX

XXXXXX XXX XXXXX XXXX XXXXXXXXX XXXX XXXXXXXXXX


             THIS IS ANOTHER MAJOR HEADING


        XXXXXXXX XXXXX XXXXXXXXX XXXX XXXXXXXX

XXXXXXXX XXXXXX XXXXX XXXX XXXXXXXXX XXXX
```

If you have a computer, you can get much fancier, of course. In fact you could have headings in different sizes and type faces.

Here are two possibilities:

Headings Using a Computer

```
XXX XXXXXXXX XXXXX XXXXXXXXX XXXX XXXXXXXX XXXX XXXXXX
XXXXX XXXX XXXXXXXXX XXXX XXXXXXXXX XXXXX
```

THIS IS A MAJOR HEADING

xxx xxxxxxxx xxxxx xxxxxxxxx xxxx xxxxxxxx xxxx xxxxxx xxxxx xxxx xxxxxxxxx xxxx xxxxxxxxxx xxxxx

This Is a Minor Heading

xxx xxxxxxxx xxxxx xxxxxxxxx xxxx xxxxxxxx xxxx xxxxxx xxxxx xxxx xxxxxxxxx xxxx xxxxxxxxxx xxxxx

This Is Another Minor Heading

xxx xxxxxxxx xxxxx xxxxxxxxx xxxx xxxxxxxx xxxx xxxxxx xxxxx xxxx xxxxxxxxx xxxx xxxxxxxxxx xxxxx

THIS IS ANOTHER MAJOR HEADING

xxx xxxxxxxx xxxxx xxxxxxxxx xxxx xxxxxxxx xxxx xxxxxx xxxxx xxxx xxxxxxxxx xxxx xxxxxxxxxx xxxxx

---

Whichever way you make headings, be sure the major heading stands out more on the page than the minor heading does.

A Practical Point About Outlines and Headings

We noted earlier that outlines rarely need to go beyond four levels of subordination. Well, headings shouldn't go even that far.

Levels of headings equate to outline levels, of course, but you have to be wary of the complexity you try to portray with levels of headings. For assignments the length of a research paper, two levels of headings will work well.

Even writers of books only occasionally go beyond two levels of headings. (You can find third- and even a few fourth-level headings in Chapter 25 of this book, for example, because the complex material there is easier to follow with the extra heading levels.)

Why not give headings to match every item in an outline? Writing with excessive headings appears choppy. Moreover, readers become confused when writers try to portray three and four levels of subordination throughout a document.

A smart writer, then, uses headings to highlight important points of a paper's organization—but only the most important points.

A TIMESAVER IN WRITING

Once you've prepared an outline, you're ready to assemble your detailed support. Arrange your notes (note cards or highlighted photocopy pages, depending on the research system you chose) to follow your outline. Use the floor, your desktop, your roommate's bed, whatever you need to spread the cards out so you can see how they fill out the outline's skeleton.

Don't let your outline keep you from moving notes around. That outline is not engraved in bronze; you can alter it as you need to. But laying out your notes will help you see where the outline may be incomplete or where you need more information. You may have more notes than you can use. Don't throw any away; you may find a place for them later.

When you are satisfied with the outline and its support, start writing. You may begin at the beginning with an introduction, then move on to the first major topic, then the second, and so on. Many writers do it this way, and it may work for you.

Or you may decide to start with the first major topic, go on to the next topics, and finish writing with the conclusion—and then the introduction. Many other writers do it this way.

The reason is simple: Frequently you're not sure what you're going to say until you've said it. You actually discover that you think as you write because the ideas take over and lead you to new discoveries. If you have already written the introduction, you may find it has little relationship to what you finally say.

Regardless of where you start writing, you'll have to use some of your notes. If you're quoting—and if you've used the traditional system with note cards—here's a trick that can save you some work: In writing your draft, when you come to a place for a quotation, don't copy it again. Just paper-clip or tape the quotation note card in place—or leave room in your draft and write in the code number for the note card (remember the code number *St7* we used on page 203?). Doing it this way will save you writing and will keep the quotations accurate, no matter how many drafts you go through.

A caution: This trick isn't intended for use with summaries and paraphrases; those notes already are in your own words, and you should be weaving the ideas and facts into the fabric of your writing in the paper's draft.

Working those quotations, summaries, and paraphrases—the material you borrow from your sources—into your writing is one of the skills you need to develop for writing a research paper. And skillful use of borrowed material is the subject of the next chapter.

ABSTRACT

Many teachers of English and other academic subjects require an abstract to be submitted with the final paper. An abstract is a brief summary of a piece of writing. Clearly, then, you should not try to write the abstract for your paper until you've finished writing the paper itself. Even though you write it last, the abstract normally appears at the beginning of a paper, like an executive summary, between the title page and the body of the paper. This type of summary is intended to tell readers what they'll find in the paper itself, letting them then judge whether they need to read the full paper. (Your instructor, of course, will read your research paper regardless of the quality of the abstract you write.)

You may be asked to write either a descriptive or an informative abstract. Descriptive abstracts are common in library reference tools, but informative abstracts are preferable when the abstract accompanies the paper itself.

DESCRIPTIVE ABSTRACT

This kind of abstract describes the paper itself; it tells readers what is covered in the study. That is, a descriptive abstract *discusses the report but not the subject.* A descriptive abstract is like a narrative form of a table of contents or topic outline: it reveals topics but not what they mean. We still have to read the report to find out what the author has to say about the subject—what conclusions the writer comes to. A descriptive abstract, then, usually is useful only for alerting readers that the report contains topics of interest to them.

Here's a descriptive abstract for our sample research paper:

> This report discusses the effects of minimum competency examinations on the education of students who are subject to the tests. It examines the social and educational causes for adoption of minimum competency testing. Then it discusses the problems for education that the tests themselves generate. Finally, it looks at the overall long-term impacts of the testing on students who undergo the education and testing programs.

INFORMATIVE ABSTRACT

This kind of abstract—the one we recommend—is more useful and complete. An informative abstract does more than merely name the topics in a report; *it tells the key ideas, summarizes basic facts, and reports major conclusions or decisions.* Because it summarizes the report, an informative abstract can serve as an executive summary at the beginning of a study.

For contrast with the descriptive abstract above, here is the informative abstract you saw earlier as a part of the sample research paper:

> Minimum competency tests are of questionable value for students; they hold at risk the quality of education of all students—not just those who fail one or more times—making them hostages to the testing system. The tests were a response to a need for simple measures of quality to restore public confidence in American education. What resulted were standardized examinations of development of minimal skills—primarily in reading, writing, and mathematics—that were linked to serious consequences. Unfortunately, the tests lead to three major drawbacks in education: class time lost to coaching, narrowing or trivialization in the curriculum, and deflection of the curriculum away from areas of value. Thus, even though minimum competency test scores have increased, these improvements are a natural result of the high stakes connected to the tests. With the tests defining both curriculum con-

tent and teacher success or failure, true education is at risk, even though there is no evidence connecting the tests to success in life.

If you compare this informative abstract with the sentence outline for the research paper, you'll see a close correspondence. Both highlight the major points of the paper, though in different ways. A hint: Pay attention to your research paper's sentence outline as you structure your informative abstract.

EXERCISE

The chapter provides a full sentence outline for the sample research paper in Chapter 19. It also shows a topic outline form of the first major idea block for the same paper. Using the format below, finish the topic outline for the sample research paper. We've supplied the major headings from the sample paper as the Roman-numeral-level entries in the outline.

II. What minimum competency tests are

   A.

   B.

   C.

III. Problems the tests generate for the classroom

   A.

      1.

      2.

   B.

      1.

      2.

      3.

   C.

      1.

      2.

      3.

IV. How minimum competency testing holds students at risk

   A.

      1.

      2.

   B.

      1.

      2.

C.

   1.

   2.

   3.

23 Using Borrowed Material in Your Paper

Skilled use of borrowed material is one mark of an accomplished writer. You can't expect just to sprinkle it on the paper in the hope it will magically create an argument for you. Good arguments with borrowed material supporting them don't just happen; they come from careful work. To make sure your borrowed material helps your argument, you must consider two key questions: whether to quote or not, and what to quote from. Answers to these questions are closely related and depend on the paper you're writing.

CHOOSING THE TYPE OF PRESENTATION

In Chapter 21 you studied three types of note cards: quotations, paraphrases, and summaries. Let's consider now why you might choose one of those types of presentation of borrowed material in preference to the others.

There are three basic reasons for choosing to quote from a source:

- A passage is worded particularly well, providing facts or opinions phrased effectively.
- A passage is written very clearly (so that paraphrasing or summarizing would provide a poor substitute).
- A passage provides the words of an authority (not necessarily someone famous, just someone in a position to know).

Paraphrases restate original source material in your own words. You interpret the technical or complex wording, but you retain the flow of the thought from the source. Thus, choose a paraphrase when the way a source presents an argument works well but the words themselves need adjustment for your purposes.

Summaries extract information from sources, capturing facts and opinions from the original but without either the original words or the original thought pattern. Choose a summary when you want only the data from a source.

We also can evaluate the three presentation types in relation to the two types of source material we discussed in Chapter 20—primary and secondary sources. Of course, there are reasons to choose a quotation, paraphrase, or summary with both primary and secondary sources. Yet, there is a difference worth noting.

Because a primary source is the origin of facts or opinions on your subject, material from it is likely to fit one or more of the criteria for quoting. For example, the excerpt from Grant's writing about the Vicksburg campaign (page 193) provides clear, effective wording. More important, it provides the words of an authority on Grant's thinking at the time of the campaign. If you were examining the successes and failures of military planners at Vicksburg, for instance, you'd be more likely to quote Grant than to paraphrase or summarize the passage.

Secondary sources select, filter, and analyze material from primary and other secondary sources. Therefore, the material itself already is pointed toward summaries. Material in secondary sources sometimes meets a criterion for quoting. As a general rule, though, you'll find fewer reasons to quote from secondary sources and more reasons to summarize or paraphrase. By no means is that an absolute rule, however.

But whether you use primary or secondary sources, whether you quote or summarize or paraphrase, you must follow three steps to use borrowed material effectively:

- *Introduce* the borrowed material.
- *Present* it.
- *Credit* the source.

INTRODUCING BORROWED MATERIAL

Perhaps the most neglected step in using borrowed material is the first one—introducing it. In this step you mention the author or title of the source before presenting the material, to signal to your readers that you are beginning the borrowed material. Here are some sample introductions:

As Grant explained in his *Memoirs.* . . .

According to the press secretary, the president decided that. . . .

Reverend Jackson was right when he said. . . .

In his essay "Here's HUD in Your Eye," Larry McMurtry reveals. . . .

The variety of introductions is almost endless, but all of them identify your source, often helping your readers judge whether the source you're citing is reputable.

Without an introduction, the borrowed material seems just spliced in; look for such an example in the following paragraph:

> Washington's victory at Yorktown was precarious almost up to the moment of the British surrender. What really defeated the British was the inability of Lord Cornwallis to move his forces away from Yorktown. "The secret of the British failure there was either the ministry's neglect in immediately securing absolute naval supremacy on this coast . . . or the over-confidence or carelessness of the admirals in command. It is the British naval administration that is to be charged with the Yorktown catastrophe" (Johnston 101). The British under Cornwallis were occupying Yorktown because it was the best available naval station, and retreat by sea would have been possible had not the French fleet kept the British fleet away from the battle area.

Readers will recognize where the borrowing begins and ends because of the quotation marks, but they will wonder who Johnston is and where the quotation comes from. Annoying, isn't it? Don't annoy your readers; don't even leave them slightly frustrated from wondering about who said what. Introduce the material:

> Washington's victory at Yorktown was precarious almost up to the moment of the British surrender. What really defeated the British was the inability of Lord Cornwallis to move his forces away from Yorktown. In *The Yorktown Campaign and the Surrender of Cornwallis,* historian Henry P. Johnston blames the British navy: "The secret of the British failure there was either the ministry's neglect in immediately securing absolute naval supremacy on this coast . . . or the over-confidence or carelessness of the admirals in command. It is the British naval administration that is to be charged with the Yorktown catastrophe" (101). The British under Cornwallis were occupying Yorktown because it was the best available naval station, and retreat by sea would have been possible had not the French fleet kept the British fleet away from the battle area.

This way, your readers know who wrote what you've quoted and where you found it. The parenthetical documentation reference, used in conjunction with the research paper's Works Cited list, gives the complete data to find the book if your readers should want to.

An introduction is even more important for a summary or paraphrase than it is for a direct quotation. Quotation marks show where a quotation begins and ends. But where does the paraphrase begin here?

> Washington's victory at Yorktown was precarious almost up to the moment of the British surrender. What really defeated the British was the inability of Lord Cornwallis to move his forces away from Yorktown. The British failed because the navy did not control the sea off the American coast or because the British admirals blundered. The British navy should be blamed for the Yorktown defeat (Johnston 101). The British under Cornwallis were occupying Yorktown because it was the best available naval station, and

retreat by sea would have been possible had not the French fleet kept the British fleet away from the battle area.

How many of the ideas come from Johnston's book? Where does the paraphrase begin? At the first word of the paragraph? Or is it only the sentence ending with the parenthetical documentation reference? Who knows? But when you introduce the paraphrase, everyone will know:

> Washington's victory at Yorktown was precarious almost up to the moment of the British surrender. What really defeated the British was the inability of Lord Cornwallis to move his forces away from Yorktown. In *The Yorktown Campaign and the Surrender of Cornwallis,* historian Henry P. Johnston asserts that the British failed because the navy did not control the sea off the American coast or because the British admirals blundered. The British navy should be blamed for the Yorktown defeat (101). The British under Cornwallis were occupying Yorktown because it was the best available naval station, and retreat by sea would have been possible had not the French fleet kept the British fleet away from the battle area.

With that simple introduction readers know where the paraphrasing begins. Be sure to introduce your summaries as well.

PRESENTING BORROWED MATERIAL

Paraphrases and summaries, no matter what their length, are fully integrated with your own writing. Introduce them, of course, and credit the source with a parenthetical reference, as we'll discuss later. But no special formatting is required for the presentation. Quotations require special presentation techniques.

Presenting Quotations in Your Final Paper

For a short quotation—*four or fewer lines of typing in your paper:*

- Type the quotation along with your own writing, without special indentation or spacing.
- Use double quotation marks (" ") to enclose your source's exact words and punctuation; if the quoted material itself includes quotation marks, use single quotation marks (' ') to enclose the interior quotation.
- Place a parenthetical reference, if required, after the quoted material and closing quotation mark but before the punctuation mark, if any, that ends the sentence, clause, or phrase with the material the reference documents. ("Placement in Text," in Chapter 24, provides a thorough explanation about placing parenthetical references in the text of your paper.)

For a long quotation—*more than four lines of typing*—in a paper with double-spaced text:

- Begin the quotation on a new line.
- Double-space before, within, and after the quotation.
- Do *not* use quotation marks for the quotation; however, if the quoted material itself includes quotation marks, use double quotation marks (" ") to enclose the interior quotation.
- Indent the quotation ten spaces from the left margin but retain the normal right margin. Indent an extra three spaces from the left for lines that begin paragraphs in the original.
- For the parenthetical reference, if required, skip two spaces after the punctuation that ends the quotation, provide the parenthetical reference, and put no punctuation after the closing parenthesis of the reference.

Here's a sample showing double-spaced text followed by a long quotation:

The integration of the Normans into the culture of England

was thorough but by no means smooth and easy. In *The History*

of England from the Accession of James the Second, Lord

Macaulay describes the degree of control the Normans achieved

after the Battle of Hastings and the opposition from Saxon

rebels:

The Battle of Hastings, and the events which

followed it, not only placed a Duke of Normandy on

the English throne, but gave up the whole

population to the tyranny of the Norman race. The

subjugation of a nation by a nation has seldom,

even in Asia, been more complete. The country was

portioned out among the captains of the invaders.

Strong military institutions, closely connected with

the institution of property, enabled the foreign

conquerors to oppress the children of the soil. A

cruel penal code, cruelly enforced, guarded the

privileges, and even the sports, of the alien tyrants.

Yet the subject race, though beaten down and

trodden underfoot, still made its sting felt. Some

bold men, the favorite heroes of our oldest ballads,

betook themselves to the woods, and there, in

defiance of curfew laws and forest laws, waged a

predatory war against their oppressors.

Assassination was an event of daily occurrence.

Many Normans suddenly disappeared, leaving no

trace. The corpses of many were found bearing the

marks of violence. Death by torture was denounced

against the murderers, and strict search was made

for them, but generally in vain; for the whole nation

was in a conspiracy to screen them. (14–15)

In less than two centuries, these different people had become

indistinguishable for the most part.

Notice that the block indentation of the long quotation substitutes for quotation marks. The indentation indicates that you are quoting.

But remember, like a short quotation, the long one needs an introduction, too. In fact, the introduction to a long quotation often tells the readers what you expect them to notice about it, thus giving them the right perspective. In the introduction to the passage from Lord Macaulay's history, we told you to watch for Norman control and Saxon opposition.

SOME FINE POINTS IN QUOTING

Be careful to quote accurately. If you need to alter a quotation, there are special techniques to show the alteration.

OMITTING WORDS

Sometimes you'll want to omit words from something you're quoting because they're irrelevant or awkward out of their original context. In addition, you may need to alter a passage so that the edited passage fits into the grammar and sense of your own writing. The device you use to show an omission is an ellipsis (. . .)—three spaced periods with a space at the beginning and the end.

When you quote only a word or phrase, you don't need to show that material has been left out before or after a quotation; the cutting is obvious. However, when your editing results in a complete sentence (or complete line of poetry), use the ellipsis to show that you've modified the original, no matter how minor the change. Of course, it's *never* acceptable to edit the original so that you change its meaning (for example, by leaving out *not* or *never*); omissions are acceptable only as a convenience to trim unnecessary words or to fit the quotation into the pattern of your writing.

When the omission occurs *inside a sentence (or line of poetry),* the remainder will look like this:

> "Fish and nuts . . . are highly complementary components of a nutritious diet."

If the omission occurs at the *end of a sentence,* use four spaced periods without a space in front of the first period (a period for the sentence plus the ellipsis):

> "The Koster people knew their food resources intimately. . . . They were not just taking foods randomly from the landscape."

An ellipsis at the end of a sentence can represent an omission of the end of that sentence, one or more sentences, or one or more paragraphs. At the end of a line of poetry, it would indicate omission of one or more lines of poetry.

Except for a block-indented quotation, if an omission at the end of a sentence precedes a parenthetical documentation reference, show the ellipsis before the ending quotation mark and parentheses and provide the sentence punctuation after:

> "The Koster people knew their food resources intimately . . ." (Struever and Holton 244).

Notice that there is a space between *intimately* and the ellipsis but not between the ellipsis and the ending quotation mark.

If that same sentence ended a block-indented quotation (which would not have quotation marks), it would look like this:

> The Koster people knew their food resources intimately. . . . (Struever and Holton 244)

Now there is no space after *intimately,* but there are two spaces between the final period and the opening parenthesis of the parenthetical reference.

ADDING WORDS

If you need to add an explanation within a quotation so that the quotation will make sense in the context of your writing, use square brackets to separate your words from those you're quoting:

> "During the occupation of Horizon 11 [circa 6400 B.C.], Early Archaic people had developed a highly selective exploitation pattern of subsistence."

Don't use parentheses instead of square brackets. If your typewriter can't make brackets, draw them neatly by hand, using black ink or pencil.

ADDING EMPHASIS

You can emphasize a portion of a quotation by underlining (or italicizing) it. However, to ensure that readers can tell who added the emphasis, provide an explanation at the end of the quotation if the emphasis is yours (no explanation is required if the emphasis is part of the original):

> "The kind of input-output analysis which was taking place was *worthy of the most sophisticated culture*" (emphasis added).

VERIFYING QUOTATION ACCURACY

If you find an error, or material that may seem to be peculiar, in the quotation you want to use, add "sic" to the quotation—in square brackets if inside the quotation or in parentheses if outside. The word *sic* (Latin for "thus") tells readers you have rendered the quotation faithfully:

> "When the Imperial Air Forces of Japan attacked Pearl Harbor on 7 December 1940 [sic], they demonstrated how vulnerable ships were to surprise air attack."

ALTERING CAPITALIZATION

If you alter the case of the initial word in a quotation, show the change in square brackets. For example, Struever and Holton actually wrote this about the long-held assumptions of archaeologists:

> "They thought it took the aborigines several thousand years . . . to learn about various foods in eastern North America and how to exploit them."

If you choose to begin your quotation and a sentence with the third word (*it*), you'll have to alter the case of that word:

> "[I]t took the aborigines several thousand years . . . to learn about various foods in eastern North America and how to exploit them"—so scientists insisted for many years before recent discoveries proved otherwise.

Of course, recasting the sentence would allow you to retain the original lowercase *it* and avoid introducing the brackets.

However, altering case is most likely to come up *within* a quotation after an ellipsis:

> According to Struever and Holton, the Koster people "calculated how to provide the community with the most nutritious foods possible. . . . [T]hey ate large quantities of fish, freshwater mussels, and nuts."

ALTERING FINAL PUNCTUATION

Within a quotation, punctuation must appear as in the original, unless properly modified through use of an ellipsis or an addition in square brackets. Final punctuation, however, will depend on how you integrate the quotation into your own writing. This quotation ends in a period:

> "They were not just taking foods randomly from the landscape."

However, you might change that period to a comma if the quotation became an internal clause in your writing:

> "They were not just taking foods randomly from the landscape," according to authorities Stuart Struever and Felicia Holton.

CREDITING YOUR SOURCE

Whenever you use borrowed material, the third step also is essential: crediting your source. You must identify the printed or spoken source of your information.

Failure to credit your source is dishonest. In Chapter 21 we discussed plagiarism—presenting someone else's words or ideas as if they were your own—in the context of notetaking. Certainly unintentional plagiarism can begin with a failure to keep track of ideas and especially words from your original sources. But plagiarism occurs if you fail to document the words or ideas of others when you use them in your writing. So to avoid plagiarism, you need to understand the mechanics of documentation.

Together, the next two chapters cover documentation. Chapter 24 explains the parenthetical documentation references that you'll place in the text of your research paper. Chapter 25 tells you how to prepare the Works Cited pages, the list of sources for your paper. In combination these in-text references and the Works Cited list make up the parenthetical documentation system.

EXERCISES

A. In Volume 2 of his memoirs (*Personal Memoirs of U. S. Grant,* published by Charles L. Webster & Company of New York in 1885), Ulysses S. Grant describes fears in the North about Sherman's army being cut off during its famous march to the sea from Atlanta and Grant's assurances to President Lincoln:

> The Southern papers in commenting upon Sherman's movements pictured him as in the most deplorable condition: stating that his men were starving, that they were demoralized and wandering about almost without object, aiming only to reach the sea coast and get under the protection of our navy. These papers got to the North and had more or less effect upon the minds of the people, causing much distress to all loyal persons—particularly to those who had husbands, sons or brothers with Sherman. Mr. Lincoln seeing these accounts, had a letter written asking me if I could give him anything that he could say to the loyal people that would comfort them. I told him there was not the slightest occasion for alarm; that with 60,000 such men as Sherman had with him, such a commanding officer as he was could not be cut off in the open country. He might possibly be prevented from reaching the point he had started out to reach, but he would get through somewhere and would finally get to his chosen destination: and even if worst came to worst he could return North. I heard afterwards of Mr. Lincoln's saying, to those who would inquire of him as to what he thought about the safety of Sherman's army, that Sherman was all right: "Grant says they are safe with such a general, and that if they cannot get out where they want to, they can crawl back by the hole they went in at."

1. Does this material represent primary or secondary source material?
2. What would be the advantages or disadvantages of quoting part or all of this material in a research paper about Sherman's march to the sea?
3. Quote at least two sentences from Grant and provide an introduction for the quotation. Be sure to quote accurately; if you alter the original material in any way, use the techniques in the chapter to show the alteration. Use (2:366–67) for the parenthetical documentation reference if your introduction contains the name of the author or (Grant 2:366–67) if it doesn't.

B. "Amazons," an article by Adrienne Mayor and Josiah Ober, originally appeared in *MHQ: The Quarterly Journal of Military History* and is one of the articles collected in *Experience of War,* edited by Robert Cowley (New York: Norton, 1992). In the following two paragraphs, Mayor and Ober discuss the possible historical foundation for the Amazons in Greek myths. Page 22 ends with "warlike," while page 23 begins with "nomadic."

What about the Amazons of Greek myth? Must they, too, be seen only as symbolic figures of psychological projection? Until quite recently, most serious historians would have had to answer yes. Yet in the 1950s large-scale Soviet archaeological excavations in the Steppes of the southern Ukraine—exactly where early versions of Amazon legends located the women's homeland—began to uncover remarkable tombs of Sarmatian warriors—warlike, nomadic horsepeople who traded with the ancient Greeks. And the archaeologists found that 20 percent of the fourth-century B.C. graves that contain weapons and armor belonged to women.

Typically, the young women's skeletons are surrounded by large iron lances; brightly painted wooden quivers and bows, and many triple-barbed bronze arrowheads; iron knives, daggers, swords, and spears; metal-plated leather armor; and horse trappings. Clear evidence of battle wounds—severe head injuries, bronze arrowheads embedded in bone—show that Sarmatian women were indeed warriors.

1. Does this passage represent primary or secondary source material?
2. Would you be more likely to quote, summarize, or paraphrase material from this passage in a research paper about Greek mythology?
3. Write a short paragraph of your own in which you summarize or paraphrase material from this passage. Be sure to introduce the borrowing. For the parenthetical documentation reference, use (22–23), (22), or (23) if your introduction contains the names of the authors; use (Mayor and Ober 22–23), (Mayor and Ober 22), or (Mayor and Ober 23) if it doesn't.

24 Parenthetical Documentation

Whether you use quotations, paraphrases, or summaries, you must document the sources of your information. In Part Three you learned a preliminary documentation system that let readers know whenever you were using outside sources for support. This chapter introduces a better system, one that not only tells readers that you are using borrowed material, but also gives them enough information to find the source.

The formats for documentation in this chapter and the next generally follow the third edition of the *MLA Handbook for Writers of Research Papers,* published by the Modern Language Association of America. This handbook is an accepted standard for documentation in many academic fields, especially the humanities. Other style guides also exist, of course, and there are differences in specific entry and presentation formats from one manual to another. We've chosen to follow MLA on most points because the guidance is thorough, reasonable, and widely accepted.

Differences Among Documentation Style Manuals

Don't be too concerned about these differences. Most of them exist to accommodate the varied needs of differing academic fields. More important, however, most documentation guides differ little on what should go into a specific documentation entry for an article or book. In practical terms, then, if you learn one system well—the one in this book, for example—you can adapt easily to the particular style in another place at another time. You'll know basically what should be included in documentation entries by anybody's standard, so you'll be able to see quickly the peculiarities of any other system you're required to follow.

PARENTHETICAL DOCUMENTATION SYSTEM

The parenthetical documentation system depends on the interaction of material you place in two portions of your research paper:

- *General source listing.* At the end of your research paper you provide an alphabetized listing, called Works Cited, with full bibliographic information about each source document you used. The list provides a general reference to your sources but, of course, doesn't identify the specific portions you used for the quotations, summaries, and paraphrases in the body of the paper.
- *Specific portion reference.* Within the body of your paper, along with each presentation of material borrowed from your sources, you include in parentheses a documentation reference to the specific portion(s) of the source or sources supporting your text. This parenthetical information provides a reference to the data in the Works Cited listing so readers can connect the general and specific documentation portions.

Interaction of References in Text and Works Cited

When readers combine the information in parentheses in the body of your paper with the full bibliographic information in your Works Cited listing, they have the data they need to locate each source and to find the specific portion you used.

Let's say this is a portion of your paper:

In the Indian pottery canteen, form and function came together. Art historians have noted the usefulness of the canteen's shape and the way it was fired. The shape of the canteen allowed it to be carried by a rider on a horse. Because of the way the pottery was fired, it was somewhat porous; as a result, the action of water seeping through to the outside, where it evaporated, cooled and sweetened the water remaining in the canteen (Clark and Ingram 47).

The *specific portion reference* is (*Clark and Ingram 47*).

- *Clark and Ingram* tells readers to look for an entry in the Works Cited listing with those names.
- The *47* indicates that the information came from that specific portion of the work.

In the Works Cited pages—the *general source listing*—readers would find this entry, alphabetized under *Clark:*

Clark, Karen, and Fred Ingram. *Acoma Canteens and Other Pottery Designs.* Washington: Steinman, 1989.

Clearly, then, you want to learn the conventions for both the general source and specific reference portions of the parenthetical documentation system. The next chapter focuses on format conventions for the Works Cited listing (the general source portion of the parenthetical documentation). The rest of this chapter treats the specific portion references that give the system its name: the parenthetical references.

PARENTHETICAL REFERENCES

BASIC CONTENT

Parenthetical references in the text of your paper should give your readers the following information:

- *A reference to the opening of the corresponding entry in the Works Cited list.* If the Works Cited entry shows only one author, you'll give that author's last name. The reference also could be two or three last names, one person's name with "et al.," the name of a group, a shortened version of the title, or a name with the title, depending in every case on what information is necessary to identify clearly the *one* work in Works Cited that you are referring to. ("Basic Forms" below details the various possibilities.)

- *Identification of the location within that work of the material you're documenting.* Normally this will be a reference to a single page or several pages. However, when your Works Cited listing gives a multivolume work, the parenthetical reference will require a volume number with the page(s). If the reference is to a one-page article, to an article in an encyclopedia that alphabetizes its articles, or to a source that has no pagination (such as a film or videocassette), there will be no place reference.

BASIC FORMS

The material required for the parenthetical reference varies somewhat with the nature of the work you refer to from your Works Cited list and how much of it you are citing. (For rules on showing inclusive page numbers, see page 266.)

Work With One Name Listed

When the Works Cited listing begins with only one person's name, use the last name and the page reference: (Brown 281) or (Brown 281–83). If the name has a qualifier such as "ed." or "trans.," you still use only the last name.

Work With Two or Three Names Listed

If the Works Cited entry opens with two or three names, include those names in the parenthetical reference: (Wesson and Jones 117) or (Stockton, Avery, and Beal 63).

Work With One Name and "et al."

If the Works Cited entry begins with a name and "et al.," which means "and others," include the "et al." in your parenthetical reference: (Steinnem et al. 92–93).

Work With Group as Author

Treat the group just like another author: (President's Commission on Energy 315). A reference such as this, of course, could easily interrupt a reader's train of thought; we'll discuss later how to avoid that problem by streamlining the parenthetical references.

Work Listed by Title

If the Works Cited entry begins with a title, use the title, or a reasonable shortened version of it, in the parenthetical reference. Be careful in shortening the title, though, because readers must find the words you give in an alphabetized list; make sure the shortened title includes the word by which the work is alphabetized in your Works Cited listing. A reference to *A Short Study of Linguistics for Beginners* might look like this: (*Short Study of Linguistics* 53). Again, streamlining might be preferable.

Multivolume Work

In reference to a multivolume work, normally you'll give a volume number with the page reference: (Martin 2:65–66). This is a reference to pages 65 to 66 of volume 2 of a multivolume work alphabetized in Works Cited under "Martin." However, if the entry in Works Cited clearly identifies only a single volume of the multivolume work, then the parenthetical reference need not include the volume number.

Multiple Works Listed for the Same Name(s)

When two or more works are alphabetized in Works Cited for the same name(s), include in the parenthetical reference the title, or a shortened version of it, of the specific work you're referring to. If two books are listed for Brian Pierce, then a reference to one of them would look like this: (Pierce, *Amateur Golfing* 27). Here's another candidate for streamlining.

Citing an Entire Work

If you need to document a textual reference to an entire work, then a page reference is inappropriate, so the parentheses would contain only the author element: (Brown). Streamlining, however, will eliminate the need for any parenthetical reference.

Indirect Reference

Although you always should attempt to find the original source for a quotation, sometimes you'll have to quote information from a source that includes the original. If you quote or paraphrase a quotation, add "qtd. in" (for "quoted in") or "paraphrased from" to the parenthetical reference, as here:

> John Harris calls literary critic Edmund Wilson a "pompous, close-minded reader" for his insistence that detective fiction is not worth reading (qtd. in Armstrong 13).

Shouldn't the indirect quotation here have both double and single quotation marks to indicate that we are quoting already quoted material? That depends on the source from which we borrow the material. If the exact words we borrow are within a direct quotation in our source, then our presentation should include both types of quotation marks. If our source shows no quotation marks, then our borrowing, as here, will have only double quotation marks.

Multiple Works in a Reference

To include two or more works in a single parenthetical reference, list each as you would for itself and use semicolons to separate them: (Jackson 53–54; Morgan 15). Again, streamlining may help reduce the interruption, but if you need to show a long, disruptive list, consider using an actual footnote instead (see the section "Notes With Parenthetical Documentation" below).

Verse Plays, Poetry, and the Bible

For verse plays, use the play's title, or a reasonable shortened form of it, followed by act and scene or by act, scene, and verse—with the parts of the play separated by periods: (*Othello* 4.2) or (*Othello* 4.2.3–4).

For poetry, again use the poem's title, or a reasonable shortened form of it, followed by the line numbers for a poem without divisions or by portions separated by periods for a long poem with major divisions: ("Coming Home" 10–12) or (*Iliad* 9.7–12.).

For the Bible, use the book title followed by chapter and verse (with a period separating chapter and verse): (John 3.16). Notice that books of the Bible, like the Bible itself, require neither underlining (italics) or quotation marks.

STREAMLINING PARENTHETICAL REFERENCES

Several times we've mentioned the possibility of streamlining. The idea is to keep the information within the parentheses as short as possible so readers are not distracted. You accomplish this by giving part or all of the needed reference in the introduction to the borrowed material. If the introduction includes the name of a book's author, then the parentheses might contain only the page reference.

> Brown notes General Grant's occasional impatience with the progress of his attrition campaign in 1864 (281).

Because Brown's name is in the introduction to the material from his book, the parenthetical reference needs only the page reference.

Especially in the case where your Works Cited list has several works by the same author and you must refer to one of those works, streamlining lessens the interruption of the parenthetical reference. Without streamlining, a reference might look like this:

> Although the Battle of the Crater, for which Union coal miners tunneled under the Confederate fortification lines near Petersburg, captures our imagination today, it has been labeled a bloody tactical blunder because of the cost in lives (Winchester, *Civil War After Gettysburg* 314).

The version below streamlines that long parenthetical reference:

> Although the Battle of the Crater, for which Union coal miners tunneled under the Confederate fortification lines near Petersburg, captures our imagination today, in *The Civil War After Gettysburg* Winchester labels it a bloody tactical blunder because of the cost in lives (314).

Keep in mind that streamlining does not permit omission of required material, but it can reduce the interruption of parenthetical references.

PLACEMENT IN TEXT

Place the parenthetical references in the text of your paper so that they interrupt the flow of thought as little as possible. Put the parentheses as close as reasonably possible after the end of the material you're documenting, but always at the end of a clause or phrase so the reference doesn't intrude. Normally, the parenthetical reference can be placed at the end of a sentence. Even with quotations, the reference doesn't have to come *immediately* after the quotation marks:

> Brown asserts that General Grant's "inability to remain patient with the pace of his attrition campaign" led to the horrendous Union losses in a mere half-hour at Cold Harbor, Virginia (281).

Of course, don't delay the parenthetical reference until the end of a sentence if readers could be confused about what material the reference documents:

> Although Brown notes Grant's occasional impatience with the progress of his attrition campaign in 1864 (281), the overall strategy of attrition—Grant against Lee's Army of Northern Virginia and Sherman against the Southern homeland supply base—brought the Union victory.

The reference here is in the middle of the sentence because only the first portion is attributable to the source. Note, however, that the parentheses do come at the end of the clause so the reference intrudes as little as possible.

POSITION RELATIVE TO SENTENCE PUNCTUATION

Notice that the parenthetical reference in the first of the two samples above preceded the period at the end of the sentence, and the parentheses in the second sample came before the comma that ended the clause. Place your parenthetical reference before the punctuation mark, if any, that ends the sentence, clause, or phrase with the material you're documenting. If a quotation ends the sentence, clause, or phrase, normally you'll place the parenthetical reference between the ending quotation marks and the punctuation for the sentence, clause, or phrase:

The Union losses at Cold Harbor, Virginia, can be attributed to General Grant's "inability to remain patient with the pace of his attrition campaign" (Brown 281).

The exception to this placement guidance is for a long quotation—one that is set off from the left margin of the rest of the paper with a block indentation. For this type of quotation, skip two spaces after the ending punctuation, provide the parenthetical reference, and put no punctuation after the closing parenthesis of the reference. Illustrations of this technique appear in the sample research paper (page 165) and in the illustrations for presenting borrowed material (page 230).

NOTES WITH PARENTHETICAL DOCUMENTATION

Parenthetical references will take care of almost all documentation references, but they don't accommodate digressions from the text. Avoid long side arguments, but if you must add notes to support your text, use standard footnote or endnote entries: That is, use parenthetical references for your normal documentation, but also use notes for the explanatory digressions, like this one:

[1]Smithson disagrees with Brown about Grant's blunder at Cold Harbor (224), but offers little support. See also Winchester 271; Souther 416–18; and Blake 76.

If you use many notes of this type, we recommend collecting them as endnotes at the end of your paper. In that case, you would include a page entitled "Notes" between the body of your paper and the Works Cited pages.

The alternative—particularly appropriate if you have only a few such notes—is to include each as a footnote at the bottom of the page on which its in-text reference number falls. In this case, separate the footnote(s) from the text by a short line (about 20 spaces long) near the bottom of the page. The sample research paper (page 171) shows a line of this sort separating a source note from the table it documents. Of course, for notes to text (rather than tables) the footnotes would end the page to which they apply, so the dividing line would always be near the bottom of the page.

EXERCISES

A. Given the Works Cited entries below as the general source listing of a research paper, write parenthetical references to show the specific portion references required for the numbered exercise items that follow. (Just show the parentheses and what would go in them; don't be concerned in this exercise with placing the references into textual passages.)

Backus, Susan B. *The Siegeworks of Petersburg.* New York: Shirlington, 1993. Vol. 3 of *Civil War Engineering.* 4 vols.

Dovberg, Walter, et al. *Under the Gun: Developments in the Use of Engineering in the Army of the Potomac.* New York: Schocken, 1993.

Jameson, F. Fitzroy. *The Letters of a Union Engineering Specialist.* Washington: Steinman, 1994.

McDonald, J. Thomas. *Engineers and Engineering During the American Civil War.* 2 vols. New York: Shirlington, 1994.

Roper, Henry Pleasants, and Sarah Jane Jefferson. "Visiting the Defenses of Washington." *Civil War Battles* 3.4 (1992): 316–32.

1. Pages 43 to 45 of *The Letters of a Union Engineering Specialist.*
2. Page 318 of the article in *Civil War Battles.*
3. Page 27 of volume 2 of *Engineers and Engineering During the American Civil War.*
4. Page 115 of *Under the Gun: Developments in the Use of Engineering in the Army of the Potomac.*
5. Pages 216 to 217 of *The Siegeworks of Petersburg.*
6. A quotation from Francis Owen's *Lincoln's Defensive Line* that is quoted on page 317 of "Visiting the Defenses of Washington."
7. Page 221 of *Under the Gun: Developments in the Use of Engineering in the Army of the Potomac* if another source by Dovberg and the same coauthors appeared in this same Works Cited listing.

B. Rewrite the following passages to streamline their parenthetical references. In your revisions, be sure to modify the material inside the parentheses to account for information you incorporate into introductions to the research material. And be sure you've followed the rules for punctuation relative to parenthetical references and quotation marks.

1. Although it is true that "most engineering in the Civil War merely repeated the tried-and-true techniques developed over the years in European wars" (McDonald, *Engineers and Engineering During the American Civil War* 1:17), the American conflict caused the growth of a new branch of wartime engineers—railroad engineers.
2. As one historian has written, "General Grant preferred to have his logistic tail covered by water lines of communication as he lacked confidence in the security of the railroads" (Franklin, "Railroad Engineers in the Union Army" 68).

25 Works Cited

As you saw in Chapter 24, parenthetical references in the body of your research paper are possible because they refer to a *general source listing* at the end of the paper. This chapter focuses on that source listing—first on the format of the pages for the list as a whole, then on the formats of the entries that appear in that list, and finally on a few special format rules that affect the appearance of parts of some entries.

WORKS CITED PAGE FORMAT

The usual name for the listing of works at the end of the paper is *Works Cited*. This title assumes that the listing contains all (and only) the works you cite in the text of your paper; it does not include others that you read but that did not account for ideas or data in your paper. Your instructor might ask you to include the other works you read during research, in which case you could change the title to *Works Consulted.*

For the Works Cited page(s), start the list on a new page, numbering that page in sequence with the rest of your paper. Here's how the page should look:

- Use the same margins as for the rest of the pages of your research paper.
- Center the title one inch from the top of the page.
- Double-space after the title to find the line on which to begin the first entry.
- Double-space both within and between entries. (*Note:* Your instructor may prefer you to single-space within individual entries and double-space only between entries.)
- Begin the first line of each entry on the left margin, but for all subsequent lines of an entry indent five spaces.
- List entries in alphabetical order.

Richards 9

Works Cited

Clark, Karen, and Fred Ingram. *Acoma Canteens and Other*
    Pottery Designs. Washington: Steinman, 1989.

Donovan, Janet. *Art of Southwest America.* New York:
    Shirlington, 1990.

Macy, Linda S. *Santa Clara Designs.* New York: Shirlington, 1988.
    Vol. 2 of *Pottery of the American Southwest.* 5 vols.

Moon, Calvin Roy, et al. *Mimbres Pottery, Decorations, and*
    Symbology. Albuquerque: La Madera, 1990.

WHAT WORKS CITED ENTRIES CONTAIN

It has become commonplace to say that Works Cited documentation entries contain three basic parts: author, title, and publication information. And that's true enough for the most simple citations, which usually make up the majority of entries in a Works Cited list. Unfortunately, there are dozens of exceptions to that basic pattern. We believe that the following six basic groups more accurately describe a documentation entry and will better help you understand the job ahead:

1. Person(s) or group responsible for the piece of material you're documenting
2. The title(s)
3. Amplifying information, to help identify or describe the work precisely
4. Publishing information, or similar information that will help someone find the work
5. Identification of the portion you are citing
6. Supplemental bibliographic information (used with *multivolume book* citations only)

Here are those groups in a simple three-part citation:

```
      1             2                    4
 ┌─────────┐┌───────────────────┐┌──────────────────────────┐
Donovan, Janet. Art of Southwest America. New York:  Shirlington, 1990.
```

Group 3 is missing because no amplifying information is necessary to describe the book; group 5 is unnecessary because the entry is for the entire book, not a portion of it; and group 6 is unnecessary because the entry is not for a multivolume book.

An entry for an essay in a collection of essays published in one volume of a multivolume work, however, has all six basic groups:

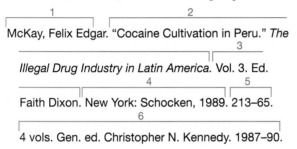

As you can see here, documentation entries can be quite complex. Yet, generally, despite complexities, the information falls into the six groups.

ENTRIES FOR BOOKS

GENERAL FORM: BOOKS

Divided here into the six basic groups are the fourteen elements you may need for a book citation. Few entries actually have all fourteen; the simple citation in the previous section has only five elements, while the sample complex citation has eleven. Obviously, you include only those elements that are appropriate for the book you're documenting.

(1) Person(s) or Group Responsible for the Piece of Material You're Documenting

- *Name(s) of individual(s) or group.* Usually this is an author, but it can be an editor, translator, or organization. The key is identifying the people *directly responsible* for the particular piece of material you're documenting. Use names as they appear on the title page of the book. Do not include professional or educational titles, such as "M.S." or "Ph.D." If the entry is to begin with a person's name, reverse the name for alphabetizing (last-first-middle instead of first-middle-last).

(2) The Title(s)

- *Title of a part of a book.* You'll need this when you're documenting an essay, a poem, a short story, and so forth, within an anthology, or when you cite a division of a book (such as the Introduction).
- *Title of the book.* If a book has both a title and a subtitle, give both with a colon and a single space between them (omit the colon if the title itself ends with punctuation, such as a question mark). (Special rules beginning on

page 264 give guidance for capitalization, quotation marks, and underlining in titles.)

(3) Amplifying Information, to Help Identify or Describe the Work Precisely

- *Translator(s).* One translation is rarely like another, so it's necessary to show the translator(s) of the work.
- *Editor(s).* The order of translator(s) and editor(s) can be reversed; show them in the order in which they appear on the book's title page.
- *Edition.* Readers will assume you're citing the first edition, without revisions, unless you indicate otherwise. Portions of different editions of the same book will be different, so you need to show exactly which one you used.
- *Volume number or number of volumes.* In a citation for a multivolume work, the number of the volume used or the number of volumes in the set can appear before the publication information, depending on how you refer to the material within your paper.
- *Series.* If the work you're citing is part of a series, give the series name and the number of the work in the series (for example, "Archaeological Studies, No. 12").

(4) Publishing Information, or Similar Information That Will Help Someone Find the Work

- *Place of publication.* Look for the place of publication on the title or copyright page or at the back of the book, especially for a book published outside the United States. If several cities are listed, use the one listed first unless you have some reason for using a different one. Give the state or country along with the city if the city is not likely to be recognized or could be confused with another city with the same name.
- *Publisher.* You need not name the publisher for a book printed before 1900. For books printed since 1900, use a shortened version of the publisher's name; for example, "Holt" rather than "Holt, Rinehart and Winston." (See pages 265–66 for special rules on dealing with publishers' names and special imprints.)
- *Date of publication.* Again, look for the publication date on the title page, on the copyright page, or at the back of the book. If no publication date appears, give the latest copyright date. Ignore dates for multiple printings; however, if you are citing a work in other than its first edition, use the publication date for the edition you're using, not the original date. For example, if a book in its third edition shows dates of 1979, 1984, and 1987, use 1987.

(5) Identification of the Portion You Are Citing

You'll use this part of an entry only when you're citing a part of a book (for example, an essay or Introduction).

- *Page numbers.* Show the *inclusive* page numbers for the portion of the book you're citing. Don't be concerned if you refer to only one or a few of those pages in the text of your paper; those specific page references will be clear in your parenthetical references in the text. Here you must show the pagination for the entire piece. (See page 266 for special rules on showing inclusive page numbers.)

(6) Supplemental Bibliographic Information

You'll use this part of an entry only when your citation is for a multivolume work—and even then only part of the time, depending on the complexity of the bibliographic information and how you refer to the material within your paper.

- *Number of volumes.* The number of volumes in a multivolume work will appear after publication and specific portion data when the earlier information in the citation is for a single volume of the set.
- *Information for the set of volumes.* Data pertaining to the set of volumes—for example, general editor and span of publication years for the set—may appear at the end of the citation for a multivolume work.

SAMPLE ENTRIES: BOOKS

Following are samples illustrating recommended formats for citations for books. A word of caution: These samples were designed to illustrate particular portions of a book citation. They do not cover every variation you may run across. (A list of samples detailing all the variations would be unbelievably long.) If the book you're citing doesn't quite fit a sample, adapt the format to fit your needs, but be sure to include all the appropriate information you've just read about in the preceding section. *Note:* Since the samples have been listed to demonstrate points about formats, no attempt has been made to alphabetize them, except for entries under "Two or More Books by the Same 'Author(s).'" In your Works Cited pages, of course, you'll list all works in alphabetical order.

One Author

Jameson, F. Fitzroy. *The Letters of a Union Engineering Specialist.* Washington: Steinman, 1994.

Two or Three Authors

Only the name of the person listed first is given out of normal order (last-first-middle rather than first-middle-last). Be sure to use authors' names as they appear on the book's title page. Do not include professional or educational titles, such as "M.S." or "Ph.D." Names of multiple authors may not be alphabetized on the title page; list them in the order in which they appear.

Clark, Karen, and Frank Ingram. *Acoma Canteens and Other Pottery Designs.* Washington: Steinman, 1989.

Hyson, Curtis F., G. Randolph Dill, and Jay H. Felmet, Jr. *Magic, Mystery, and Medicine.* Nashville: Vanderbilt UP, 1990.

More Than Three Authors

For more than three authors, give only the one listed first in the book and follow that with "et al." (for "and others").

Dovberg, Walter, et al. *Under the Gun: Developments in the Use of Engineering in the Army of the Potomac.* New York: Schocken, 1993.

Group as Author

When a group or agency is responsible for a book, treat that group as the author and list its name first, even though the group's name may appear in the book's title or may appear again as publisher. List the group or agency name in normal order. ("GPO" in this entry is the accepted abbreviation for "Government Printing Office," which prints U.S. federal publications. Note that "DC" is omitted.)

National Commission on Health Care. *Report of the National Commission on Health Care.* Washington: GPO, 1994.

Government and International Body Publications

Many government agency publications are simple enough to be treated as books with groups as authors, with the responsible agency serving as author, as in the entry above. Occasionally government publications show a specific person as author; you can begin with that person (as in the second sample below), or you can show the individual author after the title (as in the first sample).

For the *Congressional Record,* you need show only the full date and the inclusive pages for the portion being cited. For other congressional documents, give the government and body, house, committee (if appropriate), document title, number and session of Congress, and type and number of publication, followed by standard publication data. Congressional documents include bills (S 16; HR 63), resolutions (S. Res. 16; H. Res. 63), reports (S. Rept. 16; H. Rept. 63), and documents (S. Doc. 16; H. Doc. 63).

There are also state and local government documents, foreign government documents, and those of international bodies (such as the United Nations). Begin these as you would a U.S. federal publication, naming first the government or international body (for example, "Indiana. Dept. of Revenue" or "United Nations. Committee for Economic Development").

United States. Dept. of State. *Islamic Developments in Africa.* By Edan Irwin. Washington: GPO, 1989.
Irwin, Edan. *Islamic Developments in Africa.* U.S Dept. of State. Washington: GPO, 1989.
Cong. Rec. 21 Sep. 1990: 3143–45.

United States. Cong. House. Permanent Select Committee on Intelligence.
Technological Transfer Losses in the 1980s. 101st Cong., 2nd sess. H. Rept.
1122. Washington: GPO, 1990.

United Nations. Committee for Economic Cooperation. *Resource Development
in West Africa.* Elmsford: Pergamon, 1989.

Author Not Given

If no author is given in a book, begin the entry with the title. (When you alphabetize the entries for your Works Cited pages, you'll go by the first word in the title
other than an article—that is, other than *A, An,* or *The.*) Of course, treat books with
groups as authors or government and international body publications as indicated
above, even though these books frequently show no individual as author.

A Collection of Slavic Stories and Rhymes. Baltimore: Court, 1990.

Editor(s)

If your use of an edited book, for the most part, is the text of the work itself, then
the name(s) of the editor(s) ("ed." or "eds.") should appear after the title, as in the
first sample below. However, if the work of the editor(s)—including introductory or
other extratextual comments—is being cited, begin the entry with the editor(s), as in
the second sample. Moreover, if you are citing an anthology or other collection—
rather than a piece within the collection—use the second format below (for a piece in
a collection, see "Part of a Collection" below).

Kemp, Gilbert M. *Narcotics Trafficking and the Caribbean Islands.* Ed. Pamela
Hoffman. Madison: U of Wisconsin, 1990.

Hoffman, Pamela, ed. *Narcotics Trafficking and the Caribbean Islands.* By Gilbert
M. Kemp. Madison: U of Wisconsin, 1990.

Translator(s)

Normally you'll show the translator(s) of a book after the title, as in the first sample below. However, as with editors, if you are citing primarily commentary by the
translator(s), then begin with the translator(s), as in the second sample. If the book
has both a translator and an editor, show them in the order in which they appear on
the book's title page.

Gatti, Carlo. *Cats of Venice.* Trans. Rachel Hipson. New York: Shirlington, 1989.

Hipson, Rachel, trans. *Cats of Venice.* By Carlo Gatti. New York:
Shirlington, 1989.

Della Bella, Mario. *The Shores of the Adriatic.* Trans. Carl Elliot. Ed. Malcom
Hawk. Washington: Slay, 1990.

Two or More Books by the Same "Author(s)"

Sometimes two or more entries in your Works Cited listing have *exactly* the same
names at the beginning for the person(s) or group responsible for the piece you're

documenting. In such a case, give the name(s) only for the first entry; in the following entries type *three hyphens* and a period in place of the name(s). *The three hyphens signify the same name(s),* so if a person named is shown in the first entry as, say, an author and in the next as a translator, you should use the three hyphens for the name in the second entry, following the hyphens with a comma and "trans." (Notice, in the samples below, that the order is determined by the alphabetical order of the titles, since the author block is the same for each.)

Chin, Lee. *"Hong Kong Tea" and Other Stories.* Arlington: Burning Tree, 1990.
---, trans. *"The Lagoon" and More.* By Mario Della Bella. New York: Shirlington, 1989.
---. *Singapore Tales.* Arlington: Burning Tree, 1988.

However, if an entry with a single name is followed by an entry in which the first of multiple authors is that same name, do not use the three hyphens in the second entry. Three hyphens can stand for more than one name, but the name block in each case must be *exactly* the same.

Gatti, Carlo. *Cats of Venice.* Trans. Rachel Hipson. New York: Shirlington, 1989.
Gatti, Carlo, and Rachel Hipson, trans. *Carabinieri Parade.* By Luigi Mautone. Washington: Luke, 1990.
---, trans. *Neapolitan Manners.* By Rosa Valentino. New York: Shirlington, 1989.

Finally, the three hyphens also should be used when groups, governments, or international bodies serve as authors. And since government entries begin with the name of the government and the name of the body or agency sponsoring the work, you may need more than one set of three hyphens. The samples below illustrate the author blocks for several government publications.

Indiana. Dept. of Health.
---. Dept. of Revenue.
United States. Cong. House.
---. ---. Senate.
---. Dept. of Energy.

Extratextual Material

In citations for such extratextual material as an Introduction or Afterword, give the name of the author of that division of the book, followed by the name of the extratextual piece; the author of the work itself follows the book title. If the author of the extratextual material is also the author of the book, give only the last name after the book title, as in the second sample. Notice that both samples contain inclusive page numbers for the named extratextual section of the book.

Muñoz, Hector. Introduction. *Protest in the Vietnam War Years.* By David M. Ross. Washington: Luke, 1988. v–xxi.

Readman, Donna L. Afterword. *Vienna Christmas.* By Readman. Washington:
    Spinnaker, 1990. 224–32.

Part of a Collection

For parts of anthologies, collections of articles, and casebooks, the title of the
piece precedes the title of the work. Normally the title of the piece will appear in quotation marks; however, if it was published originally as a book, underline (or itali-
cize) it instead. Notice that as for an extratextual piece of a book discussed above, the
inclusive pages for the piece of the collection end the citation.

Sacco, Franco. "Umberto Eco's Labyrinth." *Contemporary European Fiction.* Ed.
    Victoria Wood. Boston: Liberty, 1990. 175–98.

Cross-References

If you're documenting multiple pieces from the same collection, you have a
choice. You can treat each piece as a part of a collection, giving full data for the collection itself each time. Or you can give one entry for the collection and then simplify
the citations for the pieces by referring to the entry for the collection. Keep in mind,
however, that each specific piece of the collection that you refer to in the text of your
paper requires its own entry in the Works Cited section. Thus, with cross-referencing
you save repeating some information in each of the citations for a piece of the collection, but you then must add an entry for the collection itself.

Fisher, Jill M. "Milan Kundera: Far From Unbearable." Wood 142–74.
Sacco, Franco. "Umberto Eco's Labyrinth." Wood 175–98.
Wood, Victoria, ed. *Contemporary European Fiction.* Boston: Liberty, 1990.

Republished Books

If you use a republished book (a new publication of an out-of-print book or a
paperback version of a book originally published in hard cover), show the original
publication date before the new publication information.

Lord, Michele I. *Mapping the Shenandoah Valley for Stonewall Jackson.* 1885.
    Baltimore: Court, 1994.

If the original book is republished under a new title, follow the original title and publication year with "Rpt. as" ("Reprinted as") and the new title. The full publication
data, as in the citation above, is for the new publication.

Ferry, R. Michael. *The Amazonia Rain Forest.* 1973. Rpt. as *Can We Save the
    Rain Forest?* Albuquerque: La Madera, 1990.

Edition Other Than First

Readers will assume the book is a first edition unless you indicate otherwise, such
as second edition ("2nd ed."), alternate edition ("Alt. ed."), revised edition ("Rev.
ed."), and so on.

Doyle, Rachel Marie. *Desktop Publishing Software.* 2nd ed. New York:
    Schocken, 1990.

Series

If a book is part of a series, give the series name and the number of the work in the series.

Mosman, Kristina J. *The Iceman and His World.* Archaeological Studies, No. 33.
    Albuquerque: La Madera, 1994.

Multivolume Work

For a specific page reference to a multivolume work, the parenthetical reference in the text of your paper will include the volume number with the page reference if you need to refer to more than one volume of the set (for example, 2:111–12 for pages 111 to 112 of volume 2). However, if in your paper you never need to document material from more than one volume of the set, you can show the specific volume number in the Works Cited entry—as in the following sample—and give only the page reference in the text of your paper (for example, 111–12 instead of 2:111–12). Notice that the sample ends with the total number of volumes in the multivolume set.

Hill, Elliot F. *History and Art of the Mayans.* Vol. 2. New York: Schocken,
    1990. 3 vols.

If the single volume you cite for your paper has its own title, include the specific volume reference between the individual publication data and the multivolume title, as in the samples below. Again, references in the text of your paper would not include the volume number. Notice that the first sample ends with the number of volumes in the set; the second sample adds inclusive years of publication for the set because not all volumes were published in the same year.

Backus, Susan B. *The Siegeworks of Petersburg.* New York: Shirlington, 1993.
    Vol. 3 of *Civil War Engineering.* 4 vols.
Moore, Donald. *Oriental Patterns in European Porcelains.* Bloomington: Indiana
    UP, 1988. Vol. 3 of *European*
    Porcelain Manufacture. 4 vols. 1985–90.

If your paper requires references to two or more volumes, then use the more general multivolume citation in your Works Cited listing (as below) and include the volume number with each parenthetical reference in the text of your paper.

Hill, Elliot F. *History and Art of the Mayans.* 3 vols. New York: Schocken, 1990.

If the multiple volumes of the set were published over a period of years, then the publication date portion shows the first and last years of the set:

Moore, Donald. *European Porcelain Manufacture.* 4 vols. Bloomington: Indiana
   UP, 1985–90.

   If the multivolume set has not been completed, include "to date" with the number
of volumes and follow the publication date of the first volume with a hyphen and a
space before the ending period.

King, Chester N. *European Chamber Music and Its Composers.* 3 vols. to date.
   Baltimore: Court, 1987– .

   When you cite a piece in a multivolume collection of pieces, show the volume
number before the publication data and both the inclusive pages for the piece and the
number of volumes in the set at the end of the entry.

Haynes, Clinton R. "Athapaskan Descendants." *Indians of the Americas.* Ed.
   Kimberly L. Dawson. Vol. 1. Austin: U of Texas P, 1989. 718–42. 3 vols.

   Depending on the factors applicable to a multivolume work, the Works Cited
entry can become quite complex. The following citation shows a piece in a volume
of a multivolume set; the volume has one editor, while the multivolume set has a general editor; the volumes of the set were published over a period of years.

McKay, Felix Edgar. "Cocaine Cultivation in Peru." *The Illegal Drug Industry in
   Latin America.* Vol. 3. Ed. Faith Dixon. New York: Schocken, 1989. 213–65. 4
   vols. Gen ed. Christopher N. Kennedy. 1987–90.

The Bible
   In the Works Cited listing, give the title and the version, but omit all publishing
information. Remember that you use neither underlining (italics) nor quotation
marks for the Bible and its books.

The Bible. New International Version.

Published Conference Proceedings
   If the book title doesn't include information about the conference, provide amplifying information after the title.

The Child '94: The Legacy of Mental, Physical, and Sexual Abuse. Proc. of a
   Conference of the Association of Social Workers and Child Care Specialists.
   23–25 May 1994. Minneapolis: U of Minnesota P, 1994.

Pamphlet
   Treat pamphlets as books.

Enos, Bernard B. *Choosing a Hard Disk.* Baltimore: Court, 1990.

Missing Publishing or Pagination Data

Use the following abbreviations for missing publication or pagination information:

no place of publication: n. p.

no publisher: n. p.

no date: n. d.

no pagination: n. pag.

The abbreviations for "no place" and "no publisher" are the same, but their positions left or right of the colon will allow readers to tell the difference. When a book has no pagination indicated, your Works Cited entry needs to contain "N. pag." so that readers will understand why parenthetical references in the text of your paper do not show page numbers.

Newsletter Design and Desktop Publishing. N.p.: n.p., 1989. N. pag.

ENTRIES FOR ARTICLES IN PERIODICALS

Periodicals are publications that are issued periodically on some sort of schedule—quarterly, bimonthly, weekly, daily, and so forth. Authorities group periodicals into three classes: journals, magazines, and newspapers. Newspapers are easy to recognize, but there isn't an absolute distinction between journals and magazines.

Many journals don't have the word *journal* in their titles, and not all periodicals with *journal* in their titles are considered journals for documentation. Nevertheless, some differentiation is necessary because the data required after the publisher in a Works Cited entry differ for the various types of periodicals. Fortunately, we don't need a scholarly distinction; instead we can make fairly simple divisions based on how the periodicals paginate their issues and on how frequently they publish issues. Therefore, the sample formats for periodicals can be distinguished on the following bases:

- *A periodical paged continuously throughout a volume is treated as a "journal, with continuous pagination."* (If, for example, the first issue of a particular volume ends with page 171 and the next issue begins with page 172, the periodical uses continuous pagination.)
- *When each issue of the periodical is paginated independently it is treated as a "journal, with issues paged independently" if it is published less frequently than once every two months.* (If each issue of a periodical begins with page 1, the issues are paginated independently.)
- *All other periodicals are distinguished by frequency of publication.*

General Form: Articles in Periodicals

(1) Person(s) or Group Responsible for the Piece of Material You're Documenting

- *Author(s).* If an article is signed, the name(s) (sometimes only initials) will appear at either the beginning or the end of the article. Treat multiple authors as you would for book entries.

(2) The Title(s)
- *Title of article.* (See pages 264–65 for guidance on capitalization, quotation marks, and underlining in titles.)

(3) Amplifying Information to Help Identify or Describe the Work Precisely
- *Type of article.* You'll need this only for editorials, letters to the editor, and reviews.

(4) Publishing Information, or Similar Information That Will Help Someone Find the Work
- *Name of periodical.* The name of the periodical itself is all the publishing information that is necessary. Drop any introductory article from the title. If readers aren't likely to recognize the title by itself, insert after the title the name of the institution or, particularly for newspapers, the city, enclosing the name in brackets.

(5) Identification of the Portion You Are Citing
- *Series number.* If a journal has been published in more than one series (for example, old and new), indicate the applicable one. Otherwise readers may have difficulty determining where to find the article you used.
- *Newspaper edition.* If a newspaper has both morning and evening or special editions, you may need to show which you used; check the masthead of the newspaper when you read it. The same article often will appear in more than one edition, but not necessarily in the same place in each.
- *Volume and/or issue number(s).* For journals, you'll include the volume and/or issue number for the issue you used.
- *Date.* All entries will include at least the year, but whether year only, month and year, or complete date depends on the type of periodical.
- *Page number(s).* (See page 266 for guidance on showing inclusive page numbers.)

SAMPLE ENTRIES: ARTICLES IN PERIODICALS

As with the samples for books, the following entries were designed to illustrate particular portions of documentation entries. You may need to adapt the formats to fit your needs, but be sure to include all pertinent information listed in the preceding discussion of general form. *Note:* The three-hyphen form for repeated authors (see "Two or More Books by the Same 'Author(s)'" on pages 251–52) applies to entries for articles in periodicals as well, but is not repeated below.

Journal, With Continuous Pagination

This type of entry includes the volume number followed by the year in parentheses, a colon, and then inclusive page numbers for the article.

Myers, Georgia. "Tellem Cliff Dwellings of Mali." *African Studies* 25 (1990): 373–92.

Journal, With Issues Paged Independently

After the volume number, add a period and the issue number.

Roper, Henry Pleasants, and Sarah Jane Jefferson. "Visiting the Defenses of Washington." *Civil War Battles* 3.4 (1992): 316–32.

Journal, With Issue Numbers Only

If a journal does not use volume numbers, use the issue number as if it were a volume number.

Bishop, Quinn T. "Progression in Regressive Pueblos in New Mexico and Colorado." *American Science* 43 (1990): 37–51.

Journal, With Series

If a journal has been published in more than one series, precede the volume number with the series. Use a numerical designator such as "4th ser." or "ns" and "os" for "new series" and "original series."

Lambert, Byron. "Draining the Aral Sea." *World Science* ns 12 (1988): 612–34.

Monthly or Bimonthly Periodical

Instead of volume and/or issue, use the month(s) and year.

Kinard, Mary Wayne. "Optical Disk Storage." *Computers at Home* May 1990: 63–78.

Weekly or Biweekly Periodical

Whether a magazine or a newspaper, for a periodical published once a week or every two weeks, give the complete date rather than volume and issue numbers.

Weinert, Garfield P. "Barbettes and Embrasures: Artillery Fortifications in the Civil War." *Museum News* 18 Jun. 1994: 17–20.

Daily Newspaper

Show the newspaper's name as it appears at the top of the first page, omitting any beginning article (*The Washington Post* becomes *Washington Post*). If the newspaper title doesn't name the city, give the city and state in brackets after the title, as in the first sample below. The first sample also illustrates how to indicate the edition for a newspaper that prints more than one edition a day (again, check the masthead on the first page to see if an edition is given).

For inclusive page numbers, check the pagination system of the newspaper carefully. If the newspaper doesn't have sections or if it numbers continuously through the edition, you'll need only the page number(s) after the date (8 Oct. 1994:38). If the newspaper includes the section number with the page number(s), the appropriate section-number combination can follow the date (8 Oct. 1994:A12–A13). But if the section designator is not combined with the page number(s), then show the section designator between the date and the page number(s) (8 Oct. 1994, sec. 3:12).

Carey, Kelly. "What's Become of the Gulags?" *Star-Herald* [St. Louis, MO] 8 Oct.
    1990, early morning ed.: A12–A13.
Sumner, Rachel. "UN Peacekeeping Efforts Flounder." *Washington Post* 21 May
    1994: A5.

Author Unknown

Whatever the type of periodical, if no author is given, begin with the article's title. The format for the rest of the entry, of course, depends on the type of periodical in which the article appears; the sample below is for a monthly magazine.

"Prehistoric Skywatchers Charted the Heavens." *Ancient History* May 1989: 53–67.

Editorial

Begin with the author if named, otherwise with the editorial's title, and follow the title with "Editorial." The rest of the entry depends on the source; our sample uses a daily newspaper.

"Is Washington a 'District of Colombia'?" Editorial. *Washington Post* 17
    Sep. 1989: A15.

Letter to the Editor

Since letters to editors can appear in any type of periodical, the portion after the title depends on the type of publication in which the letter appears. We show a journal (with continuous pagination).

Im, Lee. Letter. *Journal of Antiquity* 15 (1990): 276.

Review

Reviews may be signed or unsigned and titled or untitled, and they may appear in any type of periodical. For a signed review, use the name(s) of the reviewer(s), the review title (if there is one), and then "Rev. of. . . . " For an unsigned review, give the title (if there is one); if not, begin with "Rev. of. . . . " The first entry below shows a signed and titled review in a monthly magazine; the second sample is for an unsigned, untitled review in a daily newspaper.

Neal, Carla. "Playing and Working on the Internet." Rev. of *A Practical Guide to the
    Internet,* by Andrew Hight. *Computers at Home* Feb. 1994: 46–49.
Rev. of *Mr. Lincoln's Generals,* by Charles Barnard. *Austin Gazette* 10 Mar. 1994,
    sec. 4:3.

ENTRIES FOR OTHER SOURCES

GENERAL FORM: OTHER SOURCES

This mixed group of reference types lacks a "standard form." Still, the general idea for documentation entries applies: (1) person(s) or group responsible for the piece of material you're documenting; (2) the title(s); (3) amplifying information, to help identify or describe the work precisely; (4) publishing information, or similar information that will help someone find the work; and (5) identification of the portion you are citing.

SAMPLE ENTRIES: OTHER SOURCES

If you can't find a sample that fits your needs exactly, adapt entries or create a format, but keep the general guidelines in mind.

Speech

Use the speech title, if known; when it isn't, use in its place a designator such as Address, Keynote speech, or Lecture (titles, as below, go in quotation marks, of course, but the descriptive designators would be used without quotation marks).

Binder, Calvin. "Community Action Groups Combat Neighborhood Drug
   Trafficking." Conference of Law Enforcement Officers. Cincinnati, 10 Sep. 1990.

Class Handout or Lecture

Show class, place, and date; as appropriate and available, give speaker and title.

"Recognizing and Correcting Passive Voice." English 101 handout. Wolfram State
   College, 1993.
Unruh, Michael. Math 210 lecture. Miami U, 17 Oct. 1994.

Reference Work

Entries for items in standard reference works require less information than do basic entries for books. For a signed encyclopedia article (the first entry below), give the author, article title, encyclopedia title, and edition. For an unsigned article (the second sample), begin with the article title. Notice that neither entry includes volume and page information; these data are unnecessary for encyclopedias or dictionaries that alphabetize articles.

If the encyclopedia has separate major divisions, each of which has articles in alphabetical order, include the division title with the encyclopedia title (the third sample). This arrangement would apply as well to yearbooks issued to supplement an encyclopedia or other reference work.

The fourth sample shows an entry for an encyclopedia issued on CD-ROM. After the encyclopedia edition, provide information to identify the type of CD-ROM: operating system version (Macintosh, MS-DOS, MPC, MPC2) and release number (if known). You also can include other information that the disk's publisher used to identify the CD-ROM disk.

For other standard reference works, such as one of the *Who's Who* series, give only the edition, if applicable, and publication year after the title (for example, 14th ed. 1991–93). However, treat an article in a less common reference work as a piece in a book collection (see "Part of a Collection," page 253), and give full publication information.

Mahan, Jack S. "Balkans." *Funk & Wagnalls New Encyclopedia.* 1994 ed.

"La Brea Tar Pit." *Encyclopedia Americana.* 1993 ed.

Edmonds, Gilbert. "Islam." *Encyclopedia Britannica: Macropaedia.* 1991 ed.

"Khomeini, Ayatollah Ruhollah." *The New Grolier Multimedia Encyclopedia.* 1994
    ed. Macintosh CD-ROM version. Release 6.0.0.

Computer Software

For commercially produced computer software, begin with the writer of the program, if available; if not, begin with the title. Show the version number (for example Vers. 1.2). Label with the term "Computer software" and give as a minimum the distributor and publication year. Optional information may be added at the end of the entry—such as the computer for which the program is designed, the operating system, and the type of medium the program is recorded on (cartridge, cassette, or disk).

Filefolder Data Base Management. Vers. 1.2. Computer software. Scienobyte, 1990.
    Macintosh, disk.

Material From a Computer/Information Service

Material from an online computer information service (such as DIALOG, Data-Star, or NEXIS) or an information service such as ERIC or NTIS is like other printed material, but after the publishing information you need to add a reference to the service, giving its name and the accession or order number for the material you're citing. Thus, most of the sample entry below corresponds to a document that is part of a series, while the end of the entry refers to the information service.

Asker, James R. "U.S./Russian Satellite Maps Worst Antarctic Ozone Hole."
    Aviation Week & Space Technology 25 Oct. 1993: 72. ProQuest 00775829.

Wahlberg, Doris J. *The Effect of Mass Testing on Curriculum.* Classroom Education
    Techniques, No. 12. Syracuse: Syracuse UP, 1984. ERIC ED 043 372.

CD-ROM

Treat material compiled on a CD-ROM as you would other printed matter. That is, first document the information item—book, poem, article, and so on—as you would if you found the original. You will be limited in your ability to do this, however, by how much information the CD-ROM producer provides about the original source: some provide all the data you could wish for; others provide very little about the original source. *Time* magazine, as the first sample below shows, provides all the data about the original except for the range of pages for an article (so we used 22+ to show the article's inclusive pages, since *Time* does give the page the article began on). Indeed, pagination in an electronic source is relative to screen display (unless the electronic medium compiles copies of the original source's formatted pages), so most CD-ROMs do not provide pagination information.

After the information about the original item, provide data to identify the CD-ROM itself—at least its title and its operating system version (Macintosh, MS-DOS, MPC, MPC2). You also can provide any other information that the disk's producer used to identify the CD-ROM disk.

See "Reference Work" for a sample of an encyclopedia on CD-ROM.

Bonner, Raymond. "The Dilemma of Disarmament." *Time* 28 Dec. 1992: 22+.
   The Time Magazine Compact Almanac. 1993 multimedia edition. Macintosh
   CD-ROM.
Collelo, Thomas, et al. *Lebanon, A Country Study.* Department of the Army, 1987.
   Countries of the World on CD-ROM. Bureau Development, 1991.
   Macintosh/MS-DOS.

Unpublished Thesis or Dissertation

When a thesis or dissertation has been published, treat it as a book. However, if you use an unpublished form, show the type of work, the institution for which it was prepared, and the year it was accepted. Note that the title appears in quotation marks because the work is unpublished.

Keifer, Jesse Monroe. "Communist Command Economies and Environmental
   Destruction in Eastern Europe." Diss. U of Nebraska, 1989.

Unpublished Letter

Treat a published letter as a part of a book collection or as a letter in a periodical. The first entry below shows the format for a letter you yourself have received. The second illustrates an unpublished letter in an archive.

Acton, Anthony Norton. Letter to the author. 11 Dec. 1990.
Dean, George B. Letter to Robert James Webb. 17 Mar. 1866. Robert James Webb
   Collection. Hurley Museum Library, Huntington, SC.

Interview

To document an interview you have conducted, begin with the name of the person interviewed, show the type of interview (personal or telephone), and give the date it was held.

Fishbine, Joshua W. Personal interview. 7 Jul. 1994.

Film, Filmstrip, Slide Program, or Videocassette

For a film, usually you'll begin with the title, followed by the director, distributor, and year released. Other information (stars, writers, etc.) is optional but should be included if it bears on how you discuss the film in your paper; put this information as amplification after the director. However, if your paper deals with the work of a particular individual connected with the film, begin with that person. For a filmstrip, slide program, or videocassette, show the type of medium after the title and then follow the format for a film citation.

Braving Winter. Dir. Julia Kowalski. Panorama, 1989.
Installing Memory Chips in a Macintosh Plus. Videocassette. Dir. Jill Vantine. Video Concepts, 1990.

Radio or Television Program

As a minimum, give the program title, the network that aired it, the local station and city for the broadcast that you viewed or heard, and the broadcast date. An episode title, if available, can be shown in quotation marks preceding the program title (as in our sample), and a series title, with no special markings, can be shown after the program title. Other information may be added for amplification, and if your paper deals with the work of a particular person connected with the broadcast, begin the entry with that individual's name.

"Hotline." *Weekend Newsline.* ABC. WCAM, Cincinnati. 22 Sep. 1990.

Record or Tape

Begin the entry with the person you want to emphasize (speaker, author, composer, producer, etc.); then give the title and follow it with "Audiotape" if your source is a tape rather than a record. Show the artist(s) (along with any appropriate amplification), manufacturer, identification number, and release year.

Gatti, Carlo. *Cats of Venice.* Audiotape. Read by Veronica Erno. Recorded Books, 89172, 1989.

Legal Citation

Complex legal citations are beyond the scope of this volume. Consult the Harvard Law Review Association's *A Uniform System of Citation* for help. The sample entries below are for federal statutory material; both use section references rather than page references. Use similar entries for state constitutions and statutes.

5 US Code. Sec 522a. 1974.
US Const. Art. 3, sec. 1.

Citations for law cases show the names of first plaintiff and first defendant, the volume of the report being cited, the name of the report, the page of the report, the name of the court where the case was decided, and the year decided.

Jefferson v. Sommers. 153 AS 613. Ind. Ct. App. 1978.

SPECIAL RULES FOR TITLES

CAPITALIZATION

Do use capital letters for the *first letters* of the following types of words in titles:

- each important word in the title (see below for "unimportant" words)
- the first word in a title ("*A* House on Tatum Hill")
- the first word after a colon that joins a title and a subtitle ("Faulkner's 'Delta Autumn': *The* Fall of Idealism")
- parts of compound words that would be capitalized if they appeared by themselves ("School Declares All-*Out* War on Misspelling")

Don't use capital letters for the following "unimportant" words:

- the articles *a, an,* and *the*
- short prepositions such as *at, by, for, in, of, on, to, up*
- the conjunctions *and, as, but, if, nor, or, for, so, yet*
- the second element of a compound numeral ("Twenty-*five* Years of Tyranny")

NEITHER QUOTATION MARKS NOR UNDERLINING

Don't use either quotation marks or underlining (or italics) for the following:

- the Bible, the books of the Bible, and other sacred works such as the Talmud or the Koran
- legal references (such as acts, laws, and court cases)
- extratextual material in a book (such as the Introduction or Foreword)

UNDERLINING

Printers usually use italics, but in typing you use underlining (or italics if your typing system, such as a word processor, has this capability) for certain types of titles. Underline the title of works published separately—such as novels and poems that are entire books or pamphlets—and the titles of periodicals (magazines, journals, and newspapers). Also underline the titles of movies and radio or television programs.

QUOTATION MARKS

Use quotation marks to enclose titles of works published as parts of other works—such as short stories, most poems, and essays. Also, enclose titles of speeches and class lectures in quotation marks.

If, however, a work that has been published separately appears as part of a larger work—such as a novel as part of an anthology—underline the title. For example, underline Voltaire's *Candide* even when it is a part of an anthology entitled *Great Works of World Literature.*

MIXED QUOTATION MARKS AND UNDERLINING

You have to adapt the rules somewhat when one title appears within another. The following samples illustrate the markings for the four possible combinations of titles with quotation marks and titles with underlining (or italics):

- "Faulkner's 'Delta Autumn': The Fall of Idealism" (a short-story title within an essay title: each title without the other would have double quotation marks, but here the title within a title has single quotation marks)

- *Faulkner's "Delta Autumn" and the Myth of the Wilderness* (a short-story title within a book title: each title has its normal markings)

- "Laertes as Foil in *Hamlet*" (a play title within an essay title: each title has its normal markings)

- *Shakespeare's "Hamlet": Action Versus Contemplation* (a play title within a book title: the title within a title, which by itself would be underlined, here has double quotation marks)

SPECIAL RULES FOR PUBLISHERS' NAMES

SHORTENING

Follow these rules in shortening publishers' names for your Works Cited entries:

- Omit the articles *a, an,* and *the.*
- Omit business designators such as *Co., Inc.,* or *Ltd.*
- Omit labels such as *Books, Press,* or *Publishers. Note:* University presses create an exception. Since both universities and their presses may publish independently, use *P* for *Press* when the publisher is a university press (thus, *Indiana U* is distinct from *Indiana UP*).
- If the publisher's name includes the name of one person, use only the last name (*Alfred A. Knopf, Inc.* becomes *Knopf*).
- If the name includes several people, use only the first name (*Holt, Rinehart and Winston* becomes *Holt*).
- Use the following standard abbreviations: *UP* for University Press; *GPO* for Government Printing Office; *HMSO* for Her (His) Majesty's Stationery Office; *MLA* for The Modern Language Association of America; *NAL* for The New American Library; *NCTE* for the National Council of Teachers of English; and *NEA* for The National Education Association.

IMPRINTS

When the title page or copyright page of a book shows a publisher's special imprint, combine the imprint with a shortened version of the publisher's name: for example, a Sentry Edition published by Houghton Mifflin Company becomes Sentry-Houghton; a Mentor Book published by The New American Library becomes Mentor-NAL.

SPECIAL RULES FOR INCLUSIVE PAGE NUMBERS

When you indicate inclusive page references, often you can shorten the second number. Up to 100, show all digits (for example 3–4, 54–55). Thereafter, reduce the second number of a set to two digits (for example 253–54, 304–05, 2614–15) *unless* the hundredth or thousandth digit changes (for example 499–501, 2998–3002).

EXERCISE

Prepare a Works Cited page to include entries for the works below.

1. A book by Linda Adair entitled *People of the Desert* and subtitled *Hohokam Farmers and Craftsmen.* This book was published in 1993 by La Madera Press of Albuquerque, New Mexico.

2. An article entitled "Potters of the Rio Grande Pueblos." This article, by Clara Lee Hardin, appeared on pages 46 to 61 of volume 4, issue 7, November 1994, of *Native American Arts Today.* This magazine is published monthly.

3. An article on pages 43 to 45 of the 27 May 1994 issue of *Travel in the Southwest,* a weekly magazine. No author was shown for the article, which was entitled "New Anasazi Ruins Opened to Public."

4. Another book by Linda Adair, this one entitled *Pots That Died* and subtitled *Mimbres Ceramic Arts.* This book was published by Burning Tree Press of Arlington, Virginia, in 1994.

5. An editorial entitled "Historic Ruins vs. Jobs—Who Wins?" This unsigned editorial appeared on page A22 of the *Denver Post* on 10 October 1994.

6. A book by the Association of American Archaeologists entitled *Prehistoric Ruins in the American Southwest,* published in 1994 in Washington, DC, by Slay Press.

7. An article entitled "Chaco Canyon Petroglyphs," which appeared on pages 37 through 49 of a collection of essays entitled *Chaco Canyon Archaeology.* The article was written by Robert Ambler, Barbara Haury, Kate C. Bunzel, and Fred Avery. Margaret Moulard edited the collection of essays, which was published in 1993 by Court Printing, Inc., of Baltimore, Maryland.

8. A journal article entitled "Recent Anasazi Finds." This article, by Norma C. Tanner, appeared on pages 217 through 224 of volume 3, the Fall 1994 issue, of the *Journal of American Prehistory,* a journal that paginates continuously throughout a volume.

9. *Societies of Prehistoric America,* a three-volume work by Wesley Luckert and Perry S. Colton. All three volumes were published in 1992 by Schocken Books, Ltd., of New York City, New York.

IMPROVING YOUR
PUNCTUATION AND EXPRESSION

Punctuation

There's more to good writing than just getting commas and apostrophes in the right places—yet those commas and apostrophes are important, too.

We don't try to cover everything about punctuation in this part of the book just those rules we think will be especially helpful for you.

26 Definitions

Why begin studying punctuation with a review of grammar? If you understand the terms in this chapter, learning to punctuate a sentence will be easy, for punctuation is not really very mysterious. In fact, once you understand these terms, you probably will be surprised just how easy punctuation can be.

The catch (and, of course, there is a catch) is that you must work hard to understand them.

A Pep Talk

Skimming this chapter once, or even reading it through carefully once, will not suffice. You will have to memorize a few terms. All of this material is essential in later chapters, however, so please spend some time with it now.

1. **Clause.** *A clause is a group of words containing a subject (S) and a verb (V).*

            S   V
    Clause: Sharon ran in the New York marathon.

Sometimes people are fooled into believing a group of words is a clause simply because it contains something like a verb.

Not a clause: Running in a marathon.

The above group of words cannot be a clause for two reasons: (1) it has no subject; (2) it has no verb. Words that end in -*ing* and seem like verbs are really *verbals*. Just remember that an *-ing* word can never function by itself as a verb, and you will stay out of trouble. To be a verb, the *-ing* word must have a helper:

S   V

Rosemary is running along the beach.

The word *is* is a helping verb. Because we have added a subject and a helping verb to the *-ing* word, we now have a clause.

Clauses are either *independent* or *dependent*.

2.   **Independent clause (IC).** *An independent clause is a clause that makes a complete statement and therefore may stand alone as a sentence.*

S   V

Independent clauses: The monkey is brown.

S   V

The automobile runs smoothly.

S   V

Marilyn knows her.

S   V

(You) Close the door.

In the final example above, *you* is an unstated but understood subject. That is, readers understand the subject to be present in the sentence, even though it isn't actually there. Such understood subjects are common in imperative sentences—sentences that give commands or directions.

3.   **Dependent clause (DC).** *A dependent clause is a clause that makes an incomplete statement and therefore may not stand alone as a sentence.*

S   V

Dependent clauses: *Although* the monkey is brown. . . .

S   V

If the automobile runs smoothly. . . .

S   V

. . . *whom* Marilyn knows.

S   V

After you close the door. . . .

Dependent Clause

Notice that a dependent clause is not a sentence by itself. That is why it is dependent—it depends on an independent clause to make a complete, or even an intelligible, statement. By itself, a dependent clause doesn't make any sense.

This definition and the one above for independent clauses—though fairly standard—may not satisfy you. Fortunately, we can offer another definition that works almost all the time (and you don't need to worry about the exceptions). A *dependent clause* almost always contains a subordinating conjunction or a relative pronoun (both covered later in this chapter); we've italicized them in the examples of dependent clauses above so you can see where they are. The subordinating conjunctions and relative pronouns are like red flags signaling dependent clauses. You can recognize an *independent clause,* then, because it's a clause not containing a subordinating conjunction or relative pronoun.

4. **Sentence.** *A sentence is a group of words containing at least one independent clause.*

Sentences (independent clauses) are underlined once:

Marilyn knows her.

Although Marilyn knows her, she does not know Marilyn.

After you close the door, Susan will turn on the record player, and Sally will get the potato chips.

5. **Phrase (P).** *A phrase is a group of two or more related words not containing both a subject and a verb.*

Phrases: in the submarine

running along the beach

Remember, *-ing* words are not verbs.

6. **Subordinating conjunction (SC).** *A subordinating conjunction is a kind of word that begins a* **dependent** *clause.*

You should memorize the italicized words (which are quite common) in the list of subordinating conjunctions below.

after	how	though
although	*if*	unless
as	in order that	until
as if	inasmuch as	*when*
as long as	now that	whenever
as much as	provided that	where
as though	*since*	wherever
because	so that	whether
before	than	while

Here are examples of subordinating conjunctions beginning dependent clauses (the dependent clauses are underlined twice):

SC
Because your horse is properly registered, it may run in the race.

SC
The race will be canceled if the rain falls.

SC
Sign up for the trip to Memphis while vacancies still exist.

7. **Relative pronoun (RP).** *A relative pronoun is a kind of word that marks a* dependent *clause.*

However, like a subordinating conjunction, a relative pronoun doesn't always come at the beginning of the dependent clause, although it usually does. You should memorize these five common relative pronouns:

who, whose, whom, which, that

Here are examples of relative pronouns in dependent clauses (the dependent clauses are underlined twice):

RP
The woman who runs the bank is registering her horse.

RP
The man whose car lights are on is in the grocery store.

RP
The woman whom I met is in the broker's office.

RP
The schedule with which I was familiar is now obsolete.

RP
The schedule that I knew is now obsolete.

Sometimes, unfortunately, these same five words can function as other than relative pronouns, in which case they *do not* mark dependent clauses:

Not relative pronouns: *Who* is that masked man?

Whose golf club is this?

Whom do you wish to see?

Which car is yours?

That car is mine.

As a general rule, unless they are part of a question, the four words in our list that begin with *w* (*who, whose, whom,* and *which*) are relative pronouns. The other word, *that,* is trickier, but we can generally say that unless it is pointing out something, it is a relative pronoun. In "That car is mine," *that* points out a car, so it is not a relative pronoun.

8. **Conjunctive adverb (CA).** *A conjunctive adverb is a kind of word that marks an* **independent** *clause.*

Many students make punctuation errors because they confuse subordinating conjunctions (which mark dependent clauses) with conjunctive adverbs (which mark independent clauses). You should memorize the italicized words (which are quite common) in the list of conjunctive adverbs below:

accordingly	*however*	next
as a result	indeed	nonetheless
consequently	in fact	otherwise
first	instead	second
for example	likewise	still
for instance	meanwhile	*therefore*
furthermore	moreover	thus
hence	*nevertheless*	unfortunately

Transition Words

You may remember seeing some of these words in Chapter 5, "Coherence." A conjunctive adverb serves as a *transition,* showing the relationship between the independent clause it is in and the independent clause that preceded it.

A conjunctive adverb may not seem to mark an independent clause, but it does. The following examples are perfectly correct as sentences because they are independent clauses:

CA
Therefore, I am the winner.

CA
However, the car is red.

Often a conjunctive adverb begins the second independent clause in a sentence because that clause is closely related in meaning to the first independent clause:

CA
I finished in first place; therefore, I am the winner.

CA
You thought your new car would be blue; however, the car is metallic brown.

Sometimes a conjunctive adverb appears in the middle or even at the end of a clause (that clause, of course, is still independent):

CA
I finished in first place; I am, therefore, the winner.

CA
I finished in first place; I am the winner, therefore.

9. **Coordinating conjunction (CC).** *A coordinating conjunction is a word that joins two or more units that are grammatically alike.*

You should learn these seven coordinating conjunctions:

and	*nor*	*so*
but	*or*	*yet*
for		

A helpful learning aid is that the coordinating conjunctions are all two or three letters long.

A coordinating conjunction can do the following:

          CC
Join two or more words: Bill and Mary

                 CC
Join two or more phrases: in the car and beside the horse

                              CC
Join two or more dependent clauses: after the dance was over but before the party began

                                       CC
Join two or more independent clauses: He won the Philadelphia marathon, for he had been practicing several months.

Remember: Unlike subordinating conjunctions, relative pronouns, and conjunctive adverbs, the coordinating conjunction is not a marker for either an independent clause or a dependent clause. It simply joins two or more like items.

EXERCISE

In the sentences below, underline the independent clauses once and the dependent clauses twice. Then label all subordinating conjunctions (SC), relative pronouns (RP), conjunctive adverbs (CA), and coordinating conjunctions (CC).

1. According to the National Geographic Society, the Nile is the longest river in the world.
2. Which of the Great Lakes is smallest?
3. Unless it rains tomorrow, mow the lawn and rake the grass clippings.
4. Although he died before taking the new seat, ex-President John Tyler was elected to the Confederate House of Representatives, so the Confederates buried him with honors in Richmond while the Union ignored his death.
5. Farmers from Massachusetts brought a 1,235-pound cheese to President Thomas Jefferson in 1802, and the cheese was served at the White House until 1805.
6. Thousands of miles of wooden roads were laid in several American states in the 1840s and 1850s; most were replaced by gravel roads, however, when the wooden planks began to rot.

7. In dry areas like the Southwest desert, however, wooden roads continued in use into the 20th century.

8. David Rice Atchison became president of the United States for one day when Zachary Taylor delayed taking the oath of office for a day because Inauguration Day fell on Sunday.

9. Richard Lawrence, who was the first person to attempt to assassinate a U.S. president, fired two pistols at Andrew Jackson at point-blank range.

10. Although both weapons were properly loaded and although later tests proved both pistols functional, both misfired.

11. Lawrence was charged with simple assault, which was a misdemeanor in those days, because there was no legal precedent for dealing with a failed assassination attempt.

12. Because the prosecutor (Washington District Attorney Francis Scott Key) agreed with the defense that Lawrence was mad, Lawrence was freed on a plea of insanity and spent the rest of his life in asylums.

13. C. W. Post marketed a wheat flake cereal as "Elijah's Manna"; that name created a storm of protest from religious groups, however, so he renamed the cereal "Post Toasties."

14. Don't forget to mail your tax returns before the end of 15 April.

15. Fannie Farmer standardized measurements in the recipes in her first cookbook in 1896; to her we owe the concept of a level teaspoon.

16. Antonio López de Santa Anna, Mexican leader at the Alamo, brought to New York in 1869 a lump of chicle, the sap of the sapodilla tree; he hoped that inventor Thomas Adams could create a rubber substitute from the chicle.

17. Adams failed at inventing a rubber substitute from refined chicle; however, after seeing a girl buy paraffin to chew, he used the chicle to create chewing gum.

18. Painters Rubens, Van Dyck, and Breugel were all citizens of Belgium.

19. A band of travelers who set out on a pilgrimage from an English inn is the subject of Chaucer's *The Canterbury Tales*.

20. What endangered animal serves as the symbol for the World Wildlife Fund?

21. Milton Hersey began building his fortune by making caramels, and he produced chocolate formed as cigarettes and dominoes as a novelty.

22. Because chocolate would retain the impression of his name in hot weather, Hersey began to focus on chocolates.

23. Ray Kroc was impressed by the clean, efficient, and high-volume operations in a drive-in restaurant that the McDonald brothers owned in San Bernardino, California.

24. Kroc persuaded the McDonald brothers to let him create a franchise of their system; part of the agreement, however, retained the original McDonald's name.

25. Kroc opened his first franchise drive-in in Des Plaines, Illinois, in 1955; in 5 years there were 228 franchise operations marketing some $40 million of fast food annually.

27 Sentence Fragment

A sentence fragment is an error involving punctuation.

Sentence fragment (frag). *A sentence fragment is a group of words punctuated like a sentence but not containing an independent clause.*

Because it lacks an independent clause, a sentence fragment is just a piece of a sentence. Here are some examples:

Sentence fragments: Running along the beach.

Even though the movie won an Oscar.

See? These so-called sentences are really frauds: they begin with a capital letter and end with a period, but they don't contain an independent clause.

Usually a sentence fragment is very closely related to the sentence that preceded it. The two examples above might have appeared in the following contexts:

Sentence fragments: I finally found that stray mutt. Running along the beach.

Marie absolutely refused to go to the theater. Even though the movie had won an Oscar.

To correct a sentence fragment, either connect it to an independent clause or add a subject and a verb to convert it to an independent clause.

Fragments connected to independent clauses:

I finally found that stray mutt running along the beach.

Marie absolutely refused to go to the theater even though the movie had won an Oscar.

Fragments converted to independent clauses:

I finally found that stray mutt. It was running along the beach.

Marie absolutely refused to go to the theater. The movie had won an Oscar.

Of the two types of changes above, most readers would prefer the connection of the fragment to an independent clause. That solution provides smoother writing, avoiding the choppiness resulting from converting each fragment to its own independent clause. More important, however, the first solution increases coherence: connecting the fragment to an independent clause links the thought of the fragment to the thought of the independent clause.

Are fragments always wrong? No, of course not. Fragments are common in speech and appear in all types of writing. You'll find examples in this book because the writing was designed to communicate to you directly, as if the authors were speaking to you. Because fragments break the conventional pattern of writing, they can create a useful effect. For example, the second "sentence" of this paragraph—really a fragment—communicates the desired thought more directly and simply than would this sentence combination: "Are fragments always wrong? No, of course fragments are not always wrong." And because the fragment answers the question in the first sentence, there is no loss of coherence.

Cautions

- Fragments are never acceptable if they destroy coherence.
- Be aware of your probable readers. Some may never find fragments acceptable.
- Use fragments sparingly for good effect.

EXERCISES

A. Correct the fragments in each of the following sentence-fragment combinations in two ways.

1. The Puritans fled England to seek religious freedom. But proved intolerant of other religions in America.
2. The term *private eye* comes from the logo of Allan Pinkerton's National Detective Agency. An open eye with the words "We never sleep."
3. Thomas "Boston" Corbett, of the 16th New York Cavalry, claimed to have shot John Wilkes Booth with an Army carbine. Even though the autopsy showed Booth died from a pistol bullet.

B. For each "sentence" below, indicate whether it is a complete sentence or only a fragment.

1. Betty Grable was the top box-office attraction during World War II.
2. The hula hoop being the top-selling toy in 1957.
3. Although based on ancient games, the modern Olympics, founded by Baron Pierre de Coubertin.
4. We'll be home soon.
5. Robert Frost wrote: "Good fences make good neighbors."
6. Who played backup for Sam the Sham?
7. John Wayne, fearing being stereotyped as a cowboy, refusing the lead in *Gunsmoke.*
8. Jumbo, P.T. Barnum's giant elephant.
9. Dancer Bill Robinson's nickname was Mr. Bojangles.
10. Close the door quietly.
11. Cesar Chavez founder and first president of the United Farm Workers.
12. *Narcissism* being the psychiatric term for "self-love."
13. Switzerland remained neutral throughout both World War I and World War II.
14. The Virgin Islands were named for Queen Elizabeth I.
15. Cats having four rows of whiskers.
16. Even though each player has eight pawns at the beginning of a game of chess.
17. Both Tony Curtis and Jack Lemmon appeared in drag in the film *Some Like It Hot.*
18. Despite what popular song tells us, Lizzie Borden was found not guilty.
19. "Raindrops Keep Fallin' on My Head," the song introduced in *Butch Cassidy and the Sundance Kid.*
20. Dick Clark's *American Bandstand* originated in Philadelphia.

C. Correct the following sentence fragments.

1. The U.S. purchase of Alaska for $7.2 million in 1867 was not a widely popular move. It being called "Seward's Folly" and gaining U.S. Senate approval by only one vote.
2. The saying "buyer beware" applies to an early Sears catalog advertisement. Because it offered a sewing machine for one dollar but the buyer received only a needle and thread.
3. In 1845, New York City formed a police force with 800 officers, who soon were known as "cops." The reason being that each wore as identification a copper star.
4. Until late in the 19th century there was no such thing as standard time throughout the United States. The railroads, needing a dependable timetable for efficient operations, dividing the nation into four time zones in 1863.
5. A worldwide epidemic of influenza in 1918 killed some 27 million people. More than died in all of World War I.

28 Comma Splice and Fused Sentence

Comma splices and fused sentences are sentences that are punctuated incorrectly.

Comma splice (CS). *A comma splice occurs when two independent clauses are joined by only a comma.*

In other words, two independent clauses are "spliced" together with only a comma. Using *IC* for independent clause, we can express the comma splice as follows:

Comma splice: IC,IC.

Here are some comma splice errors:

Wrong: We hiked for three days, we were very tired.

Wrong: The television is too loud, the picture is fuzzy.

Correcting Comma Splices

There are five ways to correct a comma splice.

1. Change the comma to a period and capitalize the next word. (IC. IC.)
   Correct: We hiked for three days. We were very tired.
2. Change the comma to a semicolon. (IC;IC.)
   Correct: We hiked for three days; we were very tired.
3. Change the comma to a semicolon and add a conjunctive adverb. (IC;CA,IC.)
   Correct: We hiked for three days; hence, we were very tired.
4. Add a coordinating conjunction before the second independent clause. (IC,CC IC.)
   Correct: We hiked for three days, so we were very tired.

5. Change one independent clause to a dependent clause. (DC,IC.)
   Correct: Because we hiked for three days, we were very tired.

A very common form of comma splice occurs when only a comma precedes a conjunctive adverb at the beginning of the second independent clause in a sentence.

Wrong: Mount Rainier is beautiful, however, it is also forbidding.

The best way to correct this kind of comma splice is to change the first comma to a semicolon. (IC;CA,IC.)

Correct: Mount Rainier is beautiful; however, it is also forbidding.

Another form of comma splice occurs when two independent clauses are separated by a dependent clause but the strongest mark of punctuation is still only a comma.

Wrong: The artist is selling the portrait, because he does not have enough
       money, he has run out of paint.

How would you correct the sentence above? Does the writer mean that the artist is selling the portrait because he does not have enough money? Or does the writer mean the artist has run out of paint because he does not have enough money? Here is one instance in which correct punctuation is essential to meaning. One of several ways to correct the sentence is to place a period on the appropriate side of the dependent clause, depending on the meaning you wish to express. (IC DC.IC.) or (IC.DC,IC.)

Correct: The artist is selling the portrait because he does not have enough
         money. He has run out of paint.

Correct: The artist is selling the portrait. Because he does not have enough
         money, he has run out of paint.

Fused sentence (FS). *A fused sentence occurs when two independent clauses are joined without punctuation or a coordinating conjunction.*

In other words, a fused sentence is a comma splice without the comma.

Fused sentence: IC IC.

Here are some fused sentence errors:

Wrong: We hiked for three days we were very tired.

Wrong: The television is too loud the picture is fuzzy.

Correcting Fused Sentences

Correct a fused sentence with essentially the same methods you used to correct a comma splice:

1. Add a period after the first independent clause and capitalize the next word. (IC. IC.)

   Correct: The television is too loud. The picture is fuzzy.

2. Add a semicolon after the first independent clause. (IC;IC.)

   Correct: The television is too loud; the picture is fuzzy.

3. Add a semicolon and a conjunctive adverb after the first independent clause. (IC;CA,IC.)

   Correct: The television is too loud; furthermore, the picture is fuzzy.

4. Add a comma and a coordinating conjunction after the first independent clause. (IC,CC IC.)

   Correct: The television is too loud, and the picture is fuzzy.

5. Change one independent clause to a dependent clause. (DC,IC.)

   Correct: Whenever the television is too loud, the picture is fuzzy.

EXERCISES

A. Correct the following comma splice in five different ways:

The face of a grinning boy with big ears and one front tooth missing was used in the 1920s to advertise a dental clinic in Topeka, Kansas, some 30 years later the same face became *Mad* magazine's symbol, Alfred E. Neuman.

B. Correct the following fused sentence in five different ways:

In 1924 cartoonist Harold Gray showed Capt. J. M. Patterson, owner of the New York *Daily News*, a draft comic strip called "Little Orphan Otto" because too many other comic strips starred little boys, Patterson told Gray to make the star a girl and name her Little Orphan Annie, after the popular James Whitcomb Riley poem.

C. For each sentence below, write *CS* if the sentence is a comma splice, *FS* if it is a fused sentence, or *Correct* if it is correct.

1. ____ Workmen in New York City in 1931 erected a 16-foot Christmas tree among the rubble of their building site they were working on the future Rockefeller Center.

2. ____ They used tin cans, paper, and tinsel for decorations, two years later 700 blue and white lights adorned the first official Christmas tree at Rockefeller Center.

3. ____ During the Depression hoboes created a type of American folk art; the hoboes reworked the Indian's profile and the buffalo on nickels into other portraits and animals.

4. ____ Against the advice of advertising specialists, Leonard Odell created a unique advertising campaign for Burma-Shave, his series of small roadside signs with lighthearted rhymes spaced along the roadway caught the attention of Americans and were continued for years.

5. ____ One Burma-Shave jingle in 1936 offered a free trip to Mars in exchange for "900 empty jars" Arliss French collected the jars and demanded the trip.

6. ____ French and the company carried on well-publicized negotiations, in rhymes finally the company sent French to Moers, a tiny town in Germany whose name is pronounced "Mars."

7. ____ Many today think the Edsel failed because of the design of its grill; in truth the car failed because it was a full-sized car that hit the market just when the public was demanding smaller, more economical cars.

8. ____ In the mid-19th century, paying postage on a letter got the mail to the addressee's post office to get the letter the recipient had to pay an additional fee.

9. ____ Zachary Taylor, hero of the Mexican War, received a great deal of mail at the Baton Rouge post office, he refused to pay for it, telling the postmaster to send it all to the dead letter office.

10. ____ When the Whig Party nominated Zachary Taylor for president in 1848, they notified him by mail, Taylor didn't know he was nominated because, again, he would not pay to receive the letter.

11. ____ Calamity Jane was known for hard talk, hard drinking, hard fighting, and associating with hard characters; however, during a smallpox epidemic in Deadwood, South Dakota, she stayed with the smallpox victims in a shack outside town and nursed them through the epidemic.

12. ____ In 1874 billions of Rocky Mountain locusts arrived in the Great Plains and ravaged farms for several years a swarm would settle in an area, eat everything in sight, including clothes and curtains, and then move on.

13. ____ People hit the locusts, set out smudge pots to drive them off, burned fields where they had settled, and even fired guns at them, nothing worked.

14. ____ The Rocky Mountain locust was extinct by 1902; no reason for its extinction has been discovered.

15. ____ At a time when branding cattle was common, Sam Maverick refused to brand his, thus, *maverick* came to mean an unbranded cow.

16. ____ Today *Sooner* is a respectable name for someone from Oklahoma originally the term was applied to people who sneaked into Oklahoma territory before the start of the land rush, staked claims, and pretended to participate in the rush.

17. ____ Elisha Graves Otis, pioneer of the Otis elevator, did not invent the elevated or hoisted platform his invention was a safety device that prevented the platform from dropping if the hoist cable broke.

18. ____ The famous painting of George Washington and his army crossing the Delaware on Christmas night 1776 was painted in Germany in 1851 the boats, flag, clothing, and ice are not accurate.

19. ____ Thomas "Stonewall" Jackson was accidentally shot by his own troops at Chancellorsville, however, his bullet wounds were not what killed him.

20. ____ After his arm was amputated, Jackson asked servants to put cold towels on his body to lower his fever; he caught pneumonia and died in a week.

21. ____ After the First and Second Battles of Bull Run devastated his home and land, Wilmer McLean moved his family to Appomattox Court House, Virginia, there his home was used in 1865 for surrender talks between Generals Lee and Grant.

22. ____ Union generals bought pieces of McLean's parlor furniture for mementos much of the rest of the parlor's furnishings were broken up and stolen by souvenir hunters.

23. ____ In the weeks before D-Day, code words for four landing beaches in Normandy appeared as solutions in the London *Daily Telegraph* crossword puzzles; only four days before the landings, the operation code name, "Overlord," appeared in the puzzle.

24. ____ After Scotland Yard detectives questioned the puzzle writer, physics professor Leonard Dewes, they determined that no secrets were being passed, it was just an amazing coincidence.

25. ____ Norman Rockwell's Rosie the Riveter painting symbolized the women who filled America's factories during World War II Rockwell's Rosie has a female face but a husky masculine body, based, according to the artist, on Michelangelo's *Isaiah the Prophet*.

D. Choose three sentences with comma splices and three fused sentences from exercise C and rewrite them correctly.

29 Comma

This chapter presents the nine most important uses of the comma (,).

1. Use a comma after every item in a series except the last item.

Example: The ethics of contemporary surgery are often a problem for the
patient, the doctor, and the patient's family.

You probably already knew to put a comma after the first item (*patient* in this case),
but why do you need one after the next-to-last item (*doctor*)? Consider this example:

Example: The ethics of contemporary surgery are often a problem for the
patient, the doctor and the hospital board, and the patient's family.

Commas tell your readers that you are moving to the next item in a series. When
you omit a comma, you're telling them you're still in that same item—a compound
item—so they won't have to reread your sentence.

**2. Use a comma before a coordinating conjunction that joins two
independent clauses. (IC,CC IC.)**

Examples: I never liked parsnips, but my mother made me eat them.

She thought they were great, and she thought they would make

me grow taller.

Note: Do not confuse a coordinating conjunction that joins two verbs with a coordinating conjunction that joins two independent clauses.

The parsnips tasted awful and looked like paste.

No comma precedes the coordinating conjunction on the previous page because it connects only the two verbs *tasted* and *looked*.

3.   Use a comma after a dependent clause that begins a sentence. (DC,IC.)

Examples: Although Harriet tried as hard as she could, she could not

win even a fun-run.

Because she couldn't run fast enough, she couldn't have the free

T-shirt we awarded to the first 200 runners to cross the finish line.

4.   Use a comma after a long phrase that begins a sentence. (Long phrase,IC.)

The word *long* is rather vague, of course, but usually you will wish to place a comma after an introductory phrase of three or more words.

Examples: Even after a grueling night of writing, I couldn't finish the paper.

Running to my next class, I tried to think of an excuse to give my

professor.

5.   Use commas to set off any word, phrase, or clause that interrupts the flow of the sentence.

In other words, if you could set off a word or group of words with parentheses or dashes but do not wish to, then set off that word or group of words with commas.

Examples: My first excuse, wild as it was, didn't sound convincing.

I had thought of several good excuses for not finishing my paper, such as a computer error deleted my only draft.

The excuse I settled on was quite good, especially the part about the dog in the dormitory.

The class, together with the professor, turned their heads as I plowed into the classroom.

The professor ignored me as he finished his lecture, "Freshman English for Nonconformists."

Notice that interrupters in the middle of sentences have commas on *both* sides. You'll learn more about setting off interrupters with commas, parentheses, and dashes in Chapter 32.

6.   Use **commas to set off nonrestrictive clauses.**

This rule is actually an expansion of rule 5, because all nonrestrictive clauses are interrupters. You may wonder, however, just what restrictive and nonrestrictive clauses are.

A *restrictive clause* is essential to defining whatever it modifies. If you have only one brother, you could say, "My brother is meaner than I am." Because you have only one brother, no modifier is necessary to distinguish which brother you mean. But what if you have several brothers? Now you need to include a modifier that will restrict the meaning of *brother* to a particular one.

My brother who is wearing a red motorcycle helmet is meaner than I am.

The restrictive clause (*who is wearing a red motorcycle helmet*) is essential to defining *brother,* limiting any brother to the one wearing the helmet. You probably noticed that a restrictive clause is not an interrupter and, therefore, is not set off with commas.

A *nonrestrictive clause* is not essential to defining whatever it modifies—it just supplies additional information. Since it is not essential, you could omit it and everybody would still know who (or what) you are talking about. Thus, if you have only one brother, you could write this:

My brother, who is wearing a red motorcycle helmet, is meaner than I am.

Because you have only one brother, readers could omit the nonrestrictive clause (*who is wearing a red motorcycle helmet*) and still know who you are referring to. The word modified—*brother*—is not limited in any way by the clause; it is only described in more detail. You'll notice that we set off nonrestrictive clauses with commas (or parentheses or dashes), just as we do for other interrupters.

Thus, the presence or absence of commas with modifying clauses becomes quite important for how readers interpret what you write. For example, consider this statement:

Authorities say that truckers who drive unsafe rigs cause most of the accidents on the Beltway.

Who causes most of the accidents? All truckers? No, the absence of commas tells us that the blame falls on "truckers who drive unsafe rigs." *Who drive unsafe rigs* is a restrictive clause limiting *all truckers* to that portion with unsafe equipment.

Now consider this example:

The board members are not likely to question the Research Department's recommendations, which are generally well prepared.

A comma sets off *which are generally well prepared,* the nonrestrictive clause that provides additional detail—in this case one possible explanation for why the board members almost always accept recommendations from the Research Department. Is this essential information? No, the punctuation within the sentence indicates that the board members almost always accept recommendations from this particular department; why they do so remains speculation.

7. Use commas to set off a conjunctive adverb. (CA,IC.), (IC, CA.), (IC; CA, IC.), or (IC; IC, CA.).

This rule applies no matter where the conjunctive adverb appears within the sentence. If, as in the next-to-last example, the conjunctive adverb is in the middle of the independent clause, it will have commas on *both* sides of it.

Examples: The beautiful young princess kissed the frog. However, [IC] [CA]

his lily pad started sinking when she stepped on it. [IC]

The beautiful young princess kissed the frog; however, [IC] [CA]

his lily pad started sinking when she stepped on it. [IC]

The beautiful young princess kissed the frog; his lily pad, [IC]

however, started sinking when she stepped on it. [CA] [IC]

The beautiful young princess kissed the frog; his lily pad [IC]

started sinking when she stepped on it, however. [IC] [CA]

8. Use a comma between coordinate adjectives unless they are joined by "and."

Coordinate adjectives are sets of adjectives that independently modify a noun.

Example: The bulldog is noted for its wrinkled, flattened face.

Both *wrinkled* and *flattened* modify *face* independently. That is not the case with cumulative adjectives. When an adjective's modification is cumulative, it modifies not only the noun but also the whole adjective-noun phrase it precedes.

Example: Alicia wore a red felt hat.

Here *red* modifies not just *hat* but the phrase *felt hat*. Notice that no comma is used with cumulative adjectives.

Coordinate and Cumulative Adjectives

Distinguishing between coordinate and cumulative adjectives isn't always simple. However, because of the independence of coordinate adjectives, you can check for two characteristics that help identify them.

- Coordinate adjectives are reversible, whereas cumulative adjectives aren't. That is, *flattened, wrinkled face* works as well as *wrinkled, flattened face.* On the other hand, *felt red hat* just sounds foolish.
- *And* fits naturally between coordinate adjectives, but not between cumulative adjectives. Thus, you could write *wrinkled and flattened face* but not *red and felt hat.*

Of course, modifier chains can include both coordinate and cumulative adjectives.

Example: The stands were full for the homecoming game even though it was a cold, rainy autumn day.

Cold and *rainy* are coordinate and are separated by a comma. However, both modify *autumn day* rather than just *day,* so there is no comma after *rainy.*

9.   Use a comma to set off words in direct address.

Words in direct address normally are names but can be phrases used in place of names.

Examples: Kristina, have you washed the dishes?

Where are you going now, little sister?

You look charming, Alicia, wearing that red felt hat.

Notice that the word in direct address in the last example has commas on *both* sides because it occurs in the middle of the sentence.

EXERCISES

A. For each pair of sentences below, answer the accompanying questions.

1. Which sentence implies that there have been other helmet laws with other provisions?
   a. The helmet law, which was passed in 1993, requires bicycle riders to wear protective helmets.
   b. The helmet law that was passed in 1993 requires bicycle riders to wear protective helmets.
2. Which sentence implies that not all tourists show proper respect?
   a. Tourists who show proper respect are welcome in the churches of Italy.
   b. Tourists, who show proper respect, are welcome in the churches of Italy.
3. Which sentence implies that music does not include words?
   a. When I read I like to listen to music that has no words.
   b. When I read I like to listen to music, which has no words.

B. In the following sentences, add commas where necessary.

1. Andrea which is farther north—Helsinki Oslo or Stockholm?

2. Joseph Stalin who led the Soviet Union through World War II was *Time's* "Man of the Year" for both 1939 and 1942.

3. *Citrus paradisi* is the name for the grapefruit tree but whoever named it must not have been thinking of the acid pulp of the fruit.

4. As its name implies bone china is porcelain that includes the calcium phosphate ash from burned bones.

5. In addition to its use in ceramics bone ash is also used as a fertilizer and in cleaning and polishing compounds.

6. *Proof* designates the strength of alcoholic liquors; for example 100 proof liquor contains 50 percent ethyl alcohol.

7. Atlantic City merchants began the Miss America pageant in 1921 as a gimmick to keep tourists there after Labor Day and the first Miss America a 16-year-old schoolgirl won a golden statue of a mermaid.

8. The rotund red-cheeked man we know as Santa Claus comes from his portrayal by cartoonist Thomas Nast.

9. Although she wanted to be known for the support she gave the feminist struggle newspaper editor Amelia Jenks Bloomer is remembered for bloomers the adaptation of Turkish pantaloons she popularized.

10. Americans have been particularly disturbed by stories of clerics who are found guilty of child abuse. (Punctuate to imply that Americans are concerned about stories about all clerics.)

11. Americans have been particularly disturbed by stories of clerics who are found guilty of child abuse. (Punctuate to indicate that Americans are concerned about stories concerning those clerics who are found guilty of child abuse.)

12. Samoyeds originally were breed in northern Eurasia to have a thick long white coat; in fact the breed's name comes from the Russian version of the Lapp words for "of Lapland."

13. During Prohibition which started with the 18th Amendment and ended with its repeal it was illegal to make sell or transport liquor in the United States yet drinking liquor was not against the law.

14. As we know from books and movies about the Prohibition years public drinking moved to speakeasies but drinking also became popular at home a new habit for Americans.

15. California's wine makers produced a legal grape juice that easily became a 30-proof wine after 60 days of home fermentation.

16. Beer makers made wort which was a half-brewed beer without alcohol; likewise home fermentation would produce an alcoholic beer.

17. Information on making a home still was readily available in books and magazines and the federal government even offered a pamphlet on home brewing.

18. Prohibition Jerry was a time when much of the American public engaged in flouting the law.

19. When Tennessee passed a law forbidding the teaching of evolution the American Civil Liberties Union offered to defend anyone willing to test the law's prohibition of free speech.

20. John Scopes who taught science in a Tennessee high school was recruited to be the defendant starting the so-called "Monkey Trial" which matched William Jennings Bryan for the prosecution against Clarence Darrow for the defense.

21. In a blow against the defense the judge ruled that evolution was not an issue for the court; instead the question was simply whether Scopes had broken the law by teaching evolution.

22. Scopes told *Life* magazine after the trial that he had only substituted in the biology class and that he doubted he had really taught evolution because he knew little about it.

23. The Empire State Building originally was planned to be 1,050 feet tall only 4 feet taller than the 1,046-foot Chrysler Building but builders added a 200-foot mooring mast for dirigibles.

24. When they realized how dangerous a dirigible mast was the builders converted it into a tower with an observation deck.

25. Scraping the sky at 1,250 feet the Empire State Building remained the world's tallest building for 42 years.

26. What character has been portrayed in movies by Roger Moore George Lazenby and David Niven?

27. Although he had achieved success as a newspaper writer Mark Twain wanted to be published in a magazine so he was delighted when his "Forty-Three Days in an Open Boat" appeared in *Harper's New Monthly Magazine*.

28. Unfortunately because *Harper's* editors had trouble reading Twain's handwriting his story appeared with the author shown as Mike Swain.

29. Unable to convict Al Capone for his more notorious crimes the government finally imprisoned him in 1931 for income-tax evasion.

30. The *Batman* television series and movies featured the Riddler the Joker and the Penguin.

30 | Semicolon

The semicolon (;) is stronger than a comma but weaker than a period. This chapter presents the three most important uses of the semicolon.

1. **Use a semicolon between two independent clauses closely related in meaning but not joined by a coordinating conjunction. (IC;IC.)**

                     IC   IC

Examples: Lee won some battles; Grant won the war.

                   IC   IC

         The pale sun rose over the frozen land; the arctic fox gazed

         quietly at the sky.

2. **Use a semicolon between two independent clauses when the second independent clause is joined to the first with a conjunctive adverb. (IC;CA,IC.)**

                   IC   CA

Examples: Auto theft is a major national crime; however, people keep

                   IC

         leaving their cars unlocked.

                 IC   CA   IC

         Most stolen cars are recovered; unfortunately, many have been

         vandalized.

Note: If a conjunctive adverb is moved from the beginning of the second independent clause into the middle of it, the conjunctive adverb is then preceded by a comma instead of a semicolon; the semicolon, however, remains between the independent clauses.

```
                          IC                          CA        IC
Example: Most stolen cars are recovered; many, unfortunately, have been
```

vandalized.

3. When commas occur within one or more of the items in a series, use semicolons rather than commas to separate the items in the series.

Commas normally separate the items, with the commas clearly indicating where each portion of the series begins and ends. When any portion needs its own commas, however, readers may become confused if commas separate the portions of the series.

Confusing: Key air routes include Lisbon, Portugal, Rome, Italy, Frankfurt, Germany, and Istanbul, Turkey.

Readers with a good sense of world geography probably would understand this sample. However, you can make the readers' job easier by using semicolons to separate the major items in the series.

Better: Key air routes include Lisbon, Portugal; Rome, Italy; Frankfurt, Germany; and Istanbul, Turkey.

This way readers won't have to reread to understand the structure of the series.

EXERCISE

In the following sentences, add semicolons and commas where necessary.

1. New York City Mayor Fernando Wood was a staunch supporter of the South he proposed that the city secede declaring itself a "free city" if the South seceded.
2. In Boston in January 1919 a steel tank filled with more than 2 million gallons of molasses popped its rivets as the tank flew apart the first wave of molasses was some 30 feet high.
3. The wave of molasses swept away people and animals and crushed buildings the disaster killed 21 people and injured more than 50 others.
4. After the wave subsided some streets were left with molasses up to 3 feet deep for weeks people tracked molasses all over Boston they stuck to things they touched or sat on and the odor of molasses hung over the city.
5. Dr. James Naismith wanted a sport his students at Springfield College could play inside in the winter he hung small goals from the gym's balcony and invented basketball.
6. The first basketball game was played in Springfield in January 1892 because the goals were peach baskets a man had to climb a ladder after each goal to retrieve the ball.
7. This summer we plan to visit Philadelphia for a little sightseeing Aunt Martha who just moved to New York City and Boston where we'll look for the bar in *Cheers.*

8. Charles Willson Peale painted a tall rectangular canvas with two of his sons climbing the stairs after he mounted the canvas in a doorway and put a real step at the bottom the illusion was so effective that George Washington bowed a greeting to the boys.

9. Harry Nelson Pillsbury was proud of both his chess skills and his prodigious memory he put on performances in which he played up to 22 opponents without ever seeing any of the chess boards which meant that he had to memorize each move for each game and keep all the information in order in his head.

10. The Dust Bowl of the 1930s was centered on the area where Colorado New Mexico Texas Oklahoma and Kansas meet in all the Dust Bowl equaled an area more than twice the size of Pennsylvania.

11. The 1920s brought prosperity to the area and millions of acres of land were plowed and planted however when drought came in 1931 crop failures left nothing to hold the loose soil in place as winds swept the region.

12. In January 1933 the first great dust storm blew through the region winds blew away an estimated 850 million tons of topsoil in just 1935.

13. Unfortunately the natural conditions that led to the Dust Bowl still exist in the Southwest indeed only careful soil management and conservation keep the disaster of the 1930s from reoccurring.

14. Edith's grandchildren have moved to Tokyo Japan Palermo Italy and Cologne Germany.

15. In November 1820 a large sperm whale rammed and sank the three-masted whaleship *Essex* the tale brought back to Nantucket by the few survivors inspired Herman Melville's *Moby Dick*.

16. Sequoyah was inspired by white men's written language as a result he created a written form of the Cherokee language even though he never learned to read or write English.

17. The family of Earl K. Long Huey Long's younger brother and three-term governor of Louisiana committed Earl to an asylum when the state hospital board agreed to rule on his sanity Earl fired the superintendent and replaced him with a friend who would declare him sane.

18. *The Prison Mirror* is the oldest continuously published prison newspaper in America among its founders were Jim Bob and Cole Younger who had been part of the Jesse James Gang.

19. Almon Brown Strowger blamed the telephone operator for diverting business from his funeral parlor to that of a competitor so he invented the automated telephone exchange.

20. The battle between the *Monitor* and the *Merrimack* was the first battle between two ironclad ships though their battle was inconclusive it spelled the end of the prominence of wooden warships.

31 Colon

There are many rules for the colon, several of them relatively obscure. But there is one important rule you should know:

Use a colon after the last independent clause in a sentence to point to some more useful information about what you just said.

Virtually any grammatical unit can then follow the colon:

- a word or phrase
- a series of words or phrases
- a dependent clause
- an independent clause (or sentence)
- even a series of independent clauses or sentences

Examples:

The used car had one large defect: no engine.

The used car had three large defects: no tires, no brakes, no engine.

She sold the car for good reason: because it had no engine.

She sold the car for good reason: it had no engine.

She sold the car for three good reasons: It had no tires. It had no brakes. It had no engine.

When you have one entire sentence after the colon, should you capitalize the first letter of that sentence? There's no real standard: some people do and some people don't. (*Or* There's no real standard: *Some* people do and some people don't.) When you have a *series of sentences* after the colon, though, you should begin each with a capital letter.

The rule in this chapter says to put a colon after an independent clause. There are ways to put colons after only words, phrases, and dependent clauses. However, we suggest you learn and apply the one simple rule we give you: it can do wonderful things for your writing.

You should avoid unnecessary colons, however. If your sentence would read fine with no punctuation at all where you have a colon, simply leave the colon out. Here are some examples of incorrect colons:

He bought: two bicycle tires, a bicycle pump, and a tire repair kit.

The weather radar showed the blizzard was: crossing the Rocky Mountains, heading for Kansas, and building up strength.

EXERCISES

A. Write five sentences using a colon correctly. Follow the colon with these grammatical units (using a different grammatical unit for each of the five sentences you write):

- a word or phrase
- a series of words or phrases
- a dependent clause
- an independent clause (or sentence)
- a series of independent clauses or sentences

B. What different effects do these two sentences have?

She worked all weekend for one reason: money.
She worked all weekend for money.

C. In the following sentences, add colons where appropriate.

1. In the 14th century, Europe, Africa, and Asia were all ravaged by the same disease the Black Plague.
2. As the two players stared at each other across the net, each communicated the same message she was going to win.
3. As the two players stared at each other across the net, each communicated the message that she was going to win.
4. In 1215, King John granted a charter that guaranteed the English political and civil liberties the Magna Carta.
5. As the first of the Confederate column of troops reached the Union Army command element at Appomattox, Union Major General Joshua Chamberlain gave an unusual order he directed his soldiers to salute the Confederates as a sign of respect and peace.
6. Perhaps you know 3.14159 by its name pi.

7. At the beginning of the American Civil War many of the uniforms varied from the standard blue and gray that would predominate later a New York regiment in plaid kilts, regiments on both sides in colorful pantaloons and bright jackets of the French Zouaves, and even a Confederate unit with former prisoners in striped pants.

8. Many units in the war comprised recruits, and the fancy uniforms had a special purpose their flair generated local pride and encouraged recruitment.

9. Only two countries in South America are landlocked Bolivia and Paraguay.

10. The only countries in South America that are landlocked are Bolivia and Paraguay.

32 Dash

Years ago people considered the dash too informal for most writing other than letters home. Today, though, the dash has come into its own—it's an extremely handy mark if you want to give a slightly more personal feeling to your writing. If you want to close the gap between you and the readers, use dashes. If you want to widen the gap, don't.

We'll discuss two common rules for the dash. Notice that the first rule we discuss is identical to the one we gave you for the colon (but—yes—the dash gives a more personal feeling).

1. **Use a dash after the last independent clause in a sentence to point to some more useful information about what you just said.**

Virtually any grammatical unit can then follow the dash (though not normally a series of independent clauses):

- a word or phrase
- a series of words or phrases
- a dependent clause
- an independent clause (or sentence)

Examples:

The used car had one large defect—no engine.

The used car had three large defects—no tires, no brakes, no engine.

She sold the car for good reason—because it had no engine.

She sold the car for good reason—it had no engine.

2.   Use dashes in the same places you could use parentheses to set off some useful information in the middle of a sentence.

In the following sentences notice these points:

- The dashes add emphasis to the words they set off.
- The parentheses take emphasis away, making the words set off like a whispered aside.
- The commas provide standard emphasis.

With dashes: The store—the one around the corner—was robbed again.

With parentheses: The store (the one around the corner) was robbed again.

With commas: The store, the one around the corner, was robbed again.

Note: A dash is a line that's a little longer than a hyphen. So, how should you make a dash on a typewriter? A typewriter has only a hyphen (-) but not a dash (—). There are three ways:

- You can make a dash - which isn't on a typewriter - by using a hyphen with spaces on each side, as in this sentence.
- You can make a dash--this way--with two hyphens in a row (and no space at all on either side).
- Or you can make a dash -- this way -- with two hyphens in a row and a space before and after each set of hyphens.

Your choice.

EXERCISES

A. Write four sentences using a dash correctly. Follow the dash with these grammatical units (using a different grammatical unit for each of the four sentences you write):

- a word or phrase
- a series of words or phrases
- a dependent clause
- an independent clause (or sentence)

B. Write four sentences, with dashes, that have useful information in the middle of the sentence. The topic? Four different places you'd like to visit on a vacation.

C. What different effects do these two sentences have?

She worked all weekend for one reason—money.
She worked all weekend for one reason: money.

D. What different effects do these two sentences have?

The August breeze—surprisingly chilly—made spring seem far away.
The August breeze (surprisingly chilly) made spring seem far away.

E. In the following sentences, add dashes where appropriate.

1. Tourists visit Florence's Academy Gallery almost exclusively to see one work of art Michelangelo's *David*.
2. Florence's other main galleries the Pitti and the Uffizi contain some of the most important art works in Europe.
3. *Geheime Staatspolizei* (or "secret state police") was shortened into an infamous contraction Gestapo.
4. The Galapagos Islands known for their endangered species belong to Ecuador.
5. For the death of Sergeant Elias in Oliver Stone's *Platoon*, the music adapted from Samuel Barber's *Adagio for Strings* adds poignancy to the loss of Elias.
6. Ray Bradbury's science fiction novel about literature is named for the temperature at which paper catches fire *Fahrenheit 451*.
7. Tourists visit Florence's Academy Gallery almost exclusively to see Michelangelo's *David*.
8. Thomas Edison known for his exhaustive testing said: "Genius is 1 percent inspiration and 99 percent perspiration."
9. The next time you see an ad for the low cost of fast food today, remember what a McDonald's hamburger cost in 1963 15 cents.
10. Alfred Hitchcock's *North by Northwest* the title based on Hamlet's statement on his own madness has insanity as an underlying theme.

CHAPTER

33 Apostrophe

The apostrophe (') is, for very good reason, one of the most neglected marks of punctuation. Unlike other punctuation marks, the apostrophe can usually be omitted without any loss of meaning. Because it is still an accepted convention of our language, however, we should know its two important uses.

1. Use an apostrophe to show possession.

Examples: Sara's silver Honda
the dog's fleas

Note A: To form the possessive, follow these general rules:
(1) If the word does not end in an *s,* add an apostrophe and an *s:*

Base word: carpet

Possessive: carpet's design

(2) If the word ends in an *s,* add only an apostrophe (though adding an apostrophe and an *s* is correct, too):

Base word: dolls

Possessive: three dolls' dresses

Notice that if the word is singular, you simply apply these rules. If the word is to be plural, however, you make the word plural first, and then apply the rules.

Examples: dog (singular)
a dog's fleas (singular possessive)
two dogs (plural)
two dogs' fleas (plural possessive)

Note B: Some words—particularly those expressing units of time—may not seem possessive but still require an apostrophe:

> Examples: a day's work
> seven minutes' delay
> a month's pay

Note C: Do not use an apostrophe to show possession for personal pronouns *(yours, his, hers, its, ours, theirs).*

Wrong: It's shell is broken.

Correct: Its shell is broken.

2.   Use an apostrophe to show that letters have been left out of a word.

> Examples: *cannot* becomes *can't*
> *do not* becomes *don't*
> *does not* becomes *doesn't*
> *I will* becomes *I'll*
> *let us* becomes *let's*
> *it is* becomes *it's*

Note: The word *it's*, by the way, has only two meanings: "it is" or "it has."

EXERCISES

A. Form the singular and plural possessives of these words:

	singular possessive	plural possessive
minute	_____	_____
hobo	_____	_____
felon	_____	_____
general	_____	_____
fisherman	_____	_____
sheep	_____	_____
month	_____	_____
tomato	_____	_____
flower	_____	_____
shell	_____	_____

B. Add the necessary apostrophes to these sentences:

1. Margaret Mitchells only book was *Gone With the Wind.*
2. Tennessee Williams *A Streetcar Named Desire* places fragile Blanche DuBois, who spends too much of her life in a fantasy world, in confrontation with Stanley Kowalski, whose life is firmly rooted in reality.

3. Weve little doubt about wholl win this confrontation, but we come to realize whats lost when Blanche fails.

4. I dont know whether youll remember, but my father promised Jenifer $3,000 if she remained unmarried until she was 23.

5. *The Crucible,* Arthur Millers play about the Salem witch trials, has Puritan New England as its setting.

6. During a weeks stay in London we went to the theater every night.

7. Theres a slight buzz in one of the speakers because one of its wires is loose.

8. The eucalyptus trees leaves make up most of the koala bears diet.

9. Rose Greenhow, considered one of Washingtons most alluring hostesses, provided the Confederates one of the Civil Wars most important secrets— warning of when the Union Army was moving toward Manassas, Virginia, for the wars first battle.

10. I dont care whether that jacket is yours; just see that its put away immediately.

11. "John Browns Body" isnt about the John Brown who raided the federal arsenal at Harpers Ferry; instead, the songs John Brown was a sergeant in a Massachusetts volunteer regiment, whose friends made up the song to taunt him.

12. Karl Marx, communisms father, wasnt buried in Russia or any other of the former Soviet Unions states; you can find his grave in London.

13. For a time combination car-planes were being developed in the United States; however, they didnt fly as well as an airplane or cruise as well as an automobile, and the markets interest in them didnt last long.

14. Its been too long since we visited those relatives of yours.

15. No matter how hard Ive tried to keep the dogs toys in its box, the dog has tried harder to keep its toys wherever it wants.

CHAPTER

34 Quotation Marks

This chapter presents the two important uses of quotation marks (" ") and three rules for using other punctuation within quotation marks.

1. **Use quotation marks to enclose the exact words written or spoken by someone else.**

Example: Irving Knoke stated, "If someone is looking for an easy way to commit suicide, all he needs to do is stick his thumb out on any road."

2. **Use quotation marks to enclose the title of a poem, short story, magazine article, or newspaper article.**

In other words, use quotation marks to enclose the title of a work that is published as part of another work. Poems and short stories are rarely published separately; rather, they are usually part of a book that includes other poems or stories. Similarly, magazine articles appear as part of a magazine, and newspaper articles appear as part of a newspaper.

Note: The book, magazine, or newspaper title—that is, the title of the larger work containing the poem, short story, or article—should be underlined (or italicized).

Examples: "The Lottery," *Learning Fiction* (a short story in a collection of fiction)

"The Love Song of J. Alfred Prufrock," *Poetry for First Graders* (a poem in a collection of poetry)

"The Problems of Bigamy," *Gentlemen's Weekly Journal* (an article in a magazine)

"Mayor Silvers Wins Again!" *Cripple Creek News* (an article in a newspaper)

The following rules explain how to use other punctuation with quotation marks:

1. Always place periods and commas inside quotation marks.

Examples: I enjoyed reading "The Lottery."
I just read "The Lottery," a strange story by Shirley Jackson.

2. Always place semicolons and colons outside quotation marks.

Examples: I just read "The Lottery"; it is weird.
There are three really interesting characters in "The Lottery":
Mrs. Hutchinson, Old Man Warner, and Mr. Summers.

3. A. Place question marks and exclamation points inside quotation marks if the quotation is a question or an exclamation.

Examples: Tessie Hutchinson yelled, "That's not fair!"
The crowd answered, "Why do you say that, Tessie?"

Note: This rule applies even if the sentence is also a question or an exclamation.

Example: Was the crowd afraid of something when it asked Tessie, "Why do you say that, Tessie?"

B. Place question marks and exclamation points outside quotation marks if the sentence is a question or an exclamation but the quotation is not.

Examples: Who just said, "Steak fries are good"?
I can't believe you said, "Steak fries are better than noodles"!

EXERCISE

Add the necessary quotation marks in these sentences. Be careful to place quotation marks clearly inside or outside any other punctuation.

1. What Keats poem contains the statement: Beauty is truth, truth beauty?
2. I'm particularly fond of three short stories: Stephen Crane's The Blue Hotel, Ernest Hemingway's The Killers, and Robert Louis Stevenson's Markheim.
3. In The Blue Hotel, the Swede, who sees everyone's actions as if they were occurring in a dime novel of the Old West, says to the men playing cards, Oh, I see you are all against me.
4. The cowboy cries out in reply, say, what are you gittin' at, hey?
5. Why does the Swede jump up and shout, I don't want to fight!?
6. Why does the cowboy reply, Well, who the hell thought you did?
7. Why does the cowboy later say of the Swede, It's my opinion . . . he's some kind of a Dutchman?

8. In The Killers two gangsters arrive in the diner in Summit where Nick Adams is eating; they've come to kill Ole Anderson, who usually eats dinner at the diner.

9. George, the manager, asks, What are you going to kill Ole Anderson for? What did he ever do to you?

10. One of the gangsters, Max, replies, He never had a chance to do anything to us. He never even seen us.

11. The other gangster, Al, adds, And he's only going to see us once.

12. When George again asks why the two intend to kill Ole Anderson, Max answers, We're killing him for a friend. Just to oblige a friend, bright boy.

13. After the gangsters leave the diner, Nick goes to warn Ole Anderson, who lies listlessly in bed; Ole's response to the warning is, There ain't anything to do.

14. Why does Ole roll toward the wall and say, The only thing is . . . I just can't make up my mind to go out?

15. After trying to warn Ole Anderson, Nick Adams returns to the diner and announces, I'm going to get out of this town; when Nick tells George that he can't stand to think about Ole just waiting in his room, George tells him, Well . . . you better not think about it.

SEVEN
Expression

Your writing style is how you express yourself. Basic to that style are principles of punctuation (such as those you studied in Part Six) and of grammar—both part of the way we communicate with each other in writing.

This section presents some grammar *"do's"* and *"don't's"* to help you deal with expression problems common in the writing of college students. It also demonstrates techniques that will help you advance your style beyond the basics so that you express yourself skillfully.

CHAPTER

35 | Subordination

You probably know what *in*subordination is, but subordination is something else altogether.

When you first learned to read and write, almost every sentence was an independent clause: "Jane, see Spot." Every idea—small as it was—had exactly the same emphasis as every other idea. Of course, nobody in college writes like that, but too often college students have not progressed far enough from that grade-school style.

Your challenge is to combine related ideas into one sentence, giving them just the right emphasis. To succeed, you must learn *subordination—making less important ideas part of more important ideas.*

We all know that a subordinate is someone who ranks lower than someone else. Parts of a sentence have a rank structure, too.

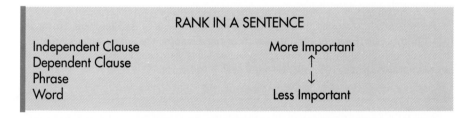

RANK IN A SENTENCE

Independent Clause	More Important
Dependent Clause	↑
Phrase	↓
Word	Less Important

Ideas expressed in an independent clause naturally seem more important than ideas expressed by only a word. Subordination, then, reduces the emphasis of an idea by lowering its position on the rank structure.

We might subordinate an idea originally in an independent clause by placing it in a dependent clause, a phrase, or—sometimes—even a word. For example:

IC   IC
Original: Art flew to Gila Bend. He arrived on time.

                                              DC   IC
Subordination   Because he flew to Gila Bend, Art arrived on time.
(a dependent clause):

                                    Phrase   IC
Subordination (a phrase):   By flying to Gila Bend, Art arrived on time.

Notice that subordination here has two effects:

- It shows what the writer believes to be the important idea: Art's arriving on time (expressed in the independent clause).
- It shows the relationship between the two ideas: the words *because* in the first revision and *by* in the second act as road signs, telling readers to be ready for a cause-effect relationship. (Because something happened, something else resulted: "Because he flew to Gila Bend, Art arrived on time.") These road signs make the readers' task much easier.

Subordination Beyond the Sentence Level

This chapter focuses on subordination at the sentence level. But subordination also is important elsewhere in the writing process—especially in prewriting when you cluster related ideas and when you develop topic sentences and a thesis statement. As you study the essay and research paper models in the first five parts of this book, you see subordination in an outline form:

- In a one-paragraph essay, related specific support ideas are clustered and then subordinated to a topic sentence idea.
- In a five-paragraph essay, related central paragraphs are clustered and subordinated to a thesis idea.
- In a research paper, related main ideas are clustered and subordinated to the research paper's thesis idea.

The relationships among the ideas vary with the patterns of development. However, for all of these increasingly complex levels of organization, the *effects of subordination* are the same as those within a sentence: *showing what the writer wishes to emphasize as most important and showing relationships among ideas.*

Now let's return to our sentence example. We could have subordinated the second independent clause if we had decided that Art's flying to Gila Bend was more important than the idea that he arrived on time.

                                    IC   IC
Original: Art flew to Gila Bend. He arrived on time.

                                              IC   DC
Subordination   Art flew to Gila Bend, where he arrived on time.
(a dependent clause):

	IC	Phrase
Subordination (a phrase):   Art flew to Gila Bend, arriving on time.

When you write, therefore, you have to decide which ideas you wish to emphasize and which you wish to subordinate.

"But," you might protest, "I use subordination all the time." Sure you do—though probably not enough. Let's express some ideas in grade-school style, early college style, and a more sophisticated style.

Degrees of Subordination

Grade-school style: The girl is playing tennis. Her name is Sally. She is a beginner. She is taking lessons. Karen is teaching her. Karen is a professional. Karen teaches at the Andromeda Club. Karen teaches every Tuesday morning.

Early college style: Sally is playing tennis. She is taking beginning lessons from Karen. Karen is a professional, and she teaches at the Andromeda Club every Tuesday morning.

Improved style: Sally is taking beginning tennis lessons from Karen, a professional who teaches at the Andromeda Club every Tuesday morning.

The last revision certainly is easier to read than either of the other versions. Why? Subordination pushes the unimportant ideas to the side of the stage so the viewers can easily see the star, the independent clause.

Apply Subordination During Editing

Here's a final tip to help you with subordination. On a first draft, you're naturally too busy thinking of ideas and how they relate to each other to worry about subordination at the sentence level. When you edit the draft—during the rewriting phase—pay attention to how you piece ideas together *within sentences*. Depending on the time you have available, you may even want to make a trip through your paper, beginning to end, just working on the best way to combine ideas into better sentences. The results will be worth the effort.

Remember, your work while you write makes your readers' work much easier. Subordination lets readers see which main ideas you consider important. And, after you finish school, that's the main reason you will write.

EXERCISES

A. Combine these simple sentences in two different ways, emphasizing a different idea each time.

1. Mary Shelly wrote a novel at the age of 19. The novel was *Frankenstein.*

   a. _____

   b. _____

2. Belize is a small country in Central America. Until 1973, it was called British Honduras.

   a. _____

   b. _____

3. The horse won the Kentucky Derby. It was draped with a blanket of roses.

   a. _____

   b. _____

4. The *Hindenburg* was the world's largest airship. It crashed at Lakehurst, New Jersey, in 1937.

   a. _____

   b. _____

5. Dr. Joyce Brothers won the grand prize, $64,000, on *The $64,000 Question.* She answered questions on boxing.

   a. _____

   b. _____

B. For each numbered exercise below, combine all the ideas in the simple sentences into one good sentence.

1. Eileen road her bike for fifteen miles.
   She was tired.
   She was thirsty.
   She was hungry.
   She finally reached the stadium.
   The stadium is near the new mall.

   _____

   _____

   _____

2. Richard Lawrence fired two pistols at Andrew Jackson.
   He fired the pistols at point-blank range.
   Both pistols misfired.

The weather probably affected the powder.
The weather was damp.

_____

_____

_____

3. Theodore Roosevelt refused to shoot a bear.
   Theodore Roosevelt was president at the time.
   Clifford Berryman drew a political cartoon about the incident.
   The bear in the cartoon was little and cute.
   Cuddly stuffed bears became known as "Teddy Bears."

_____

_____

_____

4. Thousands of miles of wooden roads were laid in several U.S. states.
   The roads were laid in the 1840s and 1850s.
   Gravel roads replaced most of the wooden roads.
   The wooden planks began to rot.

_____

_____

_____

5. In the late 1800s huge wagons hauled borax.
   They transported the borax out of Death Valley.
   Death Valley is in California.
   Eighteen mules pulled a wagon.
   Two horses also helped pull a wagon.
   The idea of freight wagons pulled by multiple teams became popular.
   The borax was called "twenty-mule team borax."

_____

_____

_____

CHAPTER

36 Sentence Variety

After the preceding chapter, you may suspect that "good" writing consists of one complicated sentence after another. Not so: you'd lose the readers after a couple of pages. On the other hand, how would you like to read sentence after sentence in grade-school or early college style?

Well, then, is the solution a compromise of all medium-length sentences? No, not really. Good writing has a mixture of:

- varied sentence lengths
- varied sentence structures

Now, variety just for the sake of variety isn't really the goal. But good sentence variety is often an indication of good coherence—of the smooth flow of ideas from one to another. So if you find yourself writing many short sentences in a row, or beginning many sentences with the subject of the independent clause, ask yourself, "Do my sentence patterns help my ideas flow smoothly? Or do they make my ideas seem fragmented, choppy?"

This chapter will give you some tips on how to vary your sentences to achieve better coherence.

SENTENCE LENGTH

Actually, not very many beginning writers have poor sentence variety from writing only long sentences. The problem is usually a series of short sentences:

The new governor was sworn in today. He is a Democrat. Ten thousand people attended the ceremony. The governor gave a brief inaugural address. The governor promised to end unemployment. He said he would reduce inflation. He also promised to improve the environment. The audience gave him a standing ovation.

Pretty dismal, right? The average sentence length is only six and a quarter words, and all the sentences except the second are either six or seven words long—not overwhelming variety. Let's use the technique of subordination we learned in the last chapter to come up with something better:

> The new Democratic governor was sworn in today. At a ceremony that ten thousand people attended, he gave a brief inaugural address, promising to end unemployment, reduce inflation, and improve the environment. The audience gave him a standing ovation.

This version is certainly much easier to read, mainly because we've eliminated choppiness and subordinated some unimportant ideas. The average sentence is now thirteen words long, within the desirable goal of twelve to twenty words per sentence.

Practical Writing: The Problem of Complex Sentences

Although beginning writers tend toward short, choppy sentences, writers in business, industry, and government sometimes tend the other way. Some even believe that writing long, complex sentences is a mark of their educational competence. They think their superiors *expect* them to write long sentences, and they aim to please.

Here's a sample of the type of writing that results:

> Whether the terrorists style themselves as separatists, anarchists, dissidents, nationalists, Marxist revolutionaries, or religious true believers, what marks them as terrorists is that they direct their violence against noncombatants with the goal of terrorizing a wider audience than the immediate victims, thereby attempting to gain political influence over the larger audience. In one variant of terrorism, organizational terrorism, represented by such groups as the Red Army Faction in Germany, the Red Brigades in Italy, Direct Action in France, and 17 November in Greece, small, tightly knit, politically homogeneous organizations that are incapable of developing popular support for their radical positions resort to terrorism to gain influence. In a second variant of terrorism, that conducted within the context of ethnic separatist or countrywide insurgencies, such as in the Philippines, El Salvador, and Colombia, groups conducting paramilitary or guerrilla operations against the established government turn to attacks on the populace at large to undermine the government's credibility, legitimacy, and public support.

These three sentences, all roughly the same length, average fifty-four words each. You can understand what they say, of course—if you read very carefully.

Yet, successful writers—and the people they work for—today are insisting on something else. They're demanding simpler writing so that busy readers don't have to struggle with the material they need to understand. Sentence averages in the twelve to twenty word range simply communicate more effectively.

SENTENCE STRUCTURE

Let's look again at the bad example that began the discussion on sentence length. Notice how many sentences begin with the subject (and its modifiers) of an independent clause:

The new governor was sworn in today. He is a Democrat. Ten thousand people attended the ceremony. The governor gave a brief inaugural address. The governor promised to end unemployment. He said he would reduce inflation. He also promised to improve the environment. The audience gave him a standing ovation.

Every sentence begins with the subject of an independent clause. Surely there is a better way to move from sentence to sentence than to begin every one with the subject. Some should begin with dependent clauses, others with phrases, and still others with transitional words. For example, look again at the revision:

The new Democratic governor was sworn in today. *At a ceremony that ten thousand people attended,* he gave a brief inaugural address, promising to end unemployment, reduce inflation, and improve the environment. The audience gave him a standing ovation.

The introduction to the second sentence provides nice relief.

Many sentences, of course, should begin with the subject of an independent clause; still, they should not all look alike. They could end with a dependent clause, they could contain a couple of independent clauses, or they could contain a series of parallel phrases or clauses (see Chapter 37). The sentences in the paragraph you are now reading, for example, all begin with the subject of an independent clause, but after that beginning, their structures vary considerably.

Apply Sentence Variety During Editing

You may think *you* would never begin a lot of sentences all the same way. And surely you'd never string together all short, choppy sentences or long, overly complex ones. Yet, in our first draft many of us write with just those patterns.

We think of an idea and write it down: "subject—verb"; we think of another idea and write it down: "subject—verb"; and so on. Similarly, we become comfortable writing sentences with much the same lengths—short ones or long ones, whichever way we're used to writing. Then, because we don't take the time to rewrite the draft, our sentences look much the same.

Check your last few pages to see if you've fallen into this bad habit.

Good writing is not an automatic process, a flow of uninterrupted inspiration flowing forth onto the page. Good writing results from a painstaking and very conscious process.

Don't just hope sentence variety will happen in your writing. After you write a draft, ask yourself these questions:

- Are my sentences different lengths?
- Do my sentences begin in a variety of ways?
- Do the sentences that begin with the subject of an independent clause have a variety of structures?

If the answers are "no," then edit your paper for sentence variety. Be careful, though, not to sacrifice clarity for the sake of variety. And don't create grotesque, unnatural sentences.

Variety is a means to achieve good writing—not the goal itself.

EXERCISES

A. Revise these paragraphs for better sentence variety. In both the original and your revision, circle the subject of the first independent clause in every sentence. Then compute the average number of words in each sentence (count all the words in the paragraph and divide by the number of sentences).

1. Original: In the early 1900s, Anthony Comstock was the secretary of New York's Society for the Suppression of Vice. Comstock displayed excessive piousness. This made him appear to many Americans as a self-righteous clown. He was quite effective at eliminating materials he and his supporters didn't like. These were materials they considered to be lewd. They particularly attacked what they saw as dirty books. They also attacked what they saw as obscene art works. Comstock attacked painter Paul Chabas' *September Morn*. *September Morn* shows a woman bathing in a lake. She is nude. However, the painting is reserved by most people's standards. It reveals very little. The painting was sure to offend Comstock. A public relations specialist decided to take advantage of this situation. He had an art dealer display a print of the painting in a shop window. He paid some young boys to stand at the window. They stared at the print. Then he notified Comstock. The response was as predicted. Chabas' painting gained national attention. The incident led to sales of millions of prints of *September Morn*. It also led to sales of dolls, calendars, and other spin-offs.

Average number of words per sentence:_____

Your revision: _____

_____

_____

_____

_____

_____

_____

_____

_____

_____

_____

Average number of words per sentence:_____

2. Original: The Whiskey Rebellion was in 1794. It was one of the greatest threats to the authority of the U.S. federal government prior to the Civil War. It began as a test of the government's ability to collect taxes. Farmers in western Pennsylvania had surplus corn. They distilled whiskey from the corn. The liquor was cheaper to transport. It also served as currency in barter for necessities. In 1791 Secretary of the Treasury Alexander Hamilton imposed a tax on stills and distilled liquors. America needed the income to pay off war debts. Many Pennsylvania farmers refused to pay the tax. They compared it to England's Stamp Act. By 1794 tax collectors in western Pennsylvania faced violent resistance. Frequently they were met with tar and feathers. In August, 5,000 armed farmers gathered at Pittsburgh. They came to protest the tax. They also talked of secession. President Washington called out the militia. He sent a force of 13,000 to suppress the insurrection. Major General Henry Lee led the militia. The militia advanced into western Pennsylvania. The resistance collapsed. The federal government had demonstrated its power.

Average number of words per sentence:_____

Your revision: _____

_____

_____

_____

_____

_____

_____

_____

_____

_____

_____

Average number of words per sentence:_____

3.   Original: Many U.S. citizens learned a story about George Washington and
     Betsy Ross. We learned that in 1776 George Washington visited Betsy Ross. He
     asked her to sew a new flag for the Continental Army. We learned that Betsy
     showed General Washington how to make a five-pointed star. Washington liked
     what he saw. Betsy Ross set to work making the Stars and Stripes. Many of us
     even have visited the Ross house. It is where the event took place. We also know
     what the resulting flag looked like. There is a famous painting called *The Spirit of
     '76*. It is by Archibald Willard. It shows two drummers and a fife player. Behind
     them is the flag we know. We're sure it flew throughout the American Revolution.
     The flag has thirteen red and white stripes. It has a blue field in the upper left
     corner. It has thirteen white stars in a circle. The stars have five points. There is
     an irony to what we know. None of these "facts" is true. Records show that Betsy
     Ross made flags. She made them for the Pennsylvania Navy. There is no evi-
     dence for the Washington-Ross story. In 1870, Betsy's grandson told the tale to
     the Pennsylvania Historical Society. He said he had heard it from Betsy. The leg-
     end found its way into popular history. It also was written down in books. There
     is no evidence that the flag Willard painted ever existed. In 1777, the Continen-
     tal Congress passed a resolution about flags. It could have led to the flag in
     Willard's painting. However, units actually flew a variety of flags. In 1783,
     Washington received a shipment of flags. They were for the Continental Army.
     The shipment came near the end of the war. The "history" we've learned about
     the Stars and Stripes seems to have a lot of romance. It doesn't seem to have a
     lot of substance.

     Average number of words per sentence:_____

     Your revision: _____

_____

_____

_____

_____

_____

_____

_____

_____

_____

Average number of words per sentence:_____

B. Revise the three sentences in the box called "Practical Writing: The Problem of Com-
    plex Sentences" for better sentence variety. Those three sentences have fifty-one, fifty-
    five, and fifty-four words, for an average of fifty-four words per sentence. The aver-
    age number of words per sentence in your revision should fall in the twelve to twenty
    word range. Although the primary purpose of this exercise is to reduce the average
    sentence length, be sure your revision also demonstrates a variety of sentence
    structures.

Average number of words per sentence:_____

Your revision: _____

_____

_____

_____

_____

_____

_____

_____

_____

_____

_____

Average number of words per sentence:_____

37 Parallelism

Now that you've studied sentence variety, you may be afraid of writing sentences that repeat simple patterns. Don't be. Some ideas work best in sentences that clearly show a pattern. When you analyze an idea, you take pains to discover similarities and differences among its parts. Whether you intend to compare or contrast those elements, you want readers to see how the parts are alike or different. Parallelism is the key.

The principle of parallel construction is simple: *be sure ideas that are similar in content and function look the same.* Parallelism works because the similarity of the appearance of the items shows clearly the pattern of the thought. The principle of parallelism applies most often to the following:

- two or more items in a series (usually with a coordinating conjunction)
- a pair of items with correlative conjunctions—a special type of series and conjunctions we'll explain later in this chapter

ITEMS IN A SERIES

The principle of parallelism requires that all items in a series must be grammatically alike. That is, all words in a series must be the same type of word, all phrases the same type of phrase, and all clauses the same type of clause. Grammatical likeness also applies to sentences in a series: each item in the series must be a *complete* sentence—not a fragment—and, therefore, the same "type" of sentence. However, the structures within these complete sentences can vary, so the patterns within the sentences may appear somewhat different, as we'll see later in this section.

Coordinating Conjunctions With a Series

Two or more items in a series within a single sentence normally use a coordinating conjunction (CC)—*and, but, or, nor, for, so,* or *yet*—before the final item.

Thus, the series looks like this:

item CC item

or this:

item, item, CC item

A series of complete sentences, however, usually will not include a coordinating conjunction before the final item.

Here are sentences with parallel constructions:

Words in series: I saw John and Mary.

I saw John, Bill, and Mary.

Phrases in series: I see him going to work and coming home.

I plan to eat in a restaurant and to see a movie.

Dependent clauses in series: The phone rang when I reached the motel but before I unpacked my suitcases.

Independent clauses in series: I liked the parrot, so I bought it for my mother.

Complete sentences in series: She sold the car for three good reasons:

It had no tires. It had no brakes. It had no engine.

Notice that each item—word, phrase, clause, or sentence—in a series has the same form as the other items in the same series.

A Reminder: Use Commas and Semicolons With Items in a Series

As you saw in Chapters 29 and 30, commas and sometimes semicolons mark the division of items in a series within a sentence. Commas are the most common dividers:

> The ethics of contemporary surgery are often a problem for the patient, the doctor, and the patient's family.
>
> When commas occur within one or more of the items in a series, semicolons mark the divisions between the items:
>
> Key air routes include Lisbon, Portugal; Rome, Italy; Frankfurt, Germany; and Istanbul, Turkey.

WORDS IN A SERIES

The words in a series of words seldom present special problems. However, the articles that appear with the series can create a minor parallelism problem.

Articles With Words in a Series

Articles are *a, an,* and *the.* When articles appear with words in a series, be sure the articles fall in one of these two patterns:

article word, word, CC word

article word, *article* word, CC *article* word

Notice the placement of the articles in these sample sentences:

Wrong: I bought food for *the* dog, cat, and *the* horse.

Correct: I bought food for *the* dog, cat, and horse.

Correct: I bought food for *the* dog, *the* cat, and *the* horse.

The correct sentences have either an article before the entire series or an article before every item in the series.

PHRASES IN A SERIES

Unlike words in a series, phrases often cause problems. Many times students mix types of phrases. Be sure that *-ing* phrases fit with other *-ing* phrases, *to* phrases with *to* phrases, and so forth.

Wrong: I like *swimming in the pond, cycling down the lane,* and *to ride horses in the pasture.*

Correct: I like *swimming in the pond, cycling down the lane,* and *riding horses in the pasture.*

Correct: I like *to swim in the pond, to cycle down the lane,* and *to ride horses in the pasture.*

Wrong: I plan *to study hard, doing well on my exams,* and *to graduate with honors.*

Correct: I plan *to study hard, to do well on my exams,* and *to graduate with honors.*

Correct: I plan on *studying hard, doing well on my exams,* and *graduating with honors.*

CLAUSES IN A SERIES

Clauses in a series seldom cause major problems. However, if the series contains dependent clauses, you can help your readers by signaling the beginning of each dependent clause. Consider this sentence:

I expect to be entertained if I'm going to pay $5 to get in a theater and I'm going to sit there for two hours.

What does the *and* join? Does it join the two independent clauses?

$\overbrace{\text{I expect to be entertained}}^{\text{item}}$ if I'm going to pay $5 to get in a theater $\overset{\text{CC}}{\text{and}}$

$\overbrace{\text{I'm going to sit there for two hours.}}^{\text{item}}$

Or does it join two dependent clauses?

I expect to be entertained if $\overbrace{\text{I'm going to pay \$5 to get in a theater}}^{\text{item}}$ $\overset{\text{CC}}{\text{and}}$

$\overbrace{\text{I'm going to sit there for two hours.}}^{\text{item}}$

The intended meaning is probably the second one: the *and* joins two dependent clauses. Readers will see the separation of the items more easily if the writer repeats the word that signals the beginning of the clauses:

I expect to be entertained if $\overbrace{\text{I'm going to pay \$5 to get in a theater}}^{\text{item}}$ $\overset{\text{CC}}{\text{and}}$

if $\overbrace{\text{I'm going to sit there for two hours.}}^{\text{item}}$

Now the meaning is clear. Here's another sample:

"I can see that you don't like the meal and that you'd rather not be here," she pouted.

Notice that the repetition of *that* (which signals the beginning of dependent clauses) makes the parallel construction clear.

Like Grammatical Units in a Series Within a Sentence

In addition to having like words, like phrases, and like clauses in a series within a sentence, be sure that the items in the series are the same type of grammatical unit. Do not, for instance, mix phrases and clauses in a series, as in this sentence:

item CC   item

Wrong: My roommate likes to sleep in bed and when he's in class.

The sentence is awkward because the writer has joined a phrase (*in bed*) with a clause (*when he's in class*). Here's what the writer should have written:

Correct: My roommate likes to sleep when he's in bed and when he's in class.

Now a clause fits with a clause. (Notice also that the sentence repeats *when*, the word that signals the beginning of each dependent clause.)

COMPLETE SENTENCES IN A SERIES

In the earlier sample of full sentences in a series, all of the sentences are quite short, and their internal structures are exactly alike: "It had no tires. It had no brakes. It had no engine." Clearly, this is a technique you have to apply sparingly. This type of series could provide a punchy variation if it were mixed in with longer sentences. Too much of it, though, could create the type of choppy, repetitive writing you learned to avoid when you studied about sentence variety in the last chapter.

However, complete sentences in a series don't have to be so much alike. Here's another sample, this time with some variation within the sentences.

> My great-grandfather wrote that Abraham Lincoln's appearance at the caucus was striking: Lincoln's beard was short and neatly trimmed. His suit was of a dark cloth that gave him a somber but dignified air and seemed to hang on his lank frame. In his hand he loosely held a black stovepipe hat.

These sentences are of varied lengths: seven, twenty-three, and ten words, respectively. Obviously their internal structures are not exactly alike. Are they parallel? Well, yes, they are. In the simplest sense, they have grammatical similarity, as each is a complete sentence. More important, each provides the same type of information—a quick, descriptive example—that answers the same question: How was Lincoln's appearance striking? And even though the structures of the sentences are not exactly alike, their basic idea patterns are similar: his beard was . . .; his suit was . . .; his hand held. . . .

Parallelism in Headings and Indented Lists

In Chapter 10 you learned about layout techniques that can make your writing look better. Two of those techniques—headings and indented lists—depend on parallelism.

Here are the headings that were added to the sample paper about the humorous things children do as they grow up:

Learning to Speak

Discovering Objects Aren't Human

Imitating Others Around Them

Notice that the headings are parallel phrases, each the same type of phrase: learning . . . , discovering . . . , imitating. . . .

Parallelism is even more important when you use indented lists. Their purpose is to *emphasize a pattern* of organization, and that is also the reason for using parallel construction. Here's a sample list without parallelism:

Desktop publishing offers our department three benefits:

- product more professional
- Production time will be cut.
- saves money

This list a jumble of styles that reminds us of the result of brainstorming, where we're interested in jotting down ideas quickly without worrying about how well they communicate. Readers will get the point—if they take the time to apply the organization that the writer has left out. Notice the difference that parallel construction makes in this revision:

Desktop publishing offers our department three benefits:

- a more professional-looking product
- reduced production time
- cost savings

PAIRS OF ITEMS WITH CORRELATIVE CONJUNCTIONS

Correlative conjunctions mate pairs of related items. The rule for parallelism with correlative conjunctions is simple: the grammatical units following each of the correlative conjunctions must be alike.

Correlative Pairs

Common correlative conjunctions are these: *either . . . or; neither . . . nor; not (only) . . . but (also); and whether . . . or.*

Items mated by correlative conjunctions (CorC) will look like this:

CorC item CorC item

Here are sentences with such pairs:

I don't like either his appearance or his manners.

Neither my aunt nor my cousin will speak to me.

Can you find the problem in this sentence?

Wrong: *Either* I go to bed early *or* get up late.

This sentence demonstrates the most common failure to maintain parallelism with correlative conjunctions: *either* precedes the subject of the sentence *(I)*, but *or* precedes the second verb *(get)*. There are two methods to deal with the problem:

Correct: I *either* go to bed early *or* get up late.

Correct: *Either* I go to bed early *or* I get up late.

The first solution moves *either* so that both correlative conjunctions precede verbs (*go* and *get*). The second solution places *either* and *or* before subjects of clauses (*I* and *I*). In both corrections, the grammatical units following each correlative conjunction are alike.

All of this may seem complicated, but it's not. You wouldn't try to compare apples and automobiles, because they're not alike. Similarly, you can't expect your readers to accept a comparison of items that don't appear to be alike. The principle of parallelism requires only that you make like items *look* alike so readers can see the similarity.

EXERCISES

A. Improve the parallelism in each of the following sentences:

1. He brought a set of clean linens, towel, and a washcloth.
2. When he visited his parents, Julio both wanted to spend time with his family and visit with old friends.
3. Greek temples for the god of medicine, Asklepios, were not only places of worship but also of healing.
4. At Christmas we like to decorate the tree, making special cookies, and singing carols.
5. Lorenzo loves hiking, climbing mountains, and especially to camp in the forest.
6. The Romans constructed their baths by elevating the floors on brick pillars, enclosing the pillars and rooms to control the air circulation, and then installed furnaces to circulate hot air.

7. Edith bought a computer, dot-matrix printer, and a popular word-processing software program.

8. Ramon never felt prepared for French class, whether he had studied the language daily or cramming several hours before class.

9. Mr. Johnston talked to a lawyer, a judge, and to his senator about the problem.

10. We like swimming in the summer, to ride horses, and cycling.

11. I didn't go to the concert because I didn't have any interest in it, the time, and I lacked the energy to go out.

12. The fountain was beautiful as the droplets spread out in the air and were made to sparkle by the sunlight.

13. The new policy upset not only the students but also those who taught them.

14. Overheated by the sun and with dehydration, I stopped running at mile seven in the July 4th road race.

15. The tomb of China's emperor Qin Shi Huangdi was protected not only by an army of over 6,000 terra-cotta soldiers but there were real drawn crossbows set to shoot intruders who set off their triggers.

16. Charles finally told his mother he wanted to go skiing, soak in the hot tub, and always avoid working.

17. Even though Marla was tired from jogging five miles and she practiced wind sprints for twenty minutes, she was ready for a night of dancing.

18. After I revised my history paper and a test in calculus, I still needed to study for a midterm in English.

19. Before going onto the stage and she heard the opening applause, Thea was very nervous.

20. Tossed by high waves and with strong winds hammering it, the small boat seemed certain to capsize.

21. I think about Grandmother's farm when I drive in rush-hour traffic or reading about crime in the streets.

22. Crane's department store is offering a special price on the towels, sheets, and the bedspreads.

23. Alex went to the party for the food, the entertainment, and to meet people who might become customers.

24. The director wanted to film scenes in the forums of ancient Rome and where the streets are narrow and crowded in Naples.

25. Dennis will go to class if it neither rains nor snows.

B. In these exercises, revise the indented lists so the items will be parallel.

1. Through his short stories and novels, Dashiell Hammett, creator of Sam Spade, Nick Charles, and other detectives, developed the typical "hard-boiled" detective:

- Crime was taken out of the drawing room of the quaint English detective story and put into the streets.
- His dialogue captured the style and rhythm of street talk.
- Tough-guy detective who lived by a code of honor of his own making.

2. Greek health-care centers, called *asklepieia,* offered a variety of services to the ill and infirm:

   - Facilities for bathing and ritual exercise.
   - There were pavilions in which patients could sleep and be visited by the god of healing, Asklepios.
   - Temples for worship of Asklepios and for handling dogs and snakes, which were associated with Asklepios, also were available.
   - Operating theaters where temple physicians performed surgery.

3. In his war with the Celtic tribes of Gaul in 52 B.C., Julius Caesar encircled the Gauls with a field of hazards:

   - The field facing the Gauls had pits with sharp stakes at the bottom—all covered with brush to hide the traps.
   - A thicket of pointed branches angled toward the Gauls.
   - Two trenches, one filled with water, came after the thicket.
   - A steep wall with towers from which Caesar's soldiers could throw spears.

38 Misused Modifiers

Dangling participle! Nothing—not even "split infinitive"—can strike such terror in the heart of an English student. But don't be afraid. Behind the fancy name is a simple concept you'll understand after studying this chapter. You won't learn the differences between dangling participles, dangling gerunds, and dangling infinitives because the differences aren't really important: we'll treat them all more simply as *dangling modifiers*. In addition to the special type of modifier problem, you'll also study *misplaced modifiers*.

What Is a Modifier?

Modifiers are words, phrases, or clauses that limit or provide additional information about other words.

In "I never saw a purple cow," the modifier *purple* limits the discussion from "all cows" to only "purple cows." (As you saw in the discussion of comma usage in Chapter 29, modifiers that limit the definition of other words are restrictive modifiers.)

In "Standing on the bridge, the captain watched his ship move slowly through the channel," the modifier *standing on the bridge* provides additional information about the captain—but it in no way limits the definition. (Modifiers that provide information but do not limit definition are nonrestrictive modifiers.)

This chapter focuses on placement of modifiers within a sentence. Because placement problems can occur with both types of modifiers, restrictive and nonrestrictive, we do not distinguish between them. However, if you study the examples carefully, you'll see that the most common problems are with placing nonrestrictive modifiers. Why? Because a nonrestrictive modifier is less essential to the point of the sentence, a writer is less likely to notice that the modifier is misplaced.

As you've seen in earlier chapters, modifiers allow you to combine several ideas into one sentence. You might write this:

Jonathan ate the doughnut. It was the only doughnut.

However, you save time and space by reducing the second sentence to a modifier:

Jonathan ate the *only* doughnut.

Still, there is a catch: word order in an English sentence often determines meaning; therefore, different word arrangements may yield different meanings. Let's see what happens if we place *only* in every possible position in "Jonathan ate the doughnut."

Only Jonathan ate the doughnut.   (No one else ate it.)

Jonathan *only* ate the doughnut.   (He didn't do anything else to it.)

Jonathan ate *only* the doughnut.   (He ate nothing else.)

Jonathan ate the *only* doughnut.   (There were no other doughnuts.)

Jonathan ate the doughnut *only.*   (He ate nothing else.)

Five combinations yield four distinctly different meanings. Play this game with other sentences and such words as *almost, every, just, merely, most, nearly, only, primarily,* and *principally.*

The game's implication is obvious, isn't it? Unless you carefully place the modifiers in your sentences, you may not write what you really mean. Modifiers are terrific savers of time and space in your writing—but they also can obscure or distort your meaning, sometimes making your writing appear ridiculous.

MISPLACED MODIFIERS

Placing a modifier in a sentence requires good judgment and careful editing. No particular place in a sentence is always right for a modifier, but this much is true: *a modifier tends to modify what it is close to.* "Close to" may be before or after the thing modified, so long as the sentence makes sense.

These sentences don't make much sense.

A jeep ran over the soldier *that had muddy tires.*

People stared in amazement *on the sidewalk.*

The accident left *neatly pressed* tire marks on the soldier's shirt.

In these sentences something comes between the modifiers and the things modified. As a result, the modifiers appear to refer to the things they are closest to: *that had muddy tires* seems to modify *soldier; on the sidewalk* seems to refer to *amazement;* and *neatly pressed* appears to modify *tire marks.*

Let's move the modifiers so they modify what they should.

A jeep *that had muddy tires* ran over the soldier.

On the sidewalk, people stared in amazement.

> or

People *on the sidewalk* stared in amazement.

The accident left tire marks on the soldier's *neatly pressed* shirt.

Notice that *on the sidewalk* works before or after *people,* whereas *that had muddy tires* works only after *jeep* and *neatly pressed* works only before *shirt.* What matters, then, is that the modifier must be close enough to the thing it modifies to complete the thought logically.

A second type of placement problem occurs when you write strings of modifiers. Consider this example:

A man *with red hair in a green suit* crossed the street.

Both *with red hair* and *in a green suit* should modify *man,* but instead *in a green suit* seems to refer to *hair.*

One solution is to put one modifier before and another after the thing modified:

A *red-haired* man *in a green suit* crossed the street.

> or

Wearing a green suit, a man *with red hair* crossed the street.

A second solution is to combine the modifiers with a coordinating conjunction:

A man *with red hair and a green suit* crossed the street.

Again, the exact position of the modifier doesn't matter if the result makes sense.

DANGLING MODIFIERS

Dangling modifiers can occur anywhere in a sentence, but the most common problem is at the beginning. A modifier that *begins* a sentence must refer to something that follows. Because of convention, readers expect an introductory word or phrase modifier to refer to the subject of the sentence.

Walking along the beach, Mary found a sand dollar.

Since we expect the opening phrase *(walking along the beach)* to modify the subject of the sentence *(Mary),* we know that Mary, not the sand dollar, was walking along the beach. But what if the sentence reads this way?

Walking along the beach, a sand dollar was found by Mary.

Again we expect the introductory phrase to modify the subject of the sentence, but sand dollars don't walk. Since the modifier cannot logically modify the subject of the sentence, we say that the modifier "dangles."

The following sentences contain dangling modifiers:

Enthusiastic, the hour seemed to pass quickly.

Finishing the game, the crowd loudly booed the home team.

After examining the data, the steam engine appeared to be the best choice.

To enjoy surfing, the waves must be high.

When only nine, John's mother took him to a circus.

Was the hour enthusiastic? Did the crowd actually finish the game? Did the steam engine examine the data? Can waves enjoy surfing? Do you really believe that John had a mother who was only nine years old? Because the modifiers above have no logical connection to the subjects of the sentences, the modifiers dangle.

You have two options to correct dangling modifiers:

- The first, the most obvious, is to recast the sentence so the subject matches the modifier.

Enthusiastic, we thought the hour passed quickly.

Finishing the game, the home team heard loud booing from the crowd.

After examining the data, we concluded that the steam engine was the best choice.

To enjoy surfing, you need high waves.

When only nine, John went to the circus with his mother.

- The second method is to change the word or phrase modifier into a clause.

Because we were enthusiastic, the hour seemed to pass quickly.

As the game ended, the crowd loudly booed the home team.

After we examined the data, the steam engine appeared to be the best choice.

If you want to enjoy surfing, the waves must be high.

When John was only nine, his mother took him to a circus.

The Bottom Line

You can avoid *both* types of problem modifiers—misplaced as well as dangling—if you keep in mind the essential relationship between modifiers and the things they modify:

- A modifier tends to modify what it is close to.
- A modifier should be close to what it must modify.

EXERCISES

A. 1. Write one sentence with a misplaced modifier and one with a dangling modifier.

a. _____

_____

b. _____

_____

2. Now correct your sentences.

a. _____

_____

b. _____

_____

B. The game at the beginning of the chapter isn't just an amusing pastime: it's based on a real and very common type of modifier placement problem in business and technical writing. Here's a sentence—less the modifier *only*—from a business report:

He has been a member of the party since 1989.

Now, place *only* in every possible position in the sentence—there are eleven—and evaluate the number of different meanings you generate. How many are there? Which do you think the author meant to write?

C. Rewrite the following sentences to eliminate the modifier problems.

1. Dressed in blue jeans and sneakers, the audience at the gala opening of the opera was appalled when Benjamin entered the lobby.
2. After being branded, the cowboy released the cow to run free in the pasture.
3. Bleating piteously, Mary allowed the lamb to follow her to school.
4. He put the cowboy hat on his head that he bought in Albuquerque.

5. The company requests that you indicate if you will accept the replacement on the enclosed card.
6. Lorenzo almost seemed disappointed about the appointment.
7. Driving through Yellowstone, the bears came right up to the car.
8. After reaching a rolling boil, the cook can skim the fat from the surface of the soup.
9. He was only a child a mother could love.
10. Opening the draperies, the snow had drifted half way up the window.
11. When completely empty, the technician should refill the tank.
12. A woman driving a half-ton pickup with a wide-brimmed hat bought the horse that won the show.
13. When cooked, pepper should be sprinkled on the chicken.
14. The coach told him frequently to run wind sprints.
15. The boy holding flowers with a shy smile approached his date.
16. The horse jumped the fence with its mane flying in the wind.
17. To ensure they arrive on time, the cards should be mailed by the first day of December.
18. Adjusting his large, red nose, the master of ceremonies announced the clown.
19. The mortician figured that he had very nearly embalmed 1,200 bodies.
20. Arriving at the campground, a campsite was rented by the weary travelers.
21. Who is the woman who told you how to find the studio in the business suit?
22. A girl in a raincoat with a Girl Scout uniform was standing outside the supermarket selling cookies in the rain.
23. Laurie borrowed an egg from Alice that was rotten.
24. The dog ate the food with brown ears.
25. Jumping high to catch the pass, the linebacker prepared to hit the wide receiver's legs as soon as he touched the football.

39 Subject-Verb Agreement

One of the most common grammar problems for students is agreement between sub-jects and verbs. The rule itself is quite simple: *a verb must agree in number with its subject.* If the subject is singular, the verb must be singular; if the subject is plural, the verb must be plural.

Singular and Plural Verbs

Usually the verb itself doesn't cause trouble. In fact, the forms for many singular and plural verbs are identical, so they can't cause a mistake in agreement. Yet, English verbs retain one peculiarity that some students find troublesome.

You know that an *-s* or *-es* ending on a noun makes the noun plural: car, car*s;* toma-to, tomato*es.* The same would seem to be true for verbs, but it isn't. An *-s* or *-es* ending on a verb makes the verb singular:

Plural	**Singular**
They run.	He run*s.*
They go.	She go*es.*
They jump.	It jump*s.*

If you understand this difference between verbs and nouns, verbs are not likely to cause you agreement problems. The problems stem from the subjects of the verbs.

Most errors in agreement occur because of some difficulty related to the subject of a sentence, particularly in:

- identifying the subject
- recognizing the subject's number

IDENTIFYING THE SUBJECT

Some agreement problems result from difficulties in finding the subject of a sentence. Two sentence structures make identifying the subject particularly troublesome:

- when the subject is delayed—so it isn't where we expect it to be
- when a phrase comes between the subject and the verb—confusing us about the subject's identity

DELAYED SUBJECT

We usually can find the subject if it comes in its ordinary place—just before the verb—but we may have trouble if it follows the verb. Watch for sentences opening with *there* or *here*. These words delay the subject so that it appears after the verb. You'll have to think through such a sentence because you won't know whether the verb should be singular or plural until you get beyond it to the subject.

       V   S
There *are* three *sailboats* at the dock.

       V   S
There *is* the *sailboat* with the sail on upside down.

    V   S
Here *are* the *supplies* you ordered.

    V   S
Here *is* the *box* you wanted first.

PHRASE BETWEEN SUBJECT AND VERB

Sometimes even when the subject comes where we expect it to be, before the verb, it is still hard to identify because of a phrase between the subject and verb. Because of the intervening phrase:

- We may think a word in the phrase is the subject.
- We may think the phrase is part of the subject, making it plural.

Let's look first at an example in which a word in the phrase might seem to be the subject:

                       S   V
Wrong: One of the Coyne *boys* *have* *climbed* the water tower.

Here the word *boys* is so close to the verb that the writer thought it was the subject. He was wrong. *Boys* is simply part of a phrase that comes between the subject and the verb. The real subject is *one:*

Correct: *One* of the Coyne boys *has climbed* the water tower.

Now let's look at a phrase that might seem to be part of the subject:

Wrong: *Martha, as well as her sisters, work* in the fields regularly.

As well as her sisters seems to be part of the subject. It seems to be equivalent to *and her sisters.* But it isn't.

Confusing Prepositional Phrases

The words here are merely prepositions; they begin phrases that have nothing to do with determining the agreement between a subject and its verb:

as well as	including
accompanied by	like
along with	together with
in addition to	with

How can we find the subject in our example above? Mentally eliminate the entire phrase:

Correct: *Martha* (~~as well as her sisters~~) *works* in the fields regularly.

The subject is now clear.

RECOGNIZING THE SUBJECT'S NUMBER

The problems we just looked at occur because the subject isn't where we expect it to be. Sometimes, though, we can find the subject and still not know whether it is singular or plural. These rules will help you:

- **Two or more subjects joined by *and* are almost always plural. The *and* joins the items—singular, plural, or mixed—into one plural unit.**

Charlotte and her *brothers drive* the metallic brown dune buggy.

That *woman* and her *husband look* a lot alike.

- **If *or* or *nor* joins subjects, the verb agrees with whichever subject is closer to the verb.**

Either *Beverly* or my other *aunts have* my thanks.

Here *aunts* is closer to the verb than is *Beverly,* so the verb is plural. What if we reverse the subjects?

         S   S   V
Either my other *aunts* or *Beverly has* my thanks.

Now *Beverly* is closer, so the verb is singular.

A Tip on Word Order

Does "Either my other aunts or Beverly has my thanks" seem awkward to you? It's technically correct. However, many readers feel uncomfortable when the singular subject (*Beverly* here) of a mixed singular-plural set forces use of a singular verb (*has* in this case). The better choice is to put the plural portion of the set closer to the verb so the verb will be plural.

The rule still applies if both items are singular or if both items are plural. If both are singular, naturally a singular subject will be next to the verb, so the verb is singular. Likewise, if both subjects are plural, a plural subject will be next to the verb, so the verb is plural.

- **Some, all, most, part, half (and other fractions) may be either singular or plural, depending on the phrase that follows them.**

You probably think we're crazy, because we told you in the first part of the chapter not to let a phrase between the subject and the verb influence subject-verb agreement. Well, here is an exception to that rule.

Many times the words in the previous list are followed by a phrase beginning with *of* ("All *of* the jurors. . . ." "Some *of* the tea . . . "). If the main word in the *of*-phrase is plural, then the verb should be plural. However, if the main word is singular or just can't be counted (we wouldn't say "one *milk*" or "thirteen *tea,*" for example), then the verb should be singular.

S   V
Some of the grapes *are* still on the table. (*Grapes* is plural, so the verb is plural.)

S   V
Some of the milk *is dripping* on the floor. (*Milk* cannot be counted, so the verb is singular.)

- **Relative pronouns (*who, whose, whom, which,* and *that*) may be singular or plural, depending on the word they refer to.**

Usually the relative pronoun refers to the word just before it:

                                     S   V
Jeannette is one of the children *who love* to read. (*Who* is a pronoun replacing *children.* Not just one child but all the children love to read.)

Again, here comes an exception. What if Jeannette is the only one in the group who loves to read? Then the pronoun *who* refers to the word *one,* not the word *children:*

<pre>S   V</pre>
Jeannette is the only one of the children *who loves* to read.

The exception, then, is that in the phrase *the only one . . . who/that,* the relative pronoun refers to the word *one,* so the verb must be singular (after all, what can be more singular than *one?*).

- **A collective noun as subject requires a singular verb when the group acts as a unit but a plural verb when the members of the group act as separate persons or things.**

A collective noun names a group: *audience, class, committee, family, jury, orchestra, team,* and so forth. The key is to determine whether the parts of the group are acting as a single body or as separate entities (that are doing the same thing).

<pre>   S   V</pre>
The *jury has been sequestered.* (The members of the collective group have been separated from the public as a single body, so the verb is singular.)

<pre>   S   V</pre>
The *jury are* unable to agree on a verdict. (Clearly, the members of the collective group are acting as separate individuals—since they can not agree as a unit—so the verb is plural.)

EXERCISES

A. Use one of the following verbs when completing this exercise:

Singular verbs: *throws, goes, misses, takes*
Plural verbs: *throw, go, miss, take*

Do not use other forms of these verbs (such as *threw, had thrown,* or the like).

1. a. Write a sentence that has the subject following the verb. Use a singular verb.

   _____

   b. Now use a plural verb.

   _____

2. Write a sentence with a singular subject and the phrase *as well as* (fill in a word) between the subject and the verb.

   _____

3. Write a sentence that has two subjects joined by *and.*

   _____

4. a. Write a sentence with two plural subjects joined by *or.*

   _____

   b. Write a sentence with two singular subjects joined by *or.*

   _____

    c. Write a sentence with a singular and a plural subject joined by *or*.

_____

    d. Rewrite sentence c but reverse the order of the subjects.

_____

5. Write a sentence with *all* as the subject and a phrase beginning with *of* between it and the verb.

_____

6. Write a sentence that contains a relative pronoun as a subject and draw an arrow to the word it refers to.

_____

7. a. Write a sentence with a collective noun as the subject and with a singular verb.

_____

    b. Write another sentence with the same collective noun as the subject and with a plural verb.

_____

B. Circle the correct verb in each set of choices below.

1. Willard is the only one of the skaters who (has, have) to be at the rink before noon.
2. One of the girls or Carlos (is, are) going to join us when we practice.
3. A fourth of the chocolates (is, are) for us; the rest (belongs, belong) to Tracy.
4. Several members of our graduating class (is, are) starting a scholarship fund.
5. The family (is, are) not likely to agree on how to divide Aunt Julia's property.
6. There (is, are) the gloves you dropped outside the door yesterday.
7. Neither the boxer nor his trainers (wants, want) him to go back into the ring.
8. Those books, including that first edition of Faulkner's *The Sound and the Fury*, (is, are) worth more that you and I can imagine.
9. Neither the bird nor the bee (has, have) to be told about people.
10. Baci is one of those dogs that (likes, like) everybody.
11. Laura together with her friends (is, are) playing Old Maid.
12. The committee (has, have) decided to decorate the gym in blue and yellow.
13. All of the milk (has, have) spoiled.
14. The team (is, are) cleaning out their lockers now that the season is over.
15. As a result, there (is, are) bloodshed and chaos.
16. Jenny is the only one of the children who (likes, like) the licorice gumdrops.
17. There (was, were), according to Senator Stevens, at least one reason to question the president's nominee.
18. The rest of the report, however, along with the drawings and photographs, (was, were) worth reading.

19. A chorus of applause and bravos (was, were) heard throughout the opera house.
20. The crowd (was, were) very quiet as Congressman Billings spoke.
21. Poverty is one of society's major failures that (causes, cause) crime.
22. Do you think the boys and Martha (realizes, realize) the mistake?
23. The first two sections of the report (was, were) uninspiring.
24. The brand of computer that man is buying for his children (carries, carry) a ninety-day warranty.
25. There (is, are) only the piano and one bed left to move.
26. Two possibilities to solve the crisis (has, have) been proposed, but so far neither (has, have) been taken seriously.
27. Each of the clerks (complains, complain) about the smoke in the office.
28. Some of the committee (is, are) waiting for the president's nominee to explain his finances.
29. Politics (is, are) a dangerous subject to discuss because everyone (has, have) an opinion.
30. Part of the barrels (has, have) been broken.

CHAPTER

40 Pronoun Agreement

This chapter deals with another agreement problem—agreement between pronouns and the things they refer to.

Pronouns and Antecedents

Pronouns replace nouns or other pronouns in sentences. A pronoun must have something to refer to—called the *antecedent* of the pronoun. Look for the antecedent for *his* in this sentence:

The boy found his dog.

Clearly, *his* refers to *boy,* so *boy* is the antecedent for *his.*

The grammar rule that students often find troublesome is this: *A pronoun must agree in number with its antecedent.* If the antecedent is singular, the pronoun must be singular; if the antecedent is plural, the pronoun must be plural.

Because the pronoun's number depends on the antecedent, our attention should be on problem antecedents. When the antecedent is simple, making the pronoun agree is a simple task. You wouldn't write this:

The *boys* looked for *his* books. (Assume all the boys are missing books.)

Boys is a plural antecedent, so you'd write this:

The *boys* looked for *their* books.

Yet, special problems do arise with two types of antecedents:

- indefinite pronoun antecedents
- compound antecedents

INDEFINITE PRONOUN ANTECEDENTS

The biggest headache connected with pronoun agreement occurs when the antecedent is an indefinite pronoun like *everyone* or *nobody*. We needn't be concerned here with all indefinite pronouns, but we must look at one problem group.

Singular Indefinite Pronouns

The following indefinite pronouns are singular and always require singular pronoun references:

each	everyone	everybody
either	someone	somebody
neither	anyone	anybody
another	no one	nobody
one		

The words formed from *-one* (like *everyone*) and from *-body* (like *everybody*) often seem to be plural, but they're not. Try thinking of them as if they had the word single in the middle, like this: *every-single-one* or *every-single-body*. Now they seem to be singular, which they really are.

An unusual mental block is associated with the indefinite pronouns above. Few people would write this:

Everyone *have* a coat.

Have just doesn't sound right following *everyone*. And for good reason. *Have* is plural, but *everyone* is singular.

Yet, often the same people who recognize *everyone* as a singular subject have trouble recognizing *everyone* as a singular antecedent. Far too often they write this:

Everyone *has their* coat.

Has, of course, is correct: the singular verb agrees with the singular subject. But plural *their* cannot refer to singular *everyone*. As illogical as this problem seems, it is still common.

Study these samples:

Wrong: Everyone wore *their* coat.

Correct: Everyone wore *his* coat.

Wrong: Nobody looked at *their* books.

Correct: Nobody looked at *his* books.

Avoiding Sexist References

You may be uneasy with the "correct" revisions above: often the *everyone* you are talking about refers to a mixed group of men and women, so *his* may seem inappropriate. You're right, of course.

Usage is changing, though in formal English the conventional use of *his* to refer to both sexes is still common. On the other extreme, some writers—particularly advertisers—are matching *their* with indefinite pronouns like *everyone.* Unfortunately, that solution would return us to the illogical agreement issue we just discussed.

So what's the solution? Well, fortunately there are a number of ways to avoid the sexist tone that comes from using only masculine pronouns—without having to match plural pronouns with singular antecedents.

Here are four techniques to avoid sexist pronoun references:

- **You can use *his or her,* as in these sentences:**

   No one can read his or her assignment.

   Everybody brought his or her book instead.

This technique works well for occasional references, but it will grow awkward and tiresome, attracting attention to itself, if you use it frequently.

- **You can alternate between *his* or *her,* so readers can perceive a balance in your treatment of the sexes.**

   No one can read his assignment.

   Everyone wore her coat.

Set together like this, the sentences seem silly, don't they? This technique is useful only in long works, where the writer can use masculine references in some passages and feminine references in others—but not close together. (For instance, this is a technique we've employed occasionally in this textbook.)

- **You can avoid the problem altogether by omitting the pronouns whenever possible.**

Instead of this:	Everyone wore his coat.
Better:	Everyone wore a coat.

Instead of this:	Each of the voters cast her ballot.
Better:	Each of the voters cast a ballot.

- **You also can avoid the problem by changing both antecedents and pronoun references to plural forms.**

Instead of this:	Everyone wore his coat.
Better:	All wore their coats.

Instead of this:	Each of the voters cast her ballot.
Better:	All of the voters cast their ballots.

For most writing, the last two methods are the techniques of choice. Considerate writers will avoid implying that the world has only masculine members (by avoiding such statements as "man's best friend is his dog"). They also will avoid implying that specific groups (such as teachers, lawyers, nurses, vice presidents, and so forth) have members of only one sex. A significant part of avoiding such gender-specific language is avoiding sexist pronoun references.

Similar problems occur with words like *each, either, neither, another,* and *one.* Usually, however, these pronouns are followed by a phrase beginning with *of* and ending with a plural noun, like these:

Each of the girls . . .

Either of the students . . .

Don't be fooled. The singular indefinite pronoun, not the word in the *of*-phrase, is the antecedent for a pronoun in the rest of the sentence.

Wrong: Each of the girls gave me *their* money.

Correct: Each of the girls gave me *her* money.

The pronoun refers to *each,* not to *girls.*

Wrong: Either of the students may bring *their* books.

Correct: Either of the students may bring *his or her* books.

His or her refers to *either,* not to *students.*

Better: Either of the students may bring the books.

COMPOUND ANTECEDENTS

Compound antecedents may be joined with *and, or,* or *nor.* And the antecedents themselves may be all singular, all plural, or a mixture of singular and plural. The rules for agreement depend on the various combinations of these factors.

- **Two or more antecedents joined by *and* require a plural pronoun.**

It makes no difference whether the antecedents are singular, plural, or mixed: The *and* makes the compound antecedent plural.

John and the other boy found *their* seats.

John and the other boys found *their* seats.

- **Plural antecedents joined by *or* or *nor* require a plural pronoun.**

Either the boys or the girls will clean *their* rooms first.

Neither the boys nor the girls want to clean *their* rooms.

- **Singular pronouns joined by *or* or *nor* require a singular pronoun.**

Either the dog or the cat will get *its* food first.

Neither the dog nor the cat will eat *its* food.

- **When *or* or *nor* joins a singular antecedent and a plural antecedent, the pronoun agrees with whichever antecedent it is closer to.**

Neither Freddy nor the other boys like *their* jobs. (The pronoun *their* agrees with *boys*.)

Neither the other boys nor Freddy likes *his* job. (*His* agrees with *Freddy*.)

A Reminder About Word Order and Agreement

"Neither the other boys nor Freddy likes his job" is technically correct, but it may seem awkward. The problem—as well as the solution—is the same as you saw with subject-verb agreement in the last chapter. The better choice is to put the plural portion of a singular-plural subject/antecedent set closer to both the verb and the pronoun reference: "Neither Freddy nor the other boys like their jobs."

EXERCISES

A. Circle the correct pronoun in each set of choices below.

1. Everyone wants to know what (his, her, his or her, their) grade will be.
2. One of the women discovered that someone had broken into (his, her, his or her, their) locker.
3. Another of the men passed (his, her, his or her, their) certification examination today.

4. Political action groups differ from political parties in (its, _their_) funding and purpose.

5. If Teresita or her sisters find the mistake, (she, _they_) will want to correct it.

6. Neither Albert nor Carlos could get (_his_, their) car started after the snow Thursday.

7. Janet and Ed spent (his, her, _his or her_, their) vacation in North Carolina again this year.

8. Someone will want to see (himself, herself, _himself or herself_, themselves) become the next lottery winner.

9. Nancy and Edgar found (his, her, _his or her_, their) seats in the field house.

10. Each car that needs a new license must have (_its_, their) exhaust inspected.

11. No one could believe it when Michele and her son arrived without (his, her, his or her, _their_) tickets.

12. Either the waiter or the waitress will seat you in (his, her, _his or her_, their) section.

13. The jury is returning to the courtroom to announce (_its_, their) verdict.

14. Members of the union will be able to vote for (his, her, his or her, _their_) choice for union president next week.

15. Everybody said (he, she, _he or she_, they) wanted a change in leadership style.

B. Correct errors in pronoun agreement in the following sentences.

1. Everyone wants to see what ~~they~~ _he/she_ can accomplish.
2. Myrna and Tina each knew her lines but neither knew ~~her~~ _each others_ stand-in part.
3. Neither of the girls can find ~~their~~ _her_ scarf.
4. Warfare and hunger savaged the people, but no one seemed able to stop ~~it~~ _them_.
5. After Martin and Lars lay in the sun all day, each had badly burned ~~their~~ _his_ arms and legs.
6. The Chamber of Commerce is seeking workers for ~~their~~ _its_ festival next Friday.
7. When our tour group arrived in London, I found my luggage, but neither Jerry nor Dennis could find ~~their~~ _his_ suitcases.
8. Economy and service may have been the garage's ideals in the beginning, but ~~it~~ _they_ won't do as the slogan today.
9. Each of the workers knew ~~their~~ _his or her_ assignments.
10. Neither Julia nor Rosemary remembered ~~their~~ _her_ new hours.

C. Revise the following sentences to eliminate the gender-specific language.

1. Another of the secretaries handed in ~~her~~ _a_ resignation today.
2. I've always wanted to thank each of my teachers for ~~his~~ _his or her_ contribution to my education.
3. Each of the team members will replay the game in ~~his~~ _his or her_ mind tonight.
4. One of the nurses tried to use ~~her~~ influence to convince the hospital management to modify the visitation rules.
5. A successful corporate executive expects ~~that he will have~~ to work long hours.

6. Can everyone finish ~~his~~ [his or her] work on schedule?
7. The pilot is responsible for ensuring that ~~his~~ [the] aircraft is serviceable before takeoff.
8. No vice president in the company will be willing to give up ~~his~~ [his or her] personal parking place.
9. Everybody thinks ~~he~~ [he or she] can be the best leader.
10. Every lawyer knows that ~~his~~ [a] summation and closing argument are crucial for the case.

41 Passive Voice

Do you ever find yourself struggling with a passage you're reading even though you know all the words? Does the phrasing seem wordy and sort of backwards? Perhaps the passage is loaded with passive voice. Like most readers, you've come to expect sentences in the active voice, although you may not know what active and passive voice are.

Active and Passive Voice

"Voice" is a grammatical term for a particular form of a verb; it refers specifically to the relationship between the subject of a sentence and the *action* of the verb.

The natural order of the English sentence—actor-action-acted upon—requires *active voice,* as in the following:

Adam	ate	the *apple.*
(actor)	(action)	(acted upon)

The subject of the sentence is the actor, the one doing the eating.

Passive voice reverses this normal, expected order. The subject is no longer the actor; the new subject is acted upon, as in this *passive voice* sentence:

The *apple*	*was eaten*	by *Adam.*
(acted upon)	(action)	(actor)

Notice that the actor now appears after the verb, in a "by" prepositional phrase.

However, a passive voice sentence may not even name the actor, as in this version:

The *apple*	*was eaten.*
(acted upon)	(action)

The subject still is acted upon, but we no longer know the identity of the actor.

Comparing even the simple active and passive sentences above allows us to see some of the disadvantages of the passive voice:

- A passive construction is *wordier* than an active one.
- Because it reverses the normal order of an action, passive voice is *indirect.*
- As its name implies, a "passive" verb *lacks the vigor* inherent in an active verb.
- And if the writer doesn't include the actor, the passive construction *may be vague.*

Passive Voice in Business and Technical Writing

Passive voice is one of the less desirable features of "bureaucratic writing" or "governmentese." Moreover, some business writers, particularly in technical fields, have developed the notion that eliminating the actor from a sentence—which often results in passive voice—will make their writing more objective. Don't be fooled. Passive constructions have a function, as we'll see later in this chapter, but usually the passive voice does more harm than good.

Why? In addition to the disadvantages of passive voice listed above, *passive constructions generate other awkward writing.* For example, if you look back at the exercises for modifiers in Chapter 38, you'll find a high incidence of passive voice attached to misplaced modifiers. Moreover, wordy sentences, such as ones beginning with *It is* and *There are* often include passive voice.

Professional editors know to look for certain wording patterns when they attack an awkward passage. They know that addressing one or two easily recognizable structures is a quick way to get at the rest of the problems in a complex passage. Of course, passive voice is chief among those structures.

Let's look at an awkward piece of bureaucratic writing and see how an editor would work with it:

There has been very little effort made by overextended police forces to attempt interdiction of drug shipments and processing laboratory destruction operations.

The beginning of the sentence combines a passive construction (*has been . . . effort made by . . . forces*) with a *There are* type of opening. Revising to eliminate the passive construction fixes both voice and wordiness problems:

Overextended police forces have done little to attempt interdiction of drug shipments and processing laboratory destruction operations.

Now the editor can focus on the wordiness and lack of parallelism in the rest of the sentence:

Overextended police forces have done little *to interdict drug shipments and destroy processing laboratories.*

The revision is simpler and certainly more clear. Of course, an editor might begin revising at the end of the sentence. Yet, editors learn to attack the simple problems in a sentence first, and revising passive voice is an easy place to begin once you know how to recognize passive voice and deal with it.

RECOGNIZING PASSIVE VOICE

Identifying passive voice is really quite simple. Only a passive sentence will receive "yes" answers in all of the following tests:

- **Is the subject of the sentence acted upon?**

In our sample sentence, *apple,* the subject of the sentence, is acted upon (eaten) by Adam.

- **Does the sentence use a form of the verb *to be* followed by the kind of main verb that almost always ends in *-ed* or *-en?***

The simple forms of *to be* are these: *is, am, are, was,* and *were.* Compound forms of *to be* use *be, being,* or *been* (for example, *will be, is being, has been*). Thus, passive verbs look like these: *is divided, was beaten,* and *will have been destroyed.* In our sample passive sentence, *was eaten* is the passive verb form.

- **If the actor appears in the sentence, is the actor in the prepositional phrase *by someone or something?* Or if the actor doesn't appear in the sentence, does the sense of the sentence imply *by someone or something?***

"The apple was eaten by Adam" ends with *by Adam,* whereas "The apple was eaten" implies *by someone.*

Passive Voice and Past Tense

Don't confuse passive voice and past tense. They sound alike, but there is no essential connection between them. Both active and passive verb forms can appear in any number of tenses, as this sample shows:

Tense	Active Voice	Passive Voice
present	takes	is being taken
past	took	was taken
future	will take	will be taken

USING PASSIVE VOICE

You may have decided by now that the passive voice was created (by someone) merely to entrap you. Not so. In fact, passive constructions have legitimate uses:

- **Passive voice is useful when the object of the action is more important than the actor.**

Residents of Sandstone, Nevada, are afraid that a lethal gas manufactured in nearby Cactus Flower may someday poison them. They fear, for example, that the *lethal gas may be released* by a defective valve or a worn gasket.

The emphasis in the last sentence is clearly on the lethal gas. That is, the context of the passage makes the gas more important than the parts that might allow a leak. Only passive voice will allow the object of the action (lethal gas) to gain emphasis by appearing first in the sentence.

- **Because passive voice can hide the actor, it is useful when the actor is obvious, unimportant, or uncertain.**

For example, if we didn't know who dropped a canister of gas, we might write this:

When a canister *was dropped,* a lethal gas enveloped the laboratory workers.

Passive Voice and Evasiveness

A strong warning is necessary here. Passive voice makes it all too easy for a writer to omit the "by" part of a thought; this evasiveness in particular is a mark of "bureaucratic writing." Imagine being told this:

Leave your application in the box. If you *are found* acceptable, you *will be notified.*

"By whom?" you want to demand. Omissions of the responsible individuals in statements like this frustrate and irritate readers.

Deciding when passive voice is a good choice requires some thought. You can stretch the justifications for its use to cover most sentences if you try hard enough. Therefore, keep in mind this general rule: *Write with the active voice unless you have an excellent reason for using the passive.*

ACTIVATING THE PASSIVE

Far too often writers use passive voice because they can't think how to write the sentence in the active voice; in such cases, the passive is more accidental than intentional. You can prevent this lack of control in your own writing by learning the following three methods to convert passive voice into active:

- **Reverse the object and the subject.**

Passive: An example *is shown* in Figure 3.

Active: Figure 3 *shows* an example.

- **Delete the main verb, leaving the sentence with a form of *to be* as the only verb.**

Passive: Your cousin *is seen* as the best candidate.

Active: Your cousin *is* the best candidate.

- **Change the verb.**

Passive: Jonathan *was given* a new book.

Active: Jonathan *received* a new book.

If you learn to recognize the passive voice and determine to avoid the passive whenever you can, these three methods will provide you the tools you need to write simple, direct, and vigorous active sentences.

EXERCISES

A. Rewrite the following sentences to eliminate the passive voice. When necessary, supply the actors.

1. Film makers like southern California because the weather is favorable, workers can be obtained at affordable prices, and local businesses are cooperative.
2. Dozens of noise makers were blown by guests at the party.
3. Some 5,000 workers are expected to be employed by the new factory.
4. The processing plants are located in the north.
5. The Special Olympics were canceled in our town when funds were not raised by the sponsors.
6. We regret to inform you that your medical records have been lost.
7. The news that a politician has been indicted by a federal grand jury no longer surprises us.
8. When the first stage of the building has been finished, the second stage may begin.
9. The third plan is viewed as the best bargain.
10. The greatest area coverage is offered by open-wire lines.
11. The pencil shaft is made of wood.
12. A welcome address will be delivered by the new chief executive tomorrow.

13. Cracks in the foundation were not considered serious until the building collapsed.
14. If you are seen as best for the job, you will be notified tomorrow.
15. The bomb was left in the office building by a short, dark-haired man with a thin mustache.
16. For once the rapist was caught before he could rape again.
17. The group is made up of several factions and fronts.
18. A dark residue is left on the cleaning rag.
19. Opposition to the tax increase was voiced by a crowd of irate citizens.
20. If the hook is placed inside the eye, the door is secure.
21. Carbon dioxide is the most commonly used lasing medium in gas lasers.
22. Once the machine is started, you must not stop it.
23. We'll begin tomorrow if the material is delivered on time.
24. The car was caused to hydroplane by a thin sheet of water on the road.
25. The end of the project was welcomed by both the executives and the workers.

B. Each of the following sentences contains a number of writing problems that need to be corrected. Those problems include at least one passive construction per sentence. Revise the passive voice first and then see what else you can do to improve the sentences.

1. The plan was designed to expand the country's agricultural base with priority being placed on the coffee-growing and the forestry segments of the economy.
2. Until an indigenous capability to produce high-technology components is attained, the nation's electronics industry will remain backward in technology.
3. The organization of the supply system is deficient in great measure because it has been severely affected by corruption in the government and also in the industries as well.
4. The use of the same pistol in each attack may be the method used by the gang in order to authenticate its responsibilities for attacks to the authorities.
5. Nontraditional machining processes can be differentiated from traditional cutting and grinding processes because the nontraditional machining processes are characterized by higher power consumption and lower material removal rates than conventional machining methods.

42 Word Choice

The French have a phrase that could be the title of this chapter. The phrase is *le mot juste,* and it means—roughly—"the right word." *Le mot juste* is often the difference between an A paper and a merely ordinary C paper—not just one good word, of course, but a lot of them. This chapter covers some basic and advanced techniques for finding those good words.

BASIC TECHNIQUES

USE PRECISE WORDS

What is a good word? Is it something really impressive, a big word that proves how educated we are? No, usually it's a word we all know. Unfortunately, even though it's a common word, we don't use it very often because we choose an even more common word instead. *See* is one of those more general words we might slap down in a rough draft. But think of all the more precise synonyms that might work better: *glimpse, gaze, stare, peer, spot,* and *witness.*

Let's take a longer example. Suppose you are reading a paragraph and run across these words:

The man walked into the room.

The words are so general they could fit into a number of strikingly different contexts:

The policeman, hidden behind a parked car, watched as *the man walked into the room.*

or

The Capitol guard smiled as *the man walked into the room.*

or

The class quieted somewhat as *the man walked into the room.*

or

The patients gasped as *the man walked into the room.*

"What a great clause!" you say. "I can use it anywhere." It's a lousy clause—you can use it anywhere. All the words are general, the kind of words that pop into your mind in a second.

Let's think a second longer and try to make the words more exact. Here are some possibilities:

man: thief, senator, English teacher, Dr. Rodney

walked: sneaked, hurried, sauntered, reeled

room: motel room, antechamber, classroom, office

Now let's rewrite that all-purpose clause using more specific words:

The policeman, hidden behind a parked car, watched as *the thief sneaked into my motel room.*

or

The Capitol guard smiled as the *senator hurried into the antechamber.*

or

The class quieted somewhat as *the English teacher sauntered into the classroom.*

or

The patients gasped as *Dr. Rodney reeled into his office.*

Each clause is better—and certainly more interesting—because the writer took the time to come up with just the right words. Try it yourself. Look for the dull, general words in your own writing and make them more specific. This technique is one of the best ways to improve your writing dramatically.

Beware of Peculiar Words

Don't become so obsessed with the idea of seeking different words that you choose them just because they're unusual. *Perambulate,* for example, means "to walk through," so we could write this:

The senator perambulated the antechamber.

Readers probably will notice the peculiarity of *perambulated* rather than its preciseness. Your goal is to get the right words—not just the unusual ones.

USE MODIFIERS

The second basic technique, in addition to using the right word, is to use modifiers. Sometimes nouns and verbs don't tell the whole story. To be really precise, you need to add some adjectives and adverbs. Let's work with one of the sentences we improved in the last section:

> The policeman, hidden behind a parked car, watched as the thief sneaked into my motel room.

From the clause we revised (*the thief sneaked into my motel room*), we can modify *thief, sneaked,* and *motel room.* Here are just a few possibilities:

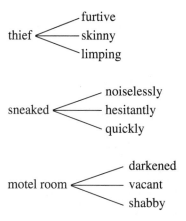

We don't want to overload the sentence with modifiers, so let's just modify *thief* and *sneaked:*

> The policeman, hidden behind a parked car, watched as the furtive thief sneaked noiselessly into my motel room.

We've come a long way from "The man walked into the room," haven't we?

Beware of Piling On

If you watch football, you've seen teams penalized for "piling on"—when players jump onto a pile of tacklers and the ball carrier after the referee has blown the play dead.

Similarly, you need to beware of piling on modifier after modifier. You have to restrain your use of modifiers to what is relevant to accomplish your purpose—and no more. Only the writer and the child's mother could love this sentence:

> The diminutive, chunky, azure-eyed, eighteen-month-old baby boy toddled to his rocking horse.

ADVANCED TECHNIQUES

USE COMPARISONS

If you really want to get your readers' attention, use a comparison. It may be the most memorable part of your theme. Remember when we said transitions are like road signs? And when we said the blueprint for your paper is like the architect's design for the structure he plans to build? These and other comparisons really help readers understand an idea.

Only one problem with comparisons: they're hard to think of, particularly good comparisons. We all can think of bad ones. The familiar phrases that come to mind almost automatically are clichés, and they are as bad as original comparisons are good. Consider this sentence:

> Although he was *blind as a bat,* Herman remained *cool as a cucumber* when he entered the arena.

See how clichés attract the wrong kind of attention to themselves? Hearing a cliché is like hearing a comedian go through the same routine time after time. After a while, nobody listens.

A good rule is that if you have heard a comparison before, don't use it. But do use original comparisons. Be daring. Try one in your next theme.

REPLACE GENERAL IDEAS WITH SPECIFIC SAMPLES

Here's something else to try in your next theme: when you want to use a general word that stands for an entire class of items—like *toys* or *vehicles* or *books*—use just one item from that class instead. Let the specific stand for the general.

Take this sentence:

> Inflation means that most Americans can hardly afford to eat, but some congressmen don't seem to care how much *food* costs.

Let's make the sentence a little more interesting by replacing the word *food* (an entire class of items) with *a loaf of bread* (one item from that class):

> Inflation means that most Americans can hardly afford to eat, but some congressmen don't seem to care how much *a loaf of bread* costs.

Here's another example:

> As a photographer she is limited. She may be able to take pictures of *nature,* but she can't take good pictures of people.

We can make the second sentence more interesting by changing the word *nature* to something more specific:

> As a photographer she is limited. She may be able to take pictures of *trees,* but she can't take good pictures of people.

See how the detail instead of the generality makes the sentence livelier?

Most college students don't use either of the advanced techniques in this section. Most of them don't get A's either. If you want to learn how to write an A paper, you might start by occasionally using a comparison or a specific word instead of a general one.

EXERCISES

A. Rewrite the following sentences two different ways, replacing the underlined general words with more precise words.

Example: The official talked to the man.
   a. The district attorney grilled the arsonist.
   b. The manager congratulated the pitcher.

1. The committee liked the idea.
   a. _The citizens favored the city beutification._
   b. _The teachers accepted the proposal._

2. The group disliked the publication.
   a. _The activists condaned the news letter._
   b. _The republicans did not consent to the newspaper._

3. The man picked up the object.
   a. _The teacher picked up some chalk._
   b. _The keeper picked up the soccerball._

4. The animal ate the food.
   a. _The dog devoured a bisquit._
   b. _The fish had some flakes._

5. The speaker spoke about the value of a good thing.
   a. _Mr. Clinton, the president preached about the value of a good voice._
   b. _The republican leader tolloff a liberal._

B. In each sentence below write a modifier in the blank. Make the modifier as colorful and specific as you can. Try to fit it into the context of the sentence.

Example: The _____ policeman arrested the mayor.

Words like *short* and *young* may not help much. On the other hand, try these choices:
The rookie policeman arrested the mayor.

   or

The bitter policeman arrested the mayor.

1. The tourists were ___amazed___ when they saw the *David.*

2. The injured guard staggered ___aimlessly.___ through the bank.

3. Fifteen of us pushed into the ___locker___ room.

4. As the ___adept___ safecracker gently touched the dial, the telephone suddenly rang.

5. The ___perfectionistic___ author was really angry about the mistake in the first printing.

6. The gardener was surprised to find such a/an ___elongated___ worm on the end of her shovel.

7. My first year in college is a/an ___alcoholic___ experience.

8. The ___rabid___ wolf stalked the reindeer.

9. The crowd shouted ___profanities___ as the diplomat's limousine passed by.

10. The ___rookie___ recruit flinched when the cannon fired.

C. We use comparisons every day, but too many of them are clichés, like "nervous as a cat on a hot tin roof" or "scared as a rabbit." For this exercise write one original comparison on any topic. (If you have trouble thinking of a topic, consider blind dates, a hobby, a famous person.)

___Blind dates are as nerve racking as___
___final exams.___

D. List three clichés other than the ones we've used as examples. (Remember, clichés are bad: avoid them like the plague.)

1. ___as soft as a babies buttocks___
2. ___as fast as a bat out of hell___
3. ___as wasted as a drunkard___

E. Improve the sentences below by changing each italicized generalization to something more specific.

Example: Small movie houses that show film classics are going out of business. After all, who wants to pay *good money* to see *an old movie?*

Revision: Small movie houses that show film classics are going out of business. After all, who wants to pay *eight dollars* to see *Humphrey Bogart?*

1. Movie reviewers complain that film makers are unwilling to take chances with new stories. They'd prefer to film a takeoff from *a TV series* or return to the characters from *a previous box office success.*

   a TV series: ___a sitcom___

   a previous box office success: ___a past thriller___

2. A *study* reported that *high-school students* could not identify where *some places are.*

A study: _a recent poll_

high-school students: _high schoolers_

some places are: _some places are located._

3. Television critics claim that viewers today are attracted to mindless programs, spending most of their time watching *situation comedies* and *sports.*

situation comedies: _sitcoms_

sports: _athletic competitions._

4. If you listen to the radio today, all you hear is *music* and *people talking.*

music: _tunes_

people talking: _yacking_

5. Opponents of colorizing movies question whether adding color to *a classic black-and-white movie* will improve or cheapen it.

a classic black-and-white movie: _an oldie_

A | Theme Format

Incredible as it may seem, English instructors are just like you and me (well—maybe a little more like me). Like you, they're human and have their little eccentricities. For example, they think that if students have done a good job writing their themes, they'll also want to make them as neat as possible. Silly idea—or is it?

That idea also has its corollary: the student who writes a theme at the last minute probably doesn't take—doesn't even *have*—the time to make it neat.

The moral is clear: be neat so that your instructors think they're looking at an A paper before they've read even the first word. Here are some guidelines, although your instructors may wish to make some changes to suit individual preferences.

- *Handwriting or typing?* Look at the two sample papers that follow. Which one would you rather read? If you can type at all, then do so. The early papers are short enough that typing them shouldn't take very long. If you don't type, use either black or blue ink. Other colors are hard to read.

- *Typing or word processing?* Should you use a typewriter or a computer with a word processing program? The answer is easy: If you have a word processor, by all means use it. It has several overwhelming advantages over the typewriter:

  - You can make corrections easily. That means you're far more likely to engage seriously in the revising process.
  - With most programs, you can use a spelling checker. That means you'll not only correct words you've misspelled but correct typos, too. By helping with the technicalities, the word processor frees you to think about the larger, more important matters of writing. Be careful, though, because spelling checkers can't catch all errors—especially when your typo results in a legitimate word.

- Most important from our point of view, the word processor helps you get words on paper easily in the first place—especially if you can compose at the keyboard. People who have become comfortable with this method know that it is one of the primary benefits of the word processor, and often they refuse to write any other way.

- *Proofreading*   Do it—*always,* but especially if you type, and even if you use a spelling checker with a word processor. Otherwise, you might be surprised by what your magic fingers did the night before.

- *Paper*   If you type, use standard-sized (8-1/2 by 11 inch) typing paper. For a standard typewriter, the erasable kind is especially good because you can make corrections easily. However, most instructors don't like to receive work on erasable paper because it's hard to write on. You can overcome this problem by typing on erasable paper and then making a photocopy to hand in (if your instructor will accept a photocopy). Do not use thin "onionskin" paper.

  For a word processor, erasing isn't required, so stick to a reasonably heavy bond paper (20-lb. paper, a good weight, is readily available in both separate sheets and continuous form, for tractor-feed printers).

  If you don't type or use a word processor, find a standard-sized tablet or pad of high-quality, lined theme paper. Don't use ordinary notebook paper (or paper torn from a spiral notebook) unless your instructor approves.

- *Corrections*   On a short assignment (like the one-paragraph essay), avoid handing in a paper with obvious corrections. If, however, you're torn between making a correction at the last minute or handing in a neat paper, of course make the correction. What good is a neat error?

- *Spacing*   If you're typing, double-space except where format requirements call for different spacing. If you're writing by hand, write on every other line.

- *Margins*   Allow an inch on the top, left, right, and bottom. On page one for a theme assignment, begin the identification block (see sample on next page) one inch from the top of the page, quadruple-space (double-space twice) to find the line for the title, and then quadruple-space again to find where to begin the first line of your theme. (For research papers, you'll probably use a title page for identification information; see the sample research paper for the format for a title page and for the first page of the paper's body. Some of the comments on the pages facing the sample research paper discuss format requirements for students who need to follow MLA page layout guidance.)

- *Page numbers*   Don't number the first page, but do count it as page one. For other pages, use Arabic numerals (2, 3, 4, and so on) and put the number in the upper right-hand corner, 1/2 inch from the top of the page and in line with the right margin. (Chapter 19 shows the MLA format, which uses a somewhat different pagination style for the research paper.)

- *Identification* Put your name, your instructor's name, the course number, and the date in the upper left-hand corner of page one, one inch from the top of the page. Your instructor may direct you to put this information on a title page for your research paper, as the sample research paper demonstrates.

- *Fastening the paper* Unless your instructor directs you to put your paper in a binder, use a stapler to fasten pages together. Paper clips are fine in theory, but in a stack of themes they tend to clip themselves onto other themes.

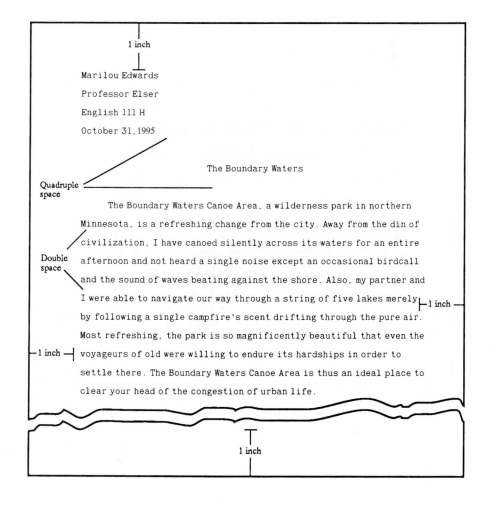

1 inch

Marilou Edwards
Professor Elser
English 111 H
October 31, 1995

The Boundary Waters

Quadruple
space

    The Boundary Waters Canoe Area, a wilderness park in northern Minnesota, is a refreshing change from the city. Away from the din of civilization, I have canoed silently across its waters for an entire afternoon and not heard a single noise except an occasional birdcall and the sound of waves beating against the shore. Also, my partner and I were able to navigate our way through a string of five lakes merely by following a single campfire's scent drifting through the pure air. Most refreshing, the park is so magnificently beautiful that even the voyageurs of old were willing to endure its hardships in order to settle there. The Boundary Waters Canoe Area is thus an ideal place to clear your head of the congestion of urban life.

Double
space

1 inch

1 inch

1 inch

Marilou Edwards
English 111 H
Professor Elser
October 31, 1988

The Boundary Waters

The Boundary Waters Canoe Area, a wilderness park in northern Minnesota, is a refreshing change from the city. Away from the din of civilization, I have canoed silently across its waters for an entire afternoon and not heard a single noise except an occasional bird call and the sound of the waves beating against the shore. Also, my partner and I were able to navigate our way through a string of five lakes merely by following a single campfire's scent drifting through the pure air. Most refreshing, the park is so magnificently beautiful that even the voyageurs of old were willing to endure its hardships in order to settle there. The Boundary Waters Canoe Area is thus an ideal place to clear your head of the congestion of urban life.

B Commonly Confused Words

These are some words college students sometimes have trouble with. The list isn't complete—we've kept it short on purpose so you can read through it rather than just use it as a reference.

Affect / Effect

Affect is almost always a verb:

"What you learn in college will *affect* your decision-making process for the rest of your life."

Effect is almost always a noun:

"What you learn in college will have an *effect* on your decision-making process for the rest of your life."

A Lot / Alot

A lot is the correct spelling.

All right / Alright

All right is the correct spelling.

Among / Between

Use *between* when you're dealing with two items; use *among* for three or more:

"*Between* you and me, I don't think there's much honor *among* all those thieves."

Complement / Compliment

Complement means to go along nicely with:

"Her scarf *complemented* her blouse."

Compliment is a nice thing to say to someone else:

"He *complimented* her on her scarf."

Disinterested / Uninterested

Disinterested means impartial; *uninterested* means bored:

"Thank goodness the referee was *disinterested* because, believe me, the fans weren't *uninterested* in the outcome of the game."

Fewer / Less

Use *fewer* to compare things you can count (like teeth, cars, glasses); use *less* for things that are amounts (like wheat, sugar, paper):

"*Fewer* people came to the fair, so we'll need *less* food to feed them."

Imply / Infer

You *imply* something to a listener when you don't quite say it explicitly; the listener *infers* what you as a speaker haven't quite said explicitly:

"The teacher *implied* that the work needs to be on time. I *inferred* that the teacher wants the work on time."

Irregardless / Regardless

Regardless is standard. *Irregardless* is nonstandard.

It's / Its' / Its

It's means "it is" or "it has"; *its'* is always incorrect; *its* shows possession (many pronouns show possession without an apostrophe: *his, hers, ours*):

"*It's* a good time to put the desk back in *its* place."

Principal / Principle

Principal can be a noun (the person who ran your high school) or an adjective (meaning "main"); *principle* is a noun that means a basic truth, rule, or law:

"The school's *principal* said that the *principal* reason for the snow holiday is that it violated her *principles* to have students traveling on dangerous roads."

Stationary / Stationery

Stationary means still; *stationery* is what you write on:

"Hold that *stationery stationary* or I'll never be able to write this letter!"

INDEX